Organizing Women

Formal and Informal Women's Groups in the Middle East

Edited by
Dawn Chatty and Annika Rabo

BERG

Oxford • New York

First published in 1997 by
Berg
Editorial offices:
150 Cowley Road, Oxford, OX4 1JJ, UK
70 Washington Square South, New York, NY 10012, USA

Berg is the imprint of Oxford International Publishers Ltd.

Library of Congress Cataloging-in-Publication Data

A catalogue record for this book is available from the Library of Congress.

British Library Cataloguing-in-Publication Data

A catalogue record for this book is available from the British Library.

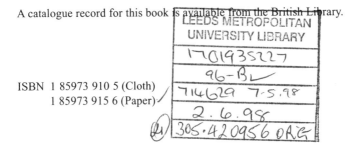

ISBN 1 85973 910 5 (Cloth)
1 85973 915 6 (Paper)

Typeset by JS Typesetting, Wellingborough, Northants.
Printed and bound in Great Britain by
Biddles Ltd, Guildford and King's Lynn

To KK, PS, AQ and ML

Contents

Preface

I have lived and worked in the Middle East for nearly twenty years and throughout that time I have only peripherally been engaged with research particularly focused on women. My own interests, first in nomadic pastoral societies, and second in general development issues, led me to view the whole, rather than focus on the particular. In the early period of women's studies, when the theory of women's universal subordination was popular, I had to follow a different line, guided by my own field data which suggested that complementarity rather than inferiority or subordination was the most promising line of inquiry when dealing with nomadic pastoral society. Such societies displayed an egalitarianism rarely found in agrarian and urban communities in the Middle East. And conducting field research among nomadic pastoral groups was never difficult. Only occasionally did a recently returned Western educated government bureaucrat question my ability, as a woman, to work with such communities. On the whole, my gender made no difference. What mattered was how I worked, the results that I produced and the relationships that I established within local government and in the field.

In 1992, Annika Rabo of Linköping University invited me to give a paper for a panel she was organizing for the annual British Society for Middle East Studies Conference at St Andrews. The panel was entitled 'State Patriarchy and State "Feminism": female perspectives on law and identity'. In the preparation of my contribution, I explored further the nomadic pastoral Harasiis women's relationship with tribal political organization and local government. A description and analysis of the independence of the women, underscored by the important economic role they played in the society formed the basis of my paper. Their political relationship with the government's local representative, the *wali*, was also explored as here was a situation where women took on commonly accepted male functions in the occasional absences of their husbands, fathers and brothers. In the main, I saw nomadic pastoral women as having an important, if informal, role both within the tribe and with the growing desert community.

At about the same time I was drawn into a spontaneous enterprise organized by a few Harasiis women to make handicrafts for sale to the small trickle of tourists and other travellers. This experience is discussed in some detail in the introduction. Here I only wish to say that it was the unexpected, and uncharacteristic difficulties, which I faced on behalf of these women that led to the workshop from which these chapters are drawn. In my frustration and exasperation, I turned to Annika Rabo and the original panellists (Seteney Shami and Eva Evers Rosander) at the St Andrews meeting and suggested we have another look at what happens when women in the Middle East try to organize themselves. A workshop on this topic was held at the Centre for Cross-Cultural Research on Women, University of Oxford in June 1995. All of the papers in this volume, except for one, were first presented at the gathering. Nancy Lindisfarne, who attended the workshop and chaired one of the sessions was then inspired to write a concluding piece which closes this collection.

Dawn Chatty

Acknowledgements

The idea for the workshop and eventually this book on the subject goes back many years and rests finally in the Sultanate of Oman where I spent over a decade working with a nomadic pastoral community. I owe much to the Harasiis tribe, particularly Mohammed and Salim Suheil for their generous support of a spontaneous income-generating project in which their wives involved themselves. Gigi Crocker Jones, Roddy Jones and Andrew Spalton encouraged this project and lent it their full support as well. In Muscat, Barka al-Bakry, then at the UNDP and Mark Mathews and Mark Pickett, at USAID, also stood behind the effort and endeavoured to turn it into a more formal association.

At Oxford, I am particularly grateful for the support and encouragement I received from the Centre for Cross-Cultural Research on Women. Shirley Ardener, Soraya Tremayne and Camillia Fawzi El-Solh gave generously of their time encouraging me and helping to plan the workshop. The actual administration and running of the workshop could not have been accomplished without the very able assistance of Lucy Butterwick, and the financial acumen of Rosemary Frances. I must also thank Kristy Sangster for her help in checking references and generally tidying up manuscripts. But the really difficult task of preparing the manuscript for submission was undertaken by Judy Mabro. To her, our grateful thanks.

The Wenner-Gren Foundation for Anthropological Research very generously provided us with a conference grant which made it possible to bring a number of our contributors to Oxford from their homes in the Middle East. OXFAM, The Overseas Development Agency, as well as Queen Elizabeth House, University of Oxford also contributed to the costs of the workshop and the added expenses incurred in preparing this manuscript for publication.

Dawn Chatty

Notes on Contributors

Nadje Sadig Al-Ali is a PhD candidate at the School of Oriental and African Studies, University of London. Her fieldwork has been conducted in Egypt and her research interests are the representation of gender in literature. She recently published *Gender Writing/Writing Gender: The Representation of Women in Modern Egyptian Literature*, Cairo: American University in Cairo Press, 1994.

Shahida El-Baz is a Researcher at the National Centre for Social and Criminological Research, Cairo. Her work has mainly centred on Egypt and she has written numerous papers in the field of political economy of development, women and NGOs.

Dawn Chatty is a social anthropologist with degrees from the University of California at Los Angeles and the Institute of Social Studies in The Hague. She has taught at the University of California at Santa Barbara, American University of Beirut, University of Damascus and Sultan Qaboos University in Oman. Currently she is Senior Research Officer at the Refugee Studies Programme, Queen Elizabeth House, University of Oxford. Her research interests include pastoral nomadic societies, the development process, gender studies, health and culture, and population displacement in the Middle East. She has published numerous articles on these subjects as well as two books, *From Camel to Truck: the Bedouin in the Modern World*, New York: Vantage Press, 1986; and *Mobile Pastoralists: Development Planning and Social Change in Oman*, New York: Columbia University Press, 1996.

Suad Joseph is Professor of Anthropology and Women's Studies at the University of California, Davis. Her research, focusing on her native Lebanon, has analysed the politicization of religion, women's local community networks, family systems, the linkages between family and state system, gender and citizenship, and the cultural construction of selfhood. Recent publications include: 'Gender and Citizenship in Middle Eastern States,' *Middle East Reports*, 1996, 26, 1; 'Problematizing Gender and

Relational Rights: Experiences from Lebanon,' *Social Politics*, 1994, 1, 3; 'Gender and Relationality Among Arab Families in Lebanon,' *Feminist Studies*, 1993, 19, 3.

Nancy Lindisfarne is Senior Lecturer in Anthropology, School of Oriental and African Studies, University of London. Her regional interests include Syria, Turkey, Iran and Afghanistan. She has written numerous papers on gender and pastoralism and Islam. She published, as Nancy Tapper, *Bartered Brides: Politics, Gender and Marriage in an Afghan Tribal Society*, Cambridge: Cambridge University Press, 1991. As Nancy Lindisfarne, coeditor with Andrea Cornwall, she published *Dislocating Masculinity*, London, Routledge, 1994. Dar al Mada will soon publish her collection of short stories, *Dancing in Damascus*, in an Arabic translation.

Valentine M. Moghadam was born in Iran and educated in Canada and the United States, where she earned a PhD in sociology in 1986. After teaching the sociology of development and Middle East Studies in New York, she joined the United Nations University. From 1990 until 1996 she was Senior Researcher and Coordinator of the Research Programme on Women and Development at the UNU's WIDER Institute in Helsinki. She is now director of Women's Studies at Illinois State University. Dr Moghadam is the author and editor of seven books and many articles on gender and development issues and has conducted research in various regions in the world, in addition to the Middle East and North Africa.

Haya al-Mughni is a sociologist who lives and works in Kuwait. Her research and writing have focused on gender politics, social movements and citizenship. She is the author of *Women in Kuwait: The Politics of Gender*, London, Al-Saqi Press, 1993.

Annika Rabo is Associate Professor in Social Anthropology, Department of Social Science at Linköping University, Sweden. Her research interests focus on Syria and Jordan. She undertook fieldwork in northern Syria analysing the impact of a huge irrigation scheme and has also worked in Jordan looking into questions of development. Her current interests focus on the interrelationships between gender, citizenship and state apparatuses. From summer of 1997 she will take up a post as Researcher on Middle Eastern Culture and Society sponsored by the Swedish Research Council for Humanities and Social Science.

Eva Evers Rosander is Associate Professor in Social Anthropology at Stockholm University and is currently employed as Senior Researcher at the Nordic Africa Institute in Uppsala, Sweden. Her regional interests include Gibraltar, Morocco and Senegal. She has published numerous studies on Islam, women, and women's associations.

May Seikaly is Associate Professor of History in the Department of Near Eastern and Asian Studies at Wayne State University, Michigan. Previously she was a visiting assistant professor of History at UCLA. She has also worked at Bahrain National University. A graduate of Oxford University, UCLA and Beirut College for Women, she has had extensive academic experience in both the Middle East and the West. Her publications include numerous articles on women in Bahrain and Palestine as well as the book *Haifa:Transformation of an Arab Society 1918–1939,* London, I.B. Tauris, 1995. She is currently working on oral history as a source for researching women's studies, communities and development of archival materials.

Seteney Shami is a Jordanian anthropologist who obtained her degrees from the American University of Beirut and the University of California, Berkeley. From 1982–1995 she taught at Yarmouk University in Jordan and was the founding chair of the Anthropology Department. She was also a visiting professor at the University of California, Berkeley, Georgetown University and the University of Chicago. Currently, she is director of MEAwards, a regional research programme in population and development administered out of the Population Council's regional office in Cairo. Her research interests include ethnicity and nationalism, urban politics and population displacement in the Arab countries, Turkey and the North Caucasus. Recent publications include 'Children of Amman: Childhood and Child Care in Squatter Areas of Amman' in E. Fernea, ed., *Children in the Muslim Middle East*, Austin, University of Texas Press, 1995; 'Transnationalism and Refugee Studies: Rethinking Forced Migration and Identity in the Middle East,' *Journal for Refugee Studies*, 9, 1, 1996; and an edited volume (with Jean Hannoyer) *Amman: The City and its Society*, Beirut, CERMOC, 1996.

1

Formal and Informal Women's Groups in the Middle East

Dawn Chatty and *Annika Rabo*

Introduction

Women everywhere have formed themselves into groups for political purposes since time immemorial. Women forming groups to protest war, to mediate conflict, to fight for a political voice or even to spearhead peace movements are common images in history. Throughout this century, in both the developed and the developing world, we see women forming groups for political expression; to participate in street demonstrations in the Egyptian Revolution of 1919 (Badran 1993, 1995; Marsot 1978), to protest about the conflict in Northern Ireland, the Israeli incursion into Southern Lebanon, and the presence of nuclear Cruise missiles at Greenham Common, United Kingdom (Jones 1987). Often Middle Eastern women have been portrayed by Westerners either as silent shadows, or as helpless victims of suppressive customs and traditions unable to organize or form groups on their own and for themselves. The last decade, however, has seen an explosion of research and publications fully acknowledging women as persons in their own right, as political and economic actors who fend and struggle and reflect on their lives and the future of their societies.[1] Yet there remains a resistance and a hesitancy on the part of Middle Eastern governments to allow women to form groups. And although a narrow range of women's associations, unions, and cooperatives do exist, these are most often created and tightly organized by men for women (e.g. Shaaban 1988; al-Mughni 1993). The 'free' association of women is notable by its glaring absence in most Middle Eastern countries.

At present some independent non-governmental women's groups do exist in Morocco, Algeria, Tunisia, Egypt, the West Bank, Kuwait and Lebanon. They are missing, however, from the basically conservative states of Qatar, the United Arab Emirates, Saudi Arabia, Oman, Jordan and Yemen as well as the radical 'socialist' states of Iraq, Libya, and Syria. Both the conservative and the socialist states seem to share a hostility to independent women's groups. Such groups are considered threatening in conservative regimes because they challenge the state's rigid control of women. Among the radical socialist regimes, the reasoning is that independent women's groups are subversive because they challenge the general consensus about which national goals are appropriate for the mobilization of women (Hatem 1993: 37–8). Hence there is a multi-layered obduracy and resistance directed at women organized in groups in the Middle East, the parameters of which may vary in time and space.

Numerous definitions of the term 'Middle East' exist to describe a region which, in contemporary usage, is understood to take in an area stretching from Morocco to Iran. In some contexts the term is extended to encompass Afghanistan and Pakistan as well (Eickelman 1989: 3–4). This collection uses the term 'Middle East' in its broadest sense, even visiting the Morocco-Senegalese borders of the region in Evers Rosander's chapter.

Background Case Study: The Sultanate of Oman[*]

Until 1970, the Sultanate of Oman could justifiably be described as the 'Tibet of Arabia' (Eickelman 1981: 68), so complete was its isolation from the rest of the world. However, after the palace coup which brought Sultan Qaboos bin Saiid to power in 1970, the state moved rapidly to make up for lost time. Schools, clinics and hospitals were commissioned and rapidly built, roads, and other infrastructural developments were begun. Omanis living abroad were encouraged to return to the country and many highly educated men and women returned from exile to work in the spirit of building up their nation after decades of stagnation. In much the same spirit that Dodd (1973) described as common during revolution or nationalist struggle, women were mobilized and took part in many aspects of Oman's development. Women were actively engaged in the armed forces, in the police force, in the civil service, in education and in radio and television. By the early 1980s the literacy rate had climbed to 20 per cent – from a single digit figure in 1970, when the country possessed only three modern schools and less than 100 places for students. A network of

---

[*] This section has been written, in parts, in the first person. It most effectively expresses the sense of impotence and frustration which Chatty experienced in trying to convince government to give de jure recognition to a de facto women's group.

tarmacked roads had been completed and Muscat, the capital, was connected by modern road to Salalah, a city 1,000 kilometres to the south. The social and economic transformation of the nation funded by the petroleum wealth of the country was staggering. However by the late 1970s and early 1980s, the numbers of returning Omanis and recently graduated male students had climbed to such a level that jobs were becoming hard to find. Women, in particular, began to feel the squeeze. The urgency of nation building was passing and women began to feel a tightening of control and the setting up of barriers making their earlier passage into the public sphere of life increasingly difficult.

During this early period of nation building, the first organization for women – the Omani Women's Association – was founded in 1970 and was registered after a decree from the Sultan to that effect in 1971. It was set up by two upper-class women desiring to support their less well off sisters. However by 1978, this organization was taken over by the government and became part of the Ministry of Social Affairs and Labour. Essentially, its activities came to be controlled and monitored by the men who ran the Ministry. In 1984 a Directorate General of Women and Child Affairs was set up, with a female member of the elite class appointed as director. A subunit for women's associations was created to supervise the creation and on-going administration of branches of the Omani Women's Association throughout the country where women could meet, learn basics of hygiene, cooking and home keeping as taught by mainly Egyptian social workers. In addition, nurseries and crèches were set up to allow women to attend these courses, as well as adult literacy classes. By the late 1980s women were being encouraged to move into the field of caring for the handicapped and disabled. A number of these government-run women's associations opened centres for handicapped children and their mothers. These were mainly in the form of day care units, giving the mothers brief respites from the continuous care their disabled or handicapped children required. By 1995 Oman had a sizeable number of non-government organizations, but the Omani Women's Association was the sole *woman only* organization in the country.

In 1981 I began a fourteen-year association with a small (3,000) nomadic pastoral tribe on the southern edge of the Empty Quarter in the Sultanate of Oman. My role during those early years was to assist the government of Oman to extend social services to this remote community without forcing them to give up their traditional way of life. This tribe, the Harasiis, survived in the extremely arid and hostile desert by raising herds of camel and goat for milk. They ranged over an area of nearly 40,000 square kilometres (about the size of Scotland). Extended family units of 10–12 people moved with their herds over the desert following the graze and browse which appeared after rain or heavy fog. A typical family kept between 100 and 200 head of goat and 20–25 camels. The smaller livestock was owned and managed by the women and older girls, while camels were nearly universally owned and managed by men and older boys (Chatty 1984). Under certain conditions, families had to split their herds, men and older boys going off with the camel herd for graze and water, while women and young children set off with the goat herds in search of the browse most suitable for them. These split households could operate for weeks and sometimes months before reconsolidating. Even when households did not split for the sake of the herds, women regularly ran households for long periods during the absences of husbands, fathers and brothers. It was not unusual for an adult male household member to be away for months at a time managing a particular herd of camel, or more recently seeking employment in adjacent countries. Women and men displayed an independence regularly described in the literature on nomadic pastoralists but not often so overtly obvious (Chatty 1996; Lancaster 1981).

When I first began working with this community, four-wheel drive vehicles had only just appeared. In 1976 the first private, off-the-road vehicle was introduced by a tribesman returning from employment abroad. Within five years 80 per cent of households had one. These modern devices were associated with men. Often camel holdings owned by men had to be sold to purchase cars and they were considered men's property. Obviously vehicles were to transform the life of the Harasiis profoundly. For the purposes of this study, I will briefly outline two aspects of the effect vehicle transport had upon the Harasiis tribe: its impact on the traditional subsistence economy; and the way in which it drew households into the national market economy.

The motor vehicle was spontaneously and universally accepted by the Harasiis tribe because it was viewed as a tremendous aid to their traditional economy. Vehicles could move men and animals around the desert to watering holes (only six in 1981) and to new pastures in incredibly short periods of time. Journeys of three weeks could be cut to nine or ten hours. But vehicles could not be run on camels' milk or goats' milk. Hence in order to operate their vehicles, men had to find paid employment. The standard rate of pay for well guard, driver, or watchman – the local jobs available to the Harasiis – was about the same sum of money needed to pay for petrol and spare parts to keep a vehicle running (Chatty 1984, 1990).

Within several years, most households had one male working for a cash wage. But this income was nearly totally tied up with the running and maintenance of vehicles. Most goods (e.g. wheat, sugar, tea, coffee, dates, manufactured items and other speciality products) from villages and town – which all pastoral groups require to survive – were being bought on a barter basis. Occasionally luxury items did find their way into pastoral households, but in the main it was a subsistence based existence with goat and camel milk at its foundation. Slowly over a period of five or six years, other items of the late twentieth-century world began to appear at campsites – gas stoves, cooking elements, thermos flasks, infant nappies, gold jewellery, watches, radios and cassette recorders. Many of these items simplified and improved activities in which women were regularly engaged. Women began to encourage further purchases along the same lines. But these were limited by the amount of money a woman could realize from the sporadic sale of her young male kids in the desert foothill market towns. Traditionally the income from these unwanted animals was sufficient to resupply the family with basic foodstuffs and a few luxury items until the next season. Gradually however, it ceased to be enough, as more and more modern goods which the Harasiis families wished to buy began to appear in the regional marketplaces.

In 1986, two women, who had particular talent twining and weaving the traditional camel straps used functionally and ornamentally for riding camels, began to make keyring holders for their men folk using the same handicraft techniques – to help them locate their keys when misplaced or dropped in soft sand. This simple idea of attaching brightly coloured braided and twined wool to a keyring became an instant success along with other less functional items made to decorate the new beasts of burden – the four-wheel drive vehicles. Within a year the keyrings were being sold locally to the occasional traveller and tourist from the only petrol station along nearly 800 kilometres of tarmacked road at Haima. With the help of a British weaving expert the Harasiis women were encouraged to produce these keyrings for sale in the capital, Muscat, 500 kilometres away. At first the number of women producing the keyring holders was no more than half a dozen. But sales soared and by 1990 there were 42 women making keyrings for two shops in the capital area. The turnover was nearly 2,000 units a year. The women were excited and wanted this venture to become something meaningful. Talk began to circulate that the government was going to open a centre for them at Haima, where they would be able to meet, to rest, or just visit with each other – just as the men already did in the reception room of the local governor. With this enthusiasm, I proposed to the women (and some husbands) that this informal cooperative working group be incorporated into a non-government association so that a request could be made to an international agency for a grant to upgrade the whole operation into a viable business managing its own marketing and book-keeping and running a revolving fund. Income from this activity would substantially boost the spending power of the women producers, in many cases allowing for the purchase of needed comestibles and in a few cases adding to the private wealth of the women. This suggestion was greeted with enthusiasm by the community as a whole. Harasiis men and women were taken with the idea of creating a viable, productive, modern commercial activity in the desert. The process of getting the group recognized by the government as an association was set into motion. Harasiis men supported wives, sisters and daughters by bringing them into the governor's office for fingerprinting and two husbands further cooperated by agreeing to sign on as officers of the association (a few of the men were literate, but none of the women). The paperwork, the drafting of by-laws and a constitution along with the fingerprinting of all the members were completed and the documentation was submitted to the Ministry of Social Affairs for approval shortly thereafter.

During this same period of time, I became aware that the UNDP offered grants for just such types of community effort under their 'Peoples' Participation Programme'. I submitted a grant proposal for £40,000 for a period of one year to set this group of women up as a self-help cooperative. The underlying assumption for all concerned was that once the project got off the ground, producing women would be able to earn in the region of £100 a month – not a substantial sum, but certainly a great improvement over their present conditions. The grant was approved in a very short period of time and all that was required was the government's rubber stamp on the documents recognizing these women as an Omani non-government association. One delay after another arose. I held talks with government legal advisors. I changed by-laws and altered the paper work as per advice from knowledgeable quarters. Still nothing happened. Finally after eighteen months of waiting and with the approval of a second grant request for £80,000 from the USAID, I sought a definitive explanation for the delay. It was obvious that the government was not going to recognize this informal collective of women as a legal entity. Without that recognition, it could not receive the two grants made to it from international non-government organizations. The unofficial, but reliable, explanation I received from a very senior level official was that the government felt these illiterate, nomadic pastoral women were like children. They needed to be supervised by the government, as a child is supervised by its father. They were simply not modern or civilized enough to accept the responsibility of being a formal association. They were vulnerable to exploitation and thus it was the government's duty to protect them. The ministry would look after them in its own way, and at the right time would set up and run a craft type income-generating activity for them but directed by men in government. With no hope of receiving official recognition, I withdrew the grant requests. But bureaucracy is not easily shut off. The £80,000 had already been allocated for this project and could not be returned. A way of using the money had to be found. A number of alternative ways of circumventing the formalization of NGO status were attempted to no avail. The Ministry of Social Affairs and Labour then tried to put forward its own proposal for taking over the funds, suggesting that it would incorporate the Harasiis nomadic pastoralists into its own on-going village community development work. This government proposal was not found to be a feasible plan and two years later the award intended for the Harasiis women's income-generating cooperative lies in a bureaucratic limbo.

Issues and Constraints

In Oman, like most of the modern nation-states of the Middle East, women have been and continue to be manipulated to symbolically represent the cultural integrity of the dominant culture in the country. Women are perceived first and foremost as wives and mothers, and gender segregation is customary. To earn status women must marry and reproduce. Their husbands control their ability to work or travel and hold unilateral right of divorce. Children belong to the husband's family and may be lost to the mother upon divorce. Family honour and good reputation – or the reverse, shame – rests mainly on the public behaviour of women, thereby reinforcing the high degree of sex segregation in the society. This is often greatly at odds with the realities of women's lives and aspirations. The individual woman though, by careful manipulation of her gender relations, often succeeds in circumventing or casting aside the culturally accepted bonds which diminish her life.

When, however, *women form groups* there appears to be little scope for interpretation. Women in formal groups are only acceptable when they conform to the cultural ideals established by the state. Hence in many countries of the Middle East, including Oman, women are only permitted to form groups which are charitable organizations concerned with the welfare of the disabled or handicapped. Any other forms of association – including self-help groups, income-generating cooperatives, and professional, skilled volunteer teams are often prohibited by law. Clearly when women organize themselves into groups they are perceived as a threat to the male dominated power structure of the state. What is this threat? Is it the actual act of being formally organized that is threatening? Does Islam – a religion so often poorly understood by Westerners – have a role to play here? Is this threat simply a gender based conflict of Arab cultural expectations and norms? Or has there been a transference of Western male ideology in the forming and running of the modern Arab nation? And finally, is it a more complex phenomenon which lies in the very nature of civil society and community self-help? Do issues of democracy or community consensus play a role in explaining this situation?

The purpose of this book is to explore the multiplicity of issues and constraints that women face when trying to organize themselves in the Middle East. The issues touched upon above, as well as others, will be addressed, analysed and interpreted in various ways by the contributors. The book presents no homogenous uniform view on the historical, current and future possibilities of Middle Eastern women's groups. But while questions, modes of analysis and possible answers differ from chapter to chapter, all authors are united in their commitment to present women in the Middle East as active agents. Asian, Latin American and African women's groups are fairly well documented, compared to those in the Middle East (see Rowbotham and Mitter 1994). Hence another purpose of this book is to document case studies from the Middle East showing that despite constraints women do form groups or act collectively for their interests.

Groups and Categories

A group can be understood as a collection of individuals who interact with each other on a regular basis thereby shaping the identities each form of themselves and of others in the group. Sociologists and anthropologists usually differentiate between social groups and social categories. While the latter is a culturally relevant conceptual entity, the former is comprised of people who themselves have some kind of common identity. A social category is constructed by an observer by choosing characteristics relevant for her or his purpose. 'Middle Eastern women' is a social category where the observer lumps people together according to the characteristics of sex and geographic background. A social group, on the other hand, would be constituted by people who see themselves and act as though sharing some sort of common identity. Social groups are often categorized by social scientists as primary or secondary. In primary groups, such as families, or members of a household, there is, in principle, face-to-face interaction between all the members. In secondary groups most members are linked to each other through more complex organizational relationships. Groups can be classified as formal or informal. The difference between the two is not always easy to determine. A formal group is usually perceived by social scientists to be fairly stable over time. An informal group, in contrast, is seen as less stable with few or no stated rules. From the point of view of the members, however, membership may be felt as exceedingly binding. Groups may also be classified as single- or multi-purpose groups. Again distinctions are not always easy to make. What may be started as a single purpose group (e.g. a support club to a soccer team) may, in fact, fulfil many purposes.

It is important, but difficult, for researchers to maintain a conceptual distinction between a social category and a social group. In our contemporary world, social categories (like 'Middle Eastern women') are often treated by outsiders as social groups with a presumed common identity. Social science researchers must not take categorizations at their face value and treat them as social groups. As human beings we all categorize and classify the world around us. A range of categorizations used in and on Middle Eastern societies are brought out in this volume. Al-Mughni and Al-Ali, for example, explore debates about women in Kuwait and Egypt. They stress how the category of 'Western women' is used by social groups in these countries as a tool for self-identity as well as an instrument by dominant male groups to shape women's social action. Hence there is an exceedingly complex relation between how human beings categorize others and how individuals form groups and for what purposes. Today the world is globally interconnected in new and different ways, and the scope of links between people without face-to-face interaction has dramatically increased. Concomitantly and to an increasing degree, social categories are coming to form and to regard themselves as social groups. Associations and organizations, furthermore, can be formed by outsiders for a collection of individuals. These individuals, initially perhaps without a sense of collectivity, common identity, or action, may develop into a social group once they begin to interact. The difference between a social category and a social group and the real development of groups from categories is a useful research tool for analysing the proliferation of formal and informal groups in the contemporary world. It also helps us to focus our inquiries and analyse the wider social context of group formation processes.

Women, Groups and Development

Third World women and the concept of development have, since the 1970s and the United Nations Decade for Women, become interlinked. The UN effort, in particular, gave recognition to female efforts and put the limelight on what were perceived to be special women's problems in development. This effort also gave opportunities to women from the Third World to speak on their own behalf. The decade opened up a sometimes heated debate between Western feminists and Third World feminists (a theme running through Al-Ali's chapter). In this period Western intellectual complacency was seriously challenged. Who had the right to speak on behalf of whom became not just an academic issue, but one which also involved a great number of special women's development projects. Hence, it involved both political power and financial resources. Women were thrown into the global world of development as practitioners, as writers and as objects to be developed.

Women in the Third World were singled out as a social category and proclaimed (by men and women) to be in need of special development efforts. At the same time women were regarded by international and national development agencies as an untapped resource for development. Thus, women were considered to be in need of development, a development problem as well as a solution to development issues, often all at the same time (Rabo 1996a).

Through the 1970s and 1980s the shifts in development vocabularies have been many. In turn such concepts as *growth, social development, alternative development, integrated development and sustainable development* have riddled development debate. Concepts such as *production, basic needs, people's participation, and structural adjustment* have been used as both catch-words and solutions for all major Third World difficulties (Sachs 1992, Evers Rosander 1992). Today we find that macroeconomists lean heavily on *the market* as a metaphor for development. The market will do what purposeful politics cannot do. The market will bring order, welfare and happiness, if not to all, at least to those who deserve it. Other social scientists instead push forward formal and informal groups and insist that development must always be promoted from the bottom up. Formal and informal groups were seen, in this perspective, to constitute both economic and political potential. By promoting and supporting such groups, economic welfare and political democracy could be firmly linked together. Propagators of such a 'bottom-up' policy for women in development began to search for groups. Previously unnoticed, these women's groups came to be seen to exhibit remarkable activity and economic potential. In this newly uncovered territory, researchers, politicians and development experts saw women as prominent actors. Women did all sorts of marvellous things like help each other in agriculture, in pastoral activities, in urban households and in business. Women could hence be targeted for special programmes and informal groups could be made into those which were more formal. Women could be selected to form groups with the support of outsiders.

There are several possible explanations why Middle Eastern women's groups are less well documented than groups in other regions. In India, for example, the prevalence and documentation of such groups can be seen as a result of the extreme poverty of many women. Some of these efforts provide women with small loans to set up businesses with which to support their families (e.g. the Grameen Bank in Bangladesh, SEWA, the Self-Employed Women's Association in India), while others give women the means to improve their skills, their diet and the health of their families (e.g. COVAC, a group of cooperatives in Mexico, and PCRW, Production, Credit for Rural Women in Nepal). In nearly the whole of the developing world, women are turning to each other for strength, support, training and ideas to improve their lives. If women do not take their destiny and that of their families into their own hands, they will simply not survive as pointed out by Evers Rosander in her chapter analysing the differences between women in Senegal and Morocco. Women in some contexts and in some countries also find it easier to organize themselves formally and informally. These cooperatives, associations and self-help groups exist in nation-states under many types of regimes. Some are monarchies, some dictatorships, others elected republican forms of government. As a whole these programmes present no threat to the state apparatus and their successes are regularly reported in development publications (e.g. International Institute of Environment and Development Sustainable Agriculture Programme). The formal political democracy of India serves as a good example.

In some countries and some contexts, alliances between women across linguistic, educational and economic barriers are also more prevalent. Yet in other regions, the very lack of any functioning formal political and economic system has opened up creative opportunities for women's informal groups, as shown by Evers Rosander in this volume. Thus a prevalence of women's groups – formal and informal – can be a healthy sign. Or it can be an indicator of extreme stress, poverty, or oppression.

What stands out most clearly is that from the 1960s until the end of the 1980s there has been a rupture in the unified global theorizing about formal and informal groups and their links to social change. We are now faced with the great challenge of trying to analyse formal and informal groups in a more global perspective and we need to 'explain the influence of local and large-scale context on each other' (Wright 1994: 16). The study of groups today entails the analysis of both discourses and social action. Important areas for empirical study include examining how social categories are talked about, and how groups are formed – voluntarily, by force, or spontaneously – through a discourse of 'us' and 'them'. We also need to analyse how activities, both directly and indirectly linked to the goals and aims of the groups studied, shape and reshape individual and collective identities. The articles in this volume are examples of both these perspectives on the study of groups. They raise a number of provocative questions which Lindisfarne's closing paper, written after reading all the chapters in the collection, takes up and discusses in the context of future lines of inquiry.

Middle Eastern Women's Groups

Middle Eastern women's groups are not, as noted above, nearly as well documented as in the rest of the world. There are several reasons for this. The UN Decade for Women resulted in women being given a role of their own to play in development. But it also resulted in a more systematic appropriation of women as symbols of the development of the whole of their societies. The Middle East as a region has not been as welcoming to First World initiated women's projects (Rabo 1996a). Many of these state apparatuses have been able to fend off close international attention. The oil-rich countries have had no need for international economic aid. Colonial relations between Europe and the Middle East also differ from those between Sub-Saharan Africa and Europe. There is, as Al-Ali stresses in her chapter, a great deal of antagonism between the Middle East and the West where the latter sees men from the Middle East as suppressing and secluding their women, and where the Middle Easterner underlines the immorality of women in the West. This conflict is one reason why women in the Middle East do not get international attention when organized in groups. As international aid to the region is limited, Middle Eastern women are not regarded as part of the international or Western discourse of 'groups'. They are instead part of a discourse on suppression and authenticity. Another reason for the lack of comparable document-ation on organized women's groups in the Middle East is that a great many of the formal ones are politically controlled. Many women's groups and organizations are state run, or owned by political parties or religious organizations (see for example, al-Mughni, Joseph, Seikaly, and El-Baz in this volume). They are either difficult to study or not really taken seriously by most researchers. In general, such organizations are felt to be too dependent on the male controlled power structure and not to merit a study on their own. And finally the lack of documentation in the Middle East can be seen as a side effect of fear. Many formal and informal groups operate under clandestine conditions, fearing that too much publicity would result in their closure or suppression (see El-Baz in this volume). Thus these groups often do not want their work to be known outside of a very small circle. Palestinian women's groups are an exception, for although many are branches of the organizing authority of the movement, Palestinian women have themselves fought for their own self-expression and this has been well documented (e.g. Peteet 1991; Sayigh 1994). We feel that, although Middle Eastern women do face great constraints when forming both formal and informal groups, the articles in these volumes clearly underline that constraints in women's daily lives are also an impetus for forming groups.

Islam

Does Islam – a religion poorly understood by Westerners – have a role to play in understanding the relative paucity of women's groups in the Middle East? A view commonly held, and often loudly proclaimed in the West, is that women's legal status and social position in Muslim countries are worse than anywhere else. We cannot, however, understand women's roles and status in the region only in terms of religion. The position of women in the Middle East cannot be attributed to the presumed intrinsic properties of Islam (see, for example, Moghadam 1993). Islam is neither more nor less patriarchal than other major religions, such as Hinduism, Judaism and Christianity, all of which share the view of woman as wife and mother.[2]

Feminists in the Arab world have gone to great lengths to separate Islam out from the patriarchal forms of social organization which have been a part of the heritage of the Middle East and the Mediterranean Rim for millennia. Their works (e.g. Ahmed 1992; Kandiyoti 1991; Badran 1995; Hatem 1986) clearly show that gender asymmetry and the status of women in the Muslim world cannot be attributed to Islam. Hence their struggle is not with religion, but with the underlying forms of social organization and its development over the centuries. The institution of veiling and segregation of women is one example of a social complex incorrectly associated with Islam. Strong evidence exists that face veiling was pre-

Islamic in origin and was used among the people of the southern Mediterranean Rim (Ahmed 1982, 1992). Historical accounts point to the fact that women just prior to and in the early days of Islam in Arabia played an active role in the social and political life of the community (Ahmed 1992) and studies of the Quran and the Hadith show that there is no particular injunction stipulating that women should be veiled or secluded from participation in public life (Abdel Kader 1984). It was only in the century after Muhammad's death that the system of veiling and seclusion came to be accepted (Ahmed 1992). Seclusion was the practice of confining women, after puberty, to their own company. Veiling, the wearing of a head and face cover in public, was the symbolic expression of that seclusion. It was an urban phenomenon as only the wealthy merchant and ruling families could afford a system where women were regarded as property, a wealth to be hidden away and kept for private pleasure and viewing. The majority of the population – the working classes, and the rural, agrarian population – could not put either veiling or seclusion into practice. They needed the women to work in order to contribute to the economic survival of the family.

By the eighteenth century, when the Middle East became increasingly dominated economically by the West, veiling came to be more than a symbolic statement of economic or political status. It took on the representation of purity and virginity. Prior to the eighteenth century, the majority of veiled women were upper class, mainly Turco-Circassian and Ethiopian, slaves and concubines. During this period, increasing numbers of prosperous middle-class households began to seclude and veil their women. For the Turco-Circassian and Ethiopian slaves seclusion and veiling had been a statement of their status as valuable property of men. But when veiling was extended to free middle-class women it was given an entirely different rationale. Whereas virginity had not been particularly important in the decision to marry or purchase a slave, it became a central concern in marriages of free (middle-class) women. Veiling, seclusion and restricted physical movement were the expression of male fears that women's chastity might be endangered – and with it the family honour.

Islam and the Colonial Narrative

By the close of the nineteenth century, the veil took on a further political dimension with the French, and then British, encounters in the Arab world. By 1892, the British occupation of Egypt had commenced. A new upper class educated in Western-type schools became the civil servants and intellectual elite. These modern men displaced the traditionally and religiously trained *ulamas* as administrators and civil servants. This new male elite began to advocate reforms of laws for women as well as the ultimate symbolic act, the abolition of the veil. The ensuing debate constituted an important moment in history. A new interpretation was coming into being in which the veil came to encompass far broader issues than merely the position of women. It now included among other conflicts, that between the colonized and the colonizers. The colonial authority's position (as expressed by Lord Cromer) was that Islam innately oppressed women, and that the veil and segregation epitomized that oppression. Only by removing the veil and changing the position of women in Islam could Egyptians be persuaded into imbibing the true spirit of Western civilization (Ahmed 1992: 153).

This colonial narrative on women and Islam became the focus of the nation and, beginning in the twentieth century, several responses arose. There was the modern intellectual approach (liberation of women through the removal of their veils and the reform of marriage and divorce laws). Then there was the nationalist conservative response which defended and upheld Islamic practices and insisted that women must veil. Eventually the veil came to symbolize the colonial resistance movement, not the inferiority of culture and the need to cast aside its customs in favour of those of the West. In the end those customs that had come under fiercest colonial attack – customs relating to women – were tenaciously affirmed by the nationalists as a means of resisting Western domination. By the second half of the twentieth century a third ideological orientation arose often in opposition to the government in power – the Islamic fundamentalists. Like the conservatives, they emphasized woman's natural domesticity, and glorified the status awarded to her in Islam, predicting certain doom if she deserted her traditional place in society (Stowasser 1993: 1–28). By the end of the twentieth century, women, their place in society, and Islam had become inextricably interwoven in the political discourses within the Middle East. This is amply illustrated in many of the chapters of this book.

Women, Men and Modern States

Informal Middle Eastern women's groups are often regarded as threatening to the state apparatus. Is this threat simply a gender based conflict of Arab cultural expectations and norms? Or has there been a transference of Western male ideology in the forming and running of the modern Arab nation? Middle Eastern societies can be classified as patrilineal and patriarchal. Polygamy is not illegal in most countries. Hence it can be argued that Middle Eastern states, in general, represent male interests. But the issue is clearly highly complex. Western industrialized society is also organized on patrilineal principles (cf Rogers 1980). Children are identified as belonging to their father's line. Residence at marriage is nearly always determined by husband's interest or work. Women are classified as 'dependants' of their husbands (especially in financial terms). And the work sphere is highly segregated. Enormous emphasis is placed on the exclusive role of the biological mother in nurturing infants and children which is closely linked with the identification of women's place in the domestic sphere. Even when a woman holds a second, salaried job outside the home, her primary occupation is considered the home. Women and the unpaid domestic or subsistence sector are separated out of the modern economy which assigns the central role of paid work to men. And finally, when women do work outside the home 'maternal deprivation' is alleged to be suffered by children. This last theory (Bowlby 1965) received massive support after the Second World War when women needed to be shifted out of the workforce to make way for returning soldiers. It is still current today and no amount of dissent from anthropologists and feminists seems to stem its popularity.

We contend that women all over the world suffered when Western ideas of gender relations were transmitted to the Third World. First it was an integral part of 'colonial rule' where male hierarchies were used for direct and indirect rule while female hierarchies atrophied (Charrad 1990; Mabro 1991). Part of the colonial narrative was the assumed inferiority of all other cultures and societies. Appended to this discourse was the language of feminism which was developing in Europe at that time. Part of this scheme was the Victorian theory of the biological inferiority of women and the Victorian ideal of the female role of domesticity. At home the Victorian male establishment derided and rejected the ideas of feminism and the notion of men's oppression of women. But overseas, in the colonies, the idea that other men were oppressing women was used as a kind of rhetoric to morally justify the project of stamping out the cultures of colonized peoples. This is nowhere more clear than in the Middle East, where Lord Cromer expressed strong views on the way in which Islam degraded women. Yet he proceeded to place restrictions on women's education in the colonies (for example, downgrading an existing women's medical college to one teaching only midwifery).[3]

New colonial institutions – army, police, civil service, political parties, schools, banks, were built up of male nationals. And much of the Western ideology of male supremacy apparently passed on intact from the Western man to his local counterparts. With the close of the colonial era and the period of independent nation statehood, this male-focused ideology became a silent element in the transfer of development assistance and technology in the second half of the twentieth century. There has been a steady development of a gendered *voice* in development policies and some plans. *Actual* practices, however, most clearly reflect the Western male ideology first exported during colonial rule and later in the post Second World War period.[4]

The Nature of Civil Society, Kinship and Community Self-help

Throughout the 1980s there was a dramatic emergence of non-governmental women's groups and organizations in the region.[5] With the encouragement of the United Nations Decade for Women (UNIFEM), there was a flurry of new activity organized around the needs of women as discussed by Moghadam in her chapter in this volume. But again these activities were in association with governmental agencies, especially ministries of social affairs, which have always held very traditional and conservative views of the needs of women. Those that challenged the male patriarchal organization of society were harassed and sometimes banned (e.g. the Arab Women's Solidarity Association in Egypt in 1991).

In trying to understand the nature of the threat with which women organizing themselves into groups are perceived we must ask whether we need to look at a more complex phenomenon which lies in the very nature of civil society and community/self-help. In the Middle East, civil society is not an organizing principle for managing or controlling groups. The family, the kin group and finally the tribe are the organizing units with other cross-cutting associations often regarded as undermining (see Joseph 1993, 1994). The voice of the individual is not important to the tribe or the kin group but it is of critical concern in civil society based on common interest groups. Organized groups, whether male or female, are regarded as threatening to the mainly oligarchic and monarchic states of the Middle East where the head of the nation is regarded as the supra-tribal leader or head of the nation family. Hence organized groups are very carefully controlled and monitored. Men are permitted sports clubs, graduate clubs, and some cultural associations; while women are generally restricted to charitable organizations in aid of the disabled or handicapped. Until very recently handicapped, disabled and mentally ill family members were kept hidden away in the bosom of the family and cared for by its womenfolk. Thus in a society where civil consensus is unimportant, where the individual voice is insignificant, where associations that cut across kin groups and tribes are feared, women who are organized in groups are considered a threat to existing institutions.

The Middle East is extremely heterogeneous. The lives of women in and from the region differ drastically in terms of access to economic and political resources and in terms of how they view themselves and are viewed by others. In all this variety, one theme seems fairly constant. Women – more than men – are enmeshed in bonds and obligations of kinship. Although men are the living symbols of agnatic ties, women are often responsible for expressing these sentiments. For most women in the Middle East 'groups of women' consist of females with whom one shares ties of kinship or affinity. In those rural areas where production is carried out within an almost exclusively kin-ordered environment, female groups obviously tend to coincide with kinship groups. But in many urban contexts, where women may work with unrelated women from many different backgrounds, kinship ties or ties expressed as kinship-like, become very important. The chapters by Evers Rosander and Joseph in this volume stress this. Many urban women in the Middle East are very poor but by setting up informal groups where members are related by kinship or affinity, they are able to help each other apart from male scrutiny. In most urban neighbourhoods informal groups emerge where women help each other on a more or less daily basis. Shami's detailed study of an upgraded quarter in Amman shows the high degree of interdependence women develop in such informal groups.

Concluding Remarks

In the last few years the issue of civil society has once again become a topic of great interest among researchers and politicians (e.g. Norton 1994; Schwedler 1995). These debates also concern issues of women organized in groups. Several aspects stand out. Firstly, civil society is often perceived to include only 'nice' voluntary associations outside of state control and repression. Secondly, civil society is regarded as gender neutral. Thirdly, 'public' and 'private' are treated as interchangeable economic or relational concepts without historical moorages (Rabo 1996b). These assumptions are both andro- and ethnocentric. We must look at the interdependencies between state and civil society. It must be stressed, that 'more' civil society does not automatically lead to democracy and development (cf. Fatton 1992: 6; Tostensen 1993; Hann 1996). It is impossible to know for certain what future developments are beneficial for women in general. The formation of some women's groups, whether formal or informal will give employment to educated and well-placed women. In other contexts an increasingly strong civil society will create opportunities for less well-to-do women to express and organize themselves for their mutual benefit. But there are grave risks that women in the Middle East will continue to be disadvantaged in this new emphasis on civil society. As long as women are seen to be exceptions to the male norm, they will be defined as 'different'. Women will continue to be singled out for special efforts in development geared towards their particular needs. From this point of view, greater efforts at organizing women will increase their dependence on the centres of power, whether these are national or international, civil or state run. Understanding the issues and constraints which women in formal and informal groups in the Middle East face is, nevertheless, one small step in the direction of helping them to control and manage their own lives.

Notes

1. See for example Ahmed 1992; Badran 1993, 1995; El Solh and Mabro 1994; Hatem 1986; Kandiyoti 1991; Moghadam 1993; Rowbotham and Mitter 1994; Tucker 1993; Yamani 1996.
2. Orthodox Jewish law of personal status, furthermore, bears many similarities to the fundamentals of Islamic laws, especially with respect to marriage and divorce.
3. Back in England his views on the subordination of women were most clearly expressed when he became the founding member of the Men's League For Opposing Women's Suffrage (see Rover 1967: 171–3).
4. This is clearly illustrated in the 1988 paper by Clare Oxby 'The Involvement of Agropastoralist Women in Livestock Programmes'. She writes, 'There is plenty of rhetoric within non-government organizations (NGOs) about the need to involve women in all their programmes, at every level of decision making, and at every stage in the process of programme design and imple-mentation. Some NGOs specifically mention agropastoral women in this respect but, despite the rhetoric, the impact so far in terms of carrying out interventions is meagre. If agropastoral women are involved at all, it is usually not in relation to animal production activities, but to other activities such as

primary health care, literacy and handicrafts. For example, a consultant's report in OXFAM's L'Affole Project, Mauritania, proposes project components for women, not in livestock related production activities, but in literacy, human health and improved stoves – even though it is clear from the same document that women play an important part in animal husbandry' (OXFAM, 1988, Mauritania: 24–7). The main exception is dairy projects. In Western eyes, milking and processing of milk is an acceptable even 'traditional' occupation for women.

5. These groups arose largely as a response to the discrediting of the official women's organizations of the 1960s and 1970s that had served as representatives of regime policies vis-à-vis women in countries like Jordan, Egypt, Tunisia, Syria and Iraq (Hatem 1993: 30).

References

Abdel Kader, S. (1984), 'A Survey of Trends in Social Science Research on Women in the Arab Region, 1960–1980,' in A. Rassam, ed., *Social Science Research and Women in the Arab World*, Paris: UNESCO.

Ahmed, L. (1982), 'Western Ethnocentrism and the Perceptions of the Harem,' in *Feminist Studies*, 8, 3: 521–34.

—— (1992), *Women and Gender in Islam: Historical Roots of a Modern Debate*, New Haven: Yale University Press.

Badran, M. (1993), 'Independent Women: More than a Century of Feminism in Egypt,' in J. Tucker, ed., *Arab Women: Old Boundaries New Frontiers*, Bloomington and Indianapolis: Indiana University Press.

—— (1995), *Feminists, Islam and Nation*, Princeton, New Jersey: Princeton University Press.

Bowlby, J. (1965), *Child Care and the Growth of Love*, Harmondsworth: Penguin.

Charrad, M. (1990), 'State and Gender in the Maghrib,' *Middle East Report*, 163: 19–23.

Chatty, D. (1984), Women's Component in Pastoral Community Assistance and Development, Sultanate of Oman: DTCD; New York: UNDP.

—— (1990), 'Tradition and Change Among the Pastoral Harasiis in Oman,' in M. Salem-Murdock, M. Horowitz, and M. Sella, eds, *Anthropology and Development in North Africa and the Middle East*, Boulder, San Francisco and Oxford: Westview Press.

—— (1996), *Mobile Pastoralists: Development Planning and Change among the Harasiis Tribe in Oman*, New York: Columbia University Press.

Dodd, P. (1973), 'Family Honour and the Forces of Change in Arab Society', in *International Journal of Middle East Studies*, 4: 40–54.

Eickelman, D. (1981),*The Middle East: An Anthropological Approach*, 2nd ed. 1989, Englewood Cliffs, New Jersey: Prentice Hall.

Evers Rosander, E. (1992), 'People's Participation as Rhetoric in Swedish Development Aid', in G. Dahl and A. Rabo, eds, *Kam-ap or Take-off: Local Notions of Development*, Stockholm: Almqvist and Wiksell.

Fatton, R. (1992), *Predatory Rules: State and Civil Society in Africa*, Boulder: Lynne Rienner.

El Guindi, F. (1981), 'Veiling Infitah with Muslim Ethics: Egypt's Contemporary Islamic Movement,' in *Social Problems,* 28, 4: 465–85.

Hann, C. (1996), 'Introduction: Political Society and Civil Anthropology,' in C. Hann and E. Dunn, eds, *Civil Society. Challenging Western Models*, London: Routledge

Hatem, M. (1986), 'The Enduring Alliance of Nationalism and Patriarchy in Muslim Personal Status Laws: the Case of Modern Egypt,' in *Feminist Issues*, Spring, 19–43.

Jones, L. (1987), 'Perceptions of "Peace Women" at Greenham Common 1981–1985,' in S. Macdonald, P. Holden, and S. Ardener, eds, *Images of Women in Peace and War*, London: Macmillan.

Joseph, S. (1993), 'Gender and Civil Society,' *Middle East Report*, 183: 22–6.

— (1994), *Gender and Family in the Arab World*, MERIP Publication.

Jowkar, F. (1986), 'Honor and Shame: a Feminist View from Within,' in *Feminist Issues,* Spring, 44–65.

Kandiyoti, D., ed. (1991), *Women, Islam and the State*, London: Macmillan.

Lancaster, W. (1981), *The Rwala Bedouin Today*, Cambridge: Cambridge University Press.

Mabro, J. (1991), *Veiled Half-Truths*, London: I.B. Tauris.

Marsot, A. (1978), 'The Revolutionary Gentlewomen in Egypt,' in L. Beck and N. Keddie, eds, *Women in the Muslim World*, Cambridge, Mass.: Harvard University Press.

Moghadam, V. (1993), *Modernizing Women: Gender and Social Change in the Middle East*, London and Boulder: Lynne Rienner Publishers.

al-Mughni, H. (1993), *Women in Kuwait: The Politics of Gender*, London: Al-Saqi Books.

Norton, A.R., ed. (1994), *Civil Society in the Middle East*, Leiden: E. J. Brill.

Oxby, C. (1991), 'The Involvement of Agropastoralist Women in Livestock Programmes,' in T. Wallace and C. March, eds, *Changing Perceptions: Writings on Gender and Development*, Oxford: Oxfam.

Oxfam (1988), 'Les femmes dans l'Affole (Mauritanie),' Oxfam Consultant's Report.

Peteet, J. (1991), *Gender in Crisis: Women and the Palestinian Resistance Movement*, New York: Columbia University Press.

Rabo, A. (1996a), 'Beyond the Veil: Gender, State and Development in Jordan and Syria,' forthcoming in S. Goodman and D. Mulinari, eds, *Women and*

Power: Research on Gender Issues in the Third World, Lund: Kvinnovetenskapligt Forum.

—— (1996b), 'Gender, State and Civil Society in Jordan and Syria,' in C. Hann and E. Dunn, eds, *Civil Society. Challenging Western Models*, London: Routledge.

Rogers, B. (1980), *The Domestication of Women: Discrimination in Developing Societies*, reprinted 1989, London: Routledge.

Rover, C. (1967), *Women's Suffrage and Party Politics in Britain, 1866–1914*, London: Routledge and Kegan Paul.

Rowbotham, S. and Mitter, S. (1994), *Dignity and Daily Bread*, London: Routledge.

Sachs, W., ed. (1992), *The Development Dictionary: A Guide to Knowledge as Power*, London: Zed Books.

Sayigh, R. (1994), *Too Many Enemies: The Palestinian Experience in Lebanon*, London: Zed Books.

Schwedler, J., ed. (1995), *Towards Civil Society in the Middle East?*, Boulder: Lynne Rienner Publishers.

Shaaban, B. (1988), *Both Right and Left Handed: Arab Women Talk About Their Lives*, Bloomington and Indianapolis: Indiana University Press.

El-Solh, C. and Mabro, J. (1994), 'Introduction: Islam and Muslim Women,' in *Muslim Women's Choices*, Oxford: Berg Publishers.

Stowasser, B. (1993), 'Women's Issues in Modern Islamic Thought,' in J. Tucker, ed., *Arab Women: Old Boundaries New Frontiers*, Bloomington and Indianapolis: Indiana University Press.

Tostensen, A. (1993), 'The Ambiguity of Civil Society in the Democratisation Process,' in A. Ofstad and A. Wiig, eds, *Development Theory: Recent Trends*, Bergen: Chr. Michelsen Institute.

Wright, S., ed. (1994), *Anthropology of Organizations*, London: Routledge.

Yamani, M., ed. (1996), *Feminism and Islam: Legal and Literary Perspectives*, London: Ithaca Press.

2

Women's NGOs in the Middle East and North Africa: Constraints, Opportunities, and Priorities

Valentine M. Moghadam

Research is proliferating on democratization and development in the Middle East, with many conferences and publications now devoted to issues such as the emergence of civil society, economic restructuring, and strategies for socio-economic revitalization in the region (see Norton 1993; Al-Sayyid 1993; Ibrahim 1993). In Cairo, the Economic Research Forum (which studies Arab countries, Iran, and Turkey, with funding from the World Bank), has organized a number of research conferences on structural adjustment, labour markets, the role of the state, financial markets, and so on.

The International Conference on Population and Development (ICPD), which took place in Cairo in September 1994, drew attention to the large numbers of Arab and especially Egyptian non-governmental organizations (NGOs). One especially interesting document, prepared by Palestinian NGOs for the ICPD NGO Forum, was entitled 'Palestinian Population Policies and Sustainable Development'; it emphasized the link between population policies and the role of NGOs, especially women's NGOs, and stressed the contributions of the Palestinian Women's Movement.[1] More recently, preparations for the Fourth World Conference on Women, which took place in Beijing in September 1995, raised further interest in the role and activities of women's NGOs in the region.

The focus of this chapter is the emergence of women's non-governmental organizations in the Middle East and North Africa, the legal and other constraints that they face, the issues to which they are orientated, and the articulation of these issues and concerns in the NGO document, 'Work Approach for the Non Government Organizations in the Arab Region', prepared in Amman in November 1994 in the context of preparations for the Beijing Conference.[2] The chapter comes in three parts. Part I discusses some of the factors behind the formation and spread of women's organizations in the region. Part 2 begins with a typology of women's NGOs in the region, and is followed by a discussion of their opportunities for growth, as well as the various constraints they face. Part 3 examines the NGO document prepared in Amman in November 1994 as a way to determine the prioritized concerns of the women's NGOs, including their articulation of the regional situation, the problems women face, and solutions to those problems. The primary focus of this paper is on the Arab countries of the region. The scope of the women's organizations includes charitable societies, professional associations, development-oriented NGOs, and feminist groups.

The Emergence and Spread of Women's Organizations

Chafetz and Dworkin (1986) in a comparative and historical study of women's movements worldwide which was completed in the mid-1980s, stated that 'independent women's movements are totally absent' in the Middle East and North Africa (p. 191). This is surprising for two reasons. First, they ignored the continuity of women's organizations in Egypt, as well as the interesting fact that the very first protest against the new revolutionary Islamic regime in Iran was carried out in March 1979 by women reacting to efforts to impose veiling. Second, Chafetz and Dworkin's explanation for the rise of women's movements centres on the expansion of female education – a process that was in full swing in the Middle East during the 1970s and 1980s. Stereotypical thinking about women in the Middle East and assumptions about their status are fairly common, and perhaps for this reason, the authors missed the opportunity to notice the dramatic rise of audacious and decidedly independent feminist groups in Algeria, who were protesting against the first draft of a very conservative Family Code in 1984.

In fact, during the 1970s and 1980s women's organizations – whether tied to political parties or independently feminist – were emerging in many countries of the region. Proposed changes to Egypt's Family Law in 1979 brought about considerable activity (Badran 1994). Moroccan, Tunisian, and Egyptian women activists and intellectuals were travelling to meet each other. In Tunisia, the feminist magazine *Nissa* was formed, the product of several years' efforts. In 1985 a broadly-based Arab Women's Solidarity Association (AWSA) was formed, headed by the well-known Egyptian writer Nawal Saadawi, in part to protect and improve Egypt's Family Law, and in part to articulate women's other problems.

At the same time, the region is home to numerous women's associations and societies that are essentially charitable in nature, providing relief, some training, and welfare for poor and rural women. The General Union of Palestinian Women, for example, has since 1965 devoted itself to charitable, social work, and nationalist endeavours. Philanthropic and charitable activity by middle-class and elite women (and men) has a long history, not only in the Middle East, but throughout the world. In the Middle East, these associations have existed since at least the 1920s, and it may be possible to view them as having legitimized a social role for women and thus prepared the way for more radical women's groups, with whom they now exist side-by-side.

In more recent years, the Middle East and North Africa (MENA) has seen the rise of numerous NGOs and PVOs (private voluntary organizations) dealing with development-related issues, provision of social services, human rights, and women's concerns. I am using the term 'NGO' broadly to describe the various organizations that have emerged outside the purview of the state – although some may have links to state agencies and of course all have to be registered under varying regulatory codes. The NGOs discussed in this paper include the numerous private voluntary associations (PVOs) that exist in Arab countries and organizations which are not directly involved in development efforts, such as human rights and women's rights organizations. Egypt has the largest number of NGOs (13,239 in 1991), of which 31.4 per cent are of a charitable nature, followed by Tunisia, with 5,186 NGOs in 1993, of which only 9.8 per cent were charitable PVOs in 1993 (Kandil 1995: 61).

The expansion of NGOs in the region is partly a function of a global trend that gained momentum in the 1980s, when donor governments and multilateral funding agencies embraced non-governmental organizations as partners in development (Edwards & Hulme 1992). At the same time, there has been a significant change in the development agenda away from a preoccupation with economic issues towards an emphasis on political and institutional problems. Human rights, good governance, participation, the environment, and gender issues have thus gained prominence. For the Middle East, this encouraged the formation of numerous NGOs that reflect both the emergence of a civil society and the new development agenda. Particularly noteworthy is the proliferation of human rights organizations and of women's organizations (Dwyer 1991; Hiltermann 1991). Although NGOs dealing with women's rights or women-in-development issues are still relatively few in number, their existence is especially significant in that they accord a recognized role for women in the development process *and* they represent changing state-society relations and definitions of citizenship. What explains the expansion of women's organizations? In the next section we consider demographic, economic, political, and international factors.

Demographic Changes

With the growth of an educated female population and the entry of women into paid labour, Middle Eastern women are now visible and vocal in public spaces that were historically the province of men. Urbanization, education and employment have had dramatic effects on the status and activities of women. These have had other important effects, including changes to the structure of the family, changing perceptions and images of women, and reaction on the part of conservative and Islamist elements (for a full discussion see Moghadam 1993 especially Chapters 4 & 5).

Increasingly large populations are now concentrated in cities, and this creates pressures for social services as well as opportunities for action. Women's enrolments at the secondary and tertiary levels of education have increased such that in some countries they represent a majority. And although the labour-force participation rates of women in the MENA region are still low in comparison with other regions, women are making headway in salaried employment. The age of first marriage for women is rising, and family size is decreasing for educated and employed women. (See Tables 1 and 2) Such demographic changes are giving these 'modernizing women' more time for other public activities, and allowing them to make demands such as the following: 'Special legislation and effective means to enforce these legislations must be developed to regulate and enforce the implementation of a minimum age of marriage – 18 years – to guarantee the rights of women within marriage, and their rights in cases of rape, abortion, family violence of all sorts, and other harmful and inhumane traditional practices against women' (Palestinian NGO paper 1994).

Economic Factors

The reduction of public spending in the areas of health, education, and social welfare, and state failures in areas such as female illiteracy, reproductive health, and legal reforms, have spurred non-governmental organizations into action and focused women's attentions on the links between development and status-of-women issues.

The 'Third World state' is shrinking in size and economic capacity

Table 1. Education indicators

	Adult literacy rate (% 15+)			Mean years of schooling (25+)			Secondary school enrollment % female		University enrollment % female	
	Total 1990	Male 1990	Female 1990	Total 1990	Male 1990	Female 1990	1980	1990	1980	1990
Algeria	57	70	46	2.6	4.4	0.8	39	43	26	–
Egypt	48	63	34	2.8	3.9	1.6	37	44	32	37
Iran	65	75	56	4.0			38	27	–	
Iraq	60	70	49	4.8	5.7	3.9	45	48	41	42
Jordan	80	89	70	5.0	6.0	4.0			36	39
Lebanon	80	88	73	4.4	5.3	3.5			25	
Libya	64	75	50	3.4	5.5	1.3	40	40	25	37
Morocco	50	61	38	2.8	4.1	1.5	38		30	47
Oman	–	–	–	0.9	1.4	0.3	24			46
Saudi Arabia	62	73	48	3.7	5.9	1.5	38	42	29	33
Syria	65	78	51	4.2	5.2	3.1		41	27	39
Tunisia	65	74	56	2.1	3.0	1.2	37	43	30	
Turkey	81	91	71	4.0						
United Arab Emirates	78	78	78	5.1	5.1	5.2	45	50	46	71
Yemen	39	53	26	0.8	1.3	0.2	21		31.5	42 (PDRY)

Sources: UNDP, *Human Development Report 1992, 1996*; UNESCO, *Education for All: Status and Trends 1994*, p. 23.

Table 2. Employment

	Labour force (as % of total population) 1990–92	Women in labour force (as % of total labour force) 1990–92	Evolution in the number of women in salaried employment 1970s–1990s		
Algeria	23.6	4.4	126,386 (1977)	523,000 (1985)	661,000 (1992)
Bahrain	45.0	10.0	14,349 (1981)*	43,531 (1991)*	
Egypt	31.0	21.0	568,520 (1976)	995,581 (1986)	1,528,500 (1990)
Iran	26.0	11.0	568,064 (1976)	504,582 (1986)	1,200,000 (1991)
Iraq	24.2	22.0	149,182 (1977)	333,233 (1987)	
Jordan	23.1	9.9	28,001 (1979)*	90,329 (1991)	
Kuwait	39.0	14.0	34,649 (1975)	61,845 (1980)	129,137 (1985)*
Lebanon	30.1	27.2			
Libya	23.7	8.7	20,967 (1973)		
Morocco	33.0	26.0	428,935 (1982)	849,768 (1991)	
Oman	28.1	8.1			
Saudi Arabia	29.1	7.1	32,326 (1974)*		
Syria	28.0	18.0	63,216 (1970)*	106,952 (1981)	292,304 (1991)
Sudan	..	29.0	67,506 (1973)		
Tunisia	29.8	21.0	168,110 (1984)	494,300 (1989)	
Turkey	35.0	30.0	876,513 (1975)	1,072,481 (1985)	1,556,904 (1993)
UAE	49.8	6.2	9,229 (1975)	27,581 (1980)	64,301 (1985)
Yemen	24.7	13.1	36,794 (1986)**	29.804 (1988)**	

Sources: UNDP, *Human Development Report 1994*, pp. 162–163; ILO, *Yearbook of Labour Statistics, Retrospective Edition on Population Censuses 1945-86*, Table 2A; *Yearbook of Labour Statistics 1994*, Table 2A; ESCWA, *Arab Women in ESCWA Member States*, (1994); Cherifati-Merabtine (1995).

* Includes non-nationals.

** YAR

•• Indicates data not available.

due to the highly competitive environment of international trade and investment, decreases in foreign aid from the North, and structural adjustment policies of the International Monetary Fund (IMF) and the World Bank (Sood 1995). This shrinkage differs across regions and countries, but the MENA region has not been immune. Structural adjustment policies (SAPs) under World Bank and IMF auspices have been adopted by a number of countries (e.g., Turkey 1980, Morocco 1983, Tunisia 1986, Egypt 1990). The countries of the Middle East and North Africa also are shifting from an *étatist* development strategy based on import-substitution industrialization to economic liberalization and a strategy for export-led growth. They have initiated privatization of state-owned enterprises and liberalization of prices and trade, as well as efforts to reduce the power of trade unions and to tie wage increases to improvements in productivity. In Egypt, for example, a programme called ERSAP is intended to transform the economy from a state-dominated model with a small formal sector and large public sector to a decentralized, market-based, open, outward-oriented economy. The government plans to reduce civil service recruitment (the principal formal-sector employer of women), end the system of guaranteed jobs for graduates (through which the vast majority of Egyptian educated women found jobs), restructure and privatize public sector enterprises (among the very few industrial jobs that offer regular employment and benefits), and revise the labour law (which at present provides generous benefits for women in the public sector). The introduction of user fees in education and healthcare, and rising prices due to liberalization, necessitates non-governmental public action.[3]

NGOs therefore provide health, educational, and social services and are catering to the basic needs of local communities, thereby filling the gaps created by recent state economic policies. A few are also working to promote women-owned businesses and to prepare women for jobs in the private sector. The growth of NGOs and PVOs has accelerated in some MENA countries either because state services are non-existent (the cases of Palestine and Lebanon) or because of widespread (and in some cases, growing) poverty, and the inaccessibility of the poor to services that are increasingly privatized (Egypt, Jordan, Yemen). Many Third World governments with shrinking budgets are privatizing social welfare or delegating it to a combination of domestic, regional, and international NGOs, who in turn attract and use domestic and international resources. In Egypt, the numerous charitable PVOs that are run by Islamist organizations receive funding through Islamic *zakat*,[4] donations from financial institutions and Islamic banks, and by some rich businessmen who are strong supporters of Islamic movements (Kandil 1995: 73). About 3,000 mosques have annexed to their premises health centres which are staffed by part-time doctors who work on a voluntary basis or receive nominal fees (p.66). The Coptic Evangelical Organization for Social Services has had a long-standing presence in Upper Egypt, where it runs income-generating, family-planning, health, and literacy projects.[5]

Contrary to the stereotype of the rich Arab country, many of the countries report large proportions of their populations as living below the poverty line, and these include Algeria, Egypt, Morocco, and Yemen. Most countries allocate a small percentage of their revenue for health, larger amounts for education, and the largest amounts on military purchases. Military expenditures have consumed a large part of the government budget and have come increasingly under criticism by, for example, the UNDP's annual *Human Development Report*. For these reasons of state failure in the provision of social services and livelihood, NGOs are expected to play an increasingly large role in the region. Women's NGOs can be expected to push for the integration of women's concerns in economic and social policies, to look out for women's interests in the provision of welfare, and to ensure that women benefit from specific development projects.

Political Factors
In addition to channelling resources, NGOs are increasingly viewed as constituting an expanding civil society, in as much as they convey the promises of development, human rights, and participation. The proliferation of NGOs in the MENA region probably reflects two parallel political developments: the rise and spread of fundamentalism, and the growth of a movement for democratization and a *civil* society.

There has been a veritable explosion in recent years in the number of NGOs advocating human rights, women's rights, and, to a lesser extent, conservation or environmental protection (for example, ENDA Inter-Arabe, based in Tunis; Lebanon's Green Line and Friends of Nature organizations). In this respect, women's NGOs are especially significant in the Middle East and North Africa, because of the historic exclusion of women from public forms of power. What is also interesting is the cross-fertilization of the environment, human rights, and women's NGOs. For example, not only are the women's NGOs and the human rights NGOs in constant contact with each other (in part because of their common interest in legal and civil rights issues) but the human rights organizations also tend to have women's committees and women in leadership positions. In this sense, women's NGOs in the MENA region and the participation of women in other NGOs are a reflection of the proactive stance of the educated female population and of the women's movement.

Another aspect to the political dimension of the expansion of women's NGOs is a defence against the rise and spread of Islamic fundamentalist movements, the failure of states to confront them (or indeed state collusion with the movements), and the conservative revision of Family Codes. These developments have alarmed many women and prompted protest action and organization on their part. One very interesting mobilizing effort on the part of women concerned about fundamentalism and conservative family codes was the establishment of the international solidarity network called Women Living Under Muslim Laws, with affiliated individuals and groups in the Middle East and North Africa. In the region itself, numerous women's rights organizations have formed to defend and expand women's rights vis-à-vis Islamist and state patriarchy. Some of the most courageous and feminist in orientation are Algerian.

International Factors

These include opportunities afforded by the UN Decade for Women (1975–85) and the Nairobi Conference (1985); the spread of global feminism; the increasing recognition of the importance of a grassroots, participatory, and bottom-up approach to development through non-governmental organizations; and the international conferences of the 1990s under the auspices of the United Nations – the International Conference on Population and Development (Cairo, 1994), the International Conference on Human Rights, and especially the Women's Tribunal (Vienna, 1994), the World Summit for Social Development (Copenhagen, March 1995), and the Fourth World Conference on Women (Beijing, 1995).

What Charlotte Bunch has called 'global feminism' – increasing understanding and cooperation between feminists in the North and South exemplified by the close connections between international feminist networks such as DAWN, WIDE, WLUML, and others – was made possible by the United Nations Decade for Women and especially the Nairobi Conference in 1985. In the period after 1985 women's organizations proliferated around the world in defence and for the extension of women's rights and advancement. The legitimacy accorded them by the United Nations and the moral and financial support they have received from certain UN agencies such as UNIFEM, UNICEF, UNFPA, and others – whether for purposes of efficiency, equity, empowerment, or national capacity-building – constitutes a significant set of factors in the emergence and spread of women's NGOs in the MENA region.

The international conferences of the 1990s under the auspices of the United Nations have spurred greater activity on the part of women's organizations, in such areas as environmental protection, human rights, reproductive rights, poverty, and employment. For the women of the Middle East (and for many democratic organizations), the ICPD, which took place in Cairo in September 1994, legitimated their existence, emboldened them, and allowed them access to international organizations which they otherwise would not easily have had. This experience was repeated at the NGO Forum of the Social Summit in March 1995, where every Middle Eastern country was represented. The largest number of registered NGOs were from Egypt (52), followed by Tunisia (41) and Algeria (22). Lebanon sent thirteen and Morocco twelve NGOs. Because of the nature and priorities of the Social Summit (poverty alleviation, productive employment, and social integration), the NGOs were largely from the fields of labour, social work, human rights, youth, and women's rights. Of the 52 Egyptian NGOs registered at the Social Summit, five were women's; of the 41 Tunisian NGOs, four were women's; and of the 12 Moroccan NGOs, three were women's.[6]

Women's NGOs in the Middle East: Classification, Opportunities, and Constraints

According to Amani Kandil, NGOs working in the field of women focus either on the protection of women's rights or in advocating the integration of women in development. She maintains that there are nineteen organizations in Morocco (12 per cent of the total number of organizations), two in Tunisia, and 22 in Egypt (1995: 67–8). If, however, we have a broader definition of NGOs, and if we include the array of rights-oriented organizations, research institutes, and social service organizations that have emerged in the past few years, then we can come up with a classification of women's organizations that includes some of the types identified by DAWN, but with some additions. DAWN is a global network of women's organizations, founded in 1986. The acronym stands for Development Alternatives with Women for a New Era (Sen & Grown 1987: 89–96; Moser 1993: 200). DAWN's six-fold classification consisted of women's organizations that are: (1) service-oriented, (2) affiliated to a political party, (3) worker-based, (4) tied to external funding, (5) grassroots, and (6) research oriented or academic.

It also added a seventh type, women's coalitions, feminist networks, or other groups that come together around specific women's issues (peace, violence against women, fundamentalism, sex tourism, and so on). For the Middle East and North Africa, I would collapse worker-based and grassroots organizations, to distinguish them from organizations whose leadership and membership are comprised mainly of middle-class, elite, and professional women; I would not distinguish outside-oriented from grassroots organizations, or even include the former at this point, because so many women's NGOs receive external funding. (This is not necessarily true of the worker-based NGOs, especially those formed during the Palestinian Intifada). I would add the following categories: professional societies, human rights/women's rights organizations, and development/women-in-development NGOs.

Of course, these categories should be regarded as fluid and perhaps as overlapping; for example, some of the service organizations are more development orientated or more feminist than others; some of the professional women's organizations also deliver services to other women and not just to their own members; some of the feminist organizations are independent while others are affiliated to political parties; some of the development and women-in-development NGOs concern themselves with health and human rights issues, in addition to their focus on community development and income-generating projects; and some of the worker-based and grassroots organizations are affiliated with political parties (as with the Palestinian women's committees that were so active during the Intifada). All combine some elements of advocacy, research, and project implementation. Their predominant (but not exclusive) policy approach may be, in Caroline Moser's terms, welfare, equity, anti-poverty, or empowerment. They may serve women's practical and basic needs, or strategic gender (feminist) interests, or both. The classification does not include the General Federations or National Unions of Women, most of which are part of the 'national women's machinery', although some, such as the General Federation of Jordanian Women, founded in 1981, is considered the largest women's NGO in Jordan. In addition to the typology, I have included some organizational examples of each.[7]

Service Organizations
Charitable organizations represent the majority or a plurality of NGOs in most MENA countries. Women's NGOs that are service oriented are the most numerous and the most traditional of the women's organizations. As in many other countries, such organizations have sometimes been criticized for having a 'welfare' approach, and they are largely

staffed by middle-class and elite women, who sometimes have a patronizing attitude towards the poor, disabled, or rural women for whom they deliver services. Nevertheless, they perform valuable functions in the areas of women's education, health (including reproductive health and family planning), and related services. Some of the more feminist social work organizations provide legal services and counselling for battered women, such as the Women's Centre for Legal Aid and Counselling, a Palestinian organization based in Jerusalem, and SOS Femmes en Détresse, based in Algiers.

In the Middle East, exemplars of women's service-oriented NGOs would be the Palestinian In'ash al-Usrah Society in al-Bireh, founded in the mid-1960s, the Women's Health Programme of the Union of Palestinian Medical Relief Committees, based in Jerusalem, and the Friends of the People Society for Social Work, based in Egypt. Service-oriented NGOs include charitable societies (e.g. Queen Alia Fund for Social Development in Jordan; Syria's Association of St Lian for Women), Red Crescent associations, YWCAs, mother-and-child welfare societies, organizations to combat illiteracy, and many family planning associations. The predominant policy approach of the service-oriented NGOs is welfare, although some include equity, anti-poverty, and even empowerment among their objectives.

Professional Associations

These include associations of professional women, and women's committees of larger professional associations. They are national but have cross-national ties and are sometimes affiliates of international professional associations. Examples are the Professional and Business Women's Association of Jordan; the Women's Committee of the Egyptian Chamber of Commerce; the Egyptian Women Writers' Association; Egyptian Women in Film; Egyptian Medical Women's Association; Egyptian Women Scientists' Society; the Women's Rights Committee of the Arab Lawyers' Union (based in Cairo); the Bahrain Society of Sociologists; the Women's Committee of the Association of Iraqi Engineers; the Women's Committee of the Iraqi Bar Association; l'Association des Journalistes Tunisiens. In Algeria, the social-professional association SEVE seeks to promote and assist women in business (Bouatta 1995).

The principal objective of these associations is to seek equity for their members within the profession and in the society; some of them also engage in charitable and welfare activities, and some include advocacy for women's rights. For example, the Women's Rights Committee of the Arab Lawyers' Union (with chapters in most Arab countries) provides legal advice and juridical aid for women; carries out research on women's legal status in the Arab world; and seeks the abrogation of existing laws that constrain women and the expansion of Arab women's political, civil, economic, social, and cultural rights (El-Messiri 1994). The women's chapter of the Egyptian Association for Industry and Environment held a national workshop in June 1995 on 'the role of women in protection of environment and natural resource conservation' (WEDO 1995).[8] Although most of the professional associations of women are elite (and sometimes elitist), they provide a role model for young women and girls and challenge patriarchal images of women.

Development Research Centres and Women's Studies Institutes

These are usually nationally based but are increasingly coordinating research activities (especially in the Maghreb). They may engage in 'pure' research of an academic nature, or combine it with advocacy for gender equity, women's empowerment, socio-economic development, and social justice. In any case, they provide useful research for other organizations involved in action. In the MENA region they include the New Woman Research and Study Centre in Cairo (research to help create 'a powerful Egyptian women's movement'); Lebanon's Centre for Strategic Studies and Research Documentation; the Cairo Institute for Human Rights Studies; Collectif Etudes Recherche Action pour le Développement, in Morocco; Centre de Recherche de Documentation et d'Information sur la Femme (CREDIF), in Tunisia; Women's Research and Education Centre, Istanbul University; the Women's Library and Information Centre, Istanbul. The Institute for Women's Studies in the Arab World, of the Lebanese American University (formerly Beirut University College), publishes a quarterly magazine called *Al-Raida*, which tackles such taboo subjects as violence within the family as well as trends in women's education, and pays close attention to literature and scholarly publications by women. The Association des Femmes Tunisiennes pour la Recherche et le Développement (AFTURD) carries out studies on women's integration in the development process with a view to enhancing women's contributions to economic and social development and calling for their participation in decision-making (UNIDO 1993).

Among the Palestinians there is the Women's Studies Programme of Birzeit University, the Women's Committee at the Beisan Centre for Research and Development in Ramallah, the Women's Affairs Centres in Gaza and Nablus, and the Women's Training and Research Society

(Women's Studies Centre) in Jerusalem. The organization Nour, located in Cairo, promotes Arab women's writings, by, *inter alia*, publishing good quality low-cost paperback editions, producing a newsletter, building links with publishing houses (El-Messiri 1994).

In the Islamic Republic of Iran, where most women's organizations are in the field of service, welfare, and charity, several groups of women are producing magazines, journals, and research papers that provide valuable information and provocative debate; most notable are *Zanan* and *Payam-e Hajjar*. The most recent addition is *Farzaneh: Journal of Women's Studies and Research,* which is published by the Centre for Women's Studies and Research, in Tehran. The extent to which these publishing collectives are feminist or contributing to women's empowerment is in dispute among Iranian feminists abroad. There is some consensus, however, that *Zanan* is especially worth following (Mir-Hosseini 1996).

Human Rights/Women's Rights Organizations

As mentioned above, the proliferation of human rights and women's rights organizations has been a striking feature of the 1990s. They have been encouraged by international conferences such as the International Conference on Human Rights and by the new development agenda that emphasizes non-economic 'conditionalities' such as good governance, democratic participation, human rights observance, and the status of women. The women's rights organizations in particular have been gearing up for the Beijing Conference and have been actively involved in the NGO preparations in New York and in the MENA region. The women's rights organizations are explicitly oriented towards women's empowerment and as such may be said to be realizing the strategic gender interests of women.

These include Egypt's Reproductive Rights Group; la Commission Femmes de la Ligue Tunisienne des Droits de l'Homme (LTDH) and l'Association Tunisienne des Femmes Démocrates; Morocco's l'Organisation Marocaine des Droits de l'Homme, l'Association Démocratique des Femmes au Maroc, and l'Union de l'Action Feminine (many of whose members are involved with the publication *8 Mars*). Egypt's New Civic Forum (in which Mona Zulfikar, a prominent women's rights lawyer, is actively involved), and the Women's Rights Committee of the Egyptian Organization for Human Rights are both active and vocal. Yemen, Lebanon, and Iraq report human rights organizations with women's committees. However, the extent to which gender equity and empowerment issues figure in these organizations is unclear. The

Palestinian Organization for Human Rights (Al-Haq), the first Palestinian human rights organization, has had a section on women's rights for a number of years. Al-Haq convened a major conference on women and the law in September 1994.[9]

Algeria is a very interesting case of mushrooming democratic, human rights, and feminist organizations (Bouatta 1995). The objectives of the Algerian women's rights organizations include some that are fairly representative and others that are specific to the Algerian case: the abolition of the Family Code; full citizenship for women; and enactment of civil laws guaranteeing equality between men and women in areas such as employment and marriage and divorce (including abolition of polygamy and unilateral male divorce, equality in division of marital property).

Development and Women-in-Development NGOs

These NGOs are newer than the older service-oriented and charity organizations, although their work is sometimes similar. Development and WID (Women in Development) NGOs provide technical assistance and expertise on such issues as sustainable development, literacy and education, health, family planning, and community development in their country or region, and implement projects such as those pertaining to income-generation and micro-enterprises, health delivery, literacy, and other development-related projects. In Egypt, many NGOs are cooperating with the Ministry of Social Affairs in implementing the 'Productive Families Project', which seeks to capitalize household resources by converting the home into a unit of production. An umbrella organization, the General Association for Vocational Training and Productive Families, coordinates NGO assistance in the provision of credits and loans, equipment, training, and marketing. Tunisia also has in place a 'productive families' programme in which NGOs are involved in poverty-alleviation and income-generating projects.

Other NGOs have evolved as the vehicle of donor funding as they are regarded as 'closer to the grassroots' or more efficient than government agencies. This category includes ENDA Inter-Arab, based in Tunis; Lebanon's Association for Popular Action, la Fondation René Moawad, and the Lebanese Women's Council. Tunisia's Association de Promotion des Projets de Femmes dans l'Economie (APROFE) was set up in 1990 and works to improve the integration of women in investment and employment, and is particularly interested in helping women to start up new projects (UNIDO 1993). In Egypt, the Association for Development and Enhancement of Women (ADEW) has projects geared to low-income women maintaining households alone (estimated to be about 18 per cent of all urban households, and consisting mainly of widows, divorcees, women with terminally ill or disabled husbands, and abandoned women), providing credit, legal assistance, and awareness of 'their importance and potential in the development process' (El-Messiri 1994).

In addition to country-based development NGOs, there are a number of regional networks or regional bodies. One is the Centre of Arab Women for Training and Research (CAWTAR), based in Tunis but acting as a regional body, and with funding from the Tunisian government, Saudi Arabia, and other Arab sources. There are also the Alliance for Arab Women (one of the two Arab focal points for the Beijing conference), AISHA – the Arab Women's Forum; and the Documentation Centre of the Arab Council for Children and Development.

AISHA is a regional NGO network established in 1993 to create a forum for exchange and cooperation for independent women's groups in the Arab world. It is comprised of fourteen organizations from Morocco, Algeria, Tunisia, Egypt, Sudan, Palestine, and Lebanon. According to the UNIFEM Western Asia newsletter of March 1995, 'AISHA guides Arab women's groups in different countries to work as a single unit through collaboration and the sharing of resources' (p. 2). It received funding from the Netherlands Embassy in Cairo to facilitate the participation of its member organizations in the Social Summit (Copenhagen, March 1995) and the Beijing Conference. The Alliance for Arab Women was founded in 1987 'to enhance the status of Arab women and enable them to play an effective role in the economic and social development of their country'. As one of the Regional NGO Focal Points (the other being the General Federation of Jordanian Women) and as organizers of the preparations for Beijing, the task of the Alliance was to incorporate the inputs of NGOs to the platform for action for the NGO Forum in Beijing. With funding from USAID through CEDPA (an American NGO),the Alliance for Arab Women conducted workshops, launched media campaigns, published a newsletter, and participated in PrepComs I, II, and the Beijing Conference.

Women's Organizations Affiliated to Political Parties

Of course, many of the General Federations of Women and National Unions of Women are affiliated to the ruling parties. For example, the Union Nationale des Femmes Tunisiennes is affiliated with the PSD, Algeria's UNFA with the FLN, the General Federation of Iraqi Women with the Iraqi Baath Party, and the Syrian Women's Federation with the

Syrian Baath Party. Other, non-governmental and non-official women's organizations may be affiliated with left-wing parties. For example, in Algeria, when Egalité was formed, its secretariat consisted almost entirely of members of the Socialist Organization of Workers (OST, Trotskyist tendency), which became the Workers' Party (PT) in 1990. According to Cherifa Bouatta, the members of Emancipation belong to the PST (Socialist Workers' Party), and those of Defense et Promotion belong largely to the PAGS (Parti de l'Avant-Garde Socialiste, or the Communist Party). These are referred to as democratic women's organizations, to distinguish them from both the state-affiliated women's groups and the pro-Islamist women's groups.

Unlike the official women's organizations, the left-wing women's groups tied to political parties tend to be more feminist in orientation, as is clearly the case in Algeria. Earlier, women's organizations tied to left-wing political parties tended to subsume 'the woman question' to larger political and party objectives. This was a reason for the tragedy of the women's organizations in Iran during and immediately after the Revolution. The side-lining of women's equity and empowerment issues in the interests of nationalist goals has also been characteristic of the Palestinian women's organizations.

Worker-based and Grassroots Women's Organizations

These organizations are concerned with the welfare and equity of women workers, and seek to empower women as workers. As such they are oriented towards meeting the practical needs of women workers rather than any explicitly feminist goals. This category includes such organizations as Egypt's Central Agricultural Cooperative Union, which has women members; and the Women's Committee of the General Federation of Agricultural Workers' Cooperatives, in Iraq. Among the Palestinians, women's grassroots organizations are especially active, and many became prominent during the Intifada, when they worked to realize the dual objectives of promoting women's productive, professional, and political activities *and* providing products and services for Palestinian families and communities to sustain the Intifada. The Women's Work Committee (WWC) was actually formed in the late 1970s by women sympathetic to the DFLP, and its members include professional, clerical, and factory workers. Subsequently, pro-Communist women in Jerusalem and Ramallah founded the Union of Palestinian Working Women's Committees, 'with branches in all the major towns in the West Bank, and later in a number of villages' (Hiltermann 1991: 134). Pro-PFLP women then formed the Union of Palestinian Women's Committees, while pro-

Fatah women founded the Women's Committee for Social Work. The WWC was renamed the Union of Women's Work Committees, and in 1989 the Federation of Palestinian Women's Action Committees.

Although the women's committees were formed by middle-class and educated women activists, their membership was popular and grassroots, with peasant and working-class women, including young women who had to drop out of school to take on a factory job as part of household survival strategies. Activities and services included income-generating projects, producer and marketing cooperatives (such as in food processing), vocational training centres, literacy classes, health education, and nurseries and child-care centres. (See Annex for details) There have been various analyses and interpretations of the social and gender impact of these committees (see Hiltermann 1991: 171; Peteet 1991; Abdo 1994). But the available evidence suggests that although the social emancipation of women was not the committees' ultimate goal – labour rights and economic self-reliance were paramount – and although many young women would drop out of the committees upon marriage, the unintended consequence was to push 'the question of women' to the fore and even to weaken some of the traditional social obstacles to women's public participation. As such, they may have paved the way for the inevitable struggle around women's full citizenship in the emerging Palestinian state.[10]

The extent of worker-based and grassroots organizations in the MENA region in which women participate or which are led by women needs further study. It is known that women's trade union participation is very weak in the region, partly a reflection of their limited participation in the formal work force, and partly a reflection of the masculinized nature of the trade unions. Nevertheless, women's committees of trade unions do exist, and women sometimes attain leadership positions within some unions and other worker-based organizations. For example, the Egyptian Trade Union Federation has a women workers' department, led by Ayse Abdel Hadi. Women have been elected officers in all 23 unions of the ETUF, although in 1990/91 they represented only 621 out of a total of 18,062 union officers.[11]

As women's employment expands in the region, especially in the context of export-led development, it will be increasingly important to monitor the way that women workers organize and mobilize in response to employment conditions and management strategies.

Opportunities for Growth

NGOs, including women's, receive funding from government sources and from international NGOs, UN bodies, or the Dutch, Canadian,

Danish, German, Swedish, and American development agencies. In Egypt, USAID is one of the principal funding sources, funding many community development and family planning projects. In 1991 it signed an agreement with the Egyptian government to channel $20 million to NGOs (Kandil 1995: 52–3). AMIDEAST funds many educational and training projects throughout the region. In Yemen, the Social Household Development Association was established in 1990 targeting the poor. With the support of international organizations such as OXFAM, the Association established a vocational training centre which provides skills-building and job placement (ibid: 63).

United Nations agencies are increasingly establishing relations with NGOs in the MENA region. Until recently, cooperation between the UNDP and Arab countries was channelled through governmental machinery. Today, the UNDP cooperates directly with NGOs. Other UN agencies with strong ties to MENA NGOs, including women's, are UNICEF, UNESCO, UNFPA, UNIFEM, and ESCWA.

Some of these agencies supported efforts on the part of MENA women's NGOs to prepare for and attend the Fourth World Conference on Women (Beijing, September 1995). UNIFEM set up a regional office for Western Asia, based in Amman, and assisted the two Arab Regional Focal Points – the Alliance for Arab Women and the General Federation of Jordanian Women – in preparations for the Beijing Conference. As a result of this and other UN and donor assistance, 52 delegates from Arab NGOs registered to participate in the Commission on the Status of Women Meeting in New York in March 1995. The largest delegation consisted of 26 members from Egypt representing fifteen NGOs (UNIFEM: 4)

Constraints and Challenges

Do the developments described above translate into a firm footing for the women's NGOs? Although external funding has facilitated NGO growth and participation in international events, it is of a limited nature, it shows signs of decreasing, and it highlights the absence of 'sustainability'. Dependence on external aid raises the question of self-reliance and the extent to which NGOs could become self-financing or obtain financing at the community, national, or regional levels. The OECD/ DAC/WID Facilitation Initiative for the 1995 Fourth World Conference on Women excluded the Middle East region, principally due to the assumption that adequate resources existed there. In fact, many women's NGOs lacked financial and other support, and not only for preparations for the Beijing conference.[12] In a show of support for Egyptian NGOs, the Danish and Netherlands embassies in Egypt established a Beijing

Trust Fund to help finance preparatory activities for the Conference. Women's NGOs are perennially plagued by funding constraints, and it is not clear that Arab sources will substitute for international ones. An additional problem is that where Arab funding is available, such as with CAWTAR, there is often a heavy-handedness that undermines the NGO's ability to act effectively.[13]

El-Messiri and Kandil have identified a number of other problems such as insufficient coordination and cooperation between NGOs, poor volunteer recruitment (except for religiously-oriented PVOs, where this is apparently not a problem), and inadequate technical abilities, especially in the fields of documentation, information retrieval, and computerization. Organizational and managerial problems are known to hamper the activities of women's organizations, as discussed by Sen and Grown and reiterated by Moser. Although little is known about the internal structures and leadership styles of women's NGOs in MENA countries, the dissolution of the Tunisian feminist journal *Nissa* and the controversy around the AWSA and its style of work suggest that dissent, conflict, power struggles and 'uses and abuses of charisma' may be present.[14]

NGOs also face legal constraints and restrictions on their activities in some countries. In Egypt, Law 32 of 1964 provides a comprehensive regulatory scheme for NGOs (called PVOs) in which the Ministry of Social Affairs (MOSA) is empowered to do the following: prescribe the charter and the bylaws; review and approve board membership, and appoint up to 50 per cent of the board members; dissolve an association without court order, or decree that two or more NGOs should be amalgamated; restrict association activities to one category of a prescribed list of eight activities (expanded to twelve in 1986). MOSA may also strike down any decision of an NGO board of directors that it considers in violation of Law 32. This law is considered extremely onerous by individuals who in early 1995 were trying to establish a new women's NGO focused on research and training geared to working-class women. These individuals initially sought to set up the NGO as a 'special project' of a UN agency, but were unsuccessful.

Palestinian NGOs have also encountered difficulties. A draft law circulated by the Palestinian Authority governing relations between the authority and the NGOs met with strong protests, spearheaded by the Palestinian NGO Network. As of late 1995, the draft law had been 'frozen', but it remains a cause for concern.[15]

To the extent that women's NGOs – and others – contribute to the democratization process, the creation of a democratic civil society and a civic culture, and seek to participate in the development process, they are important in and of themselves. The opening up of political space and the diffusion of once centralized economic power and resources will allow for the articulation of more feminist demands, including women's perspectives on economic policy and planning. However, for the time being the NGOs face many constraints. These arise partly from the nature of the political and social structures in which they are situated. The women's NGOs are not mass movements and do not include the participation of urban poor, working-class, and rural women as they do in, for example, India and some Latin American countries. Their constituency is limited and it is possible that in the case of some women's NGOs, their *raison d'être* is rather self-interested. Although there are good reasons why Middle Eastern feminists have been wary of socialist and nationalist parties and correctly regard the labour movements as male movements, there is a need to address the concerns of disadvantaged social groups and to make feminist issues relevant and comprehensible to them. The challenge for Middle Eastern feminists is to integrate theory and action around strategic gender interests and around the practical and very often basic needs of working-class, peasant, and urban poor women.

That many women's NGOs are essentially elite, professional, and middle-class bodies does not mean that they do not have a wider impact. In Middle Eastern societies, where the public sphere has historically been the province of men, where male–female gaps are still huge (except in higher education), where economic decision-making is entirely male, and where women's participation in formal political structures and in elections, whether as candidates or as voters, is still low and in some cases declining, in Egypt for example (Zulfikar: 7–9), the very existence of women's NGOs challenges the patriarchal order in rather profound ways. They may also be paving the way for more concerted collective action on the part of women. Throughout the world, women's organizations are active around such issues as structural adjustment and economic policy, employment opportunities for women and support structures for working mothers, violence against women, peace and security issues, environmental protection, quotas to ensure women's political participation, and reproductive rights for women. Women's NGOs in the MENA region can be expected to take on these issues in a more concerted fashion.

NGO Priorities: The Work Plan Document

Some of the above issues were discussed at the Conference of the Non-Government Organizations, held in Amman in November 1994. They are reflected in the document entitled 'Work Approach for the Non-Government Organizations in the Arab Region'. The document is very interesting both for what it contains and what it leaves out of its considerations. In terms of its contents, the attention and priority it gives to some issues is intriguing.[16]

The document begins by highlighting some of the positive and negative developments as these have affected the status of women globally and especially in the Arab region. Positive developments include 'the transformation towards democracy' and respect for human rights (p. 2); and the recent growth and activity of women's NGOs, which is attributed to 'government encouragement' and to 'the United Nations and World community encouragement' (p. 12). It is later stated that women's NGOs, including the regional networks, 'must enhance the struggle towards democracy, political pluralism and strengthening the role of national institutions and the State of Law' (p. 8).

Negative developments include: (1) the economic crisis caused by indebtedness, poverty, out-migration in search of employment; submission to dictates of the IMF; unemployment; inadequate health and social services, including those cut by structural adjustment policies; (2) wars and conflicts, such as the continuing Arab-Palestinian-Israeli conflict. The document takes a strong stand against invasion, occupation, and evacuation, and declares: 'People should never be subject to economic sanctions and starvation' (p. 4). These are references to Kuwait and Iraq alike.

The NGO document characterizes Arab women's situation as follows: absence of real equality; absence of effective participation in development; absence of a just and comprehensive peace (again a reference to Palestine); increasing violence against women; and lack of socio-economic security. Elsewhere the document notes that only eight Arab countries (Egypt, Iraq, Jordan, Kuwait, Libya, Morocco, Tunisia, Yemen) have signed the UN Convention on the Elimination of All Forms of Discrimination Against Women, but even they have done so with reservations that impede implementation. Women are still not involved in political decision-making, and there remain 'concepts and traditions which prevent women from assuming high positions in the legislative and judicial fields' (p. 11). The poor state of statistics and data on women and gender issues is also noted, and the document states several times that women's multiple roles, especially their care giving responsibility, are onerous.

Importance of the Palestinian Question, Lebanon, and Sanctions

Early in the document a paragraph establishes these priority goals: a 'just and comprehensive peace to liberate the land, alleviate the economic sanctions, and to provide all types of security' (p. 6). This priority theme is repeated several times in the course of the document, for example, on p. 20, which mentions the suffering of Palestinian women and Lebanese women, sanctions imposed on the Iraqis and the Libyans, and the 'selection [selectivity] and dual standards in the application of the Security Council resolutions'.

The document takes an anti-militarism stand at times, by asking for the allocation of 'some of the armament budget for on-going development projects to alleviate poverty in the region' (p. 9). Elsewhere, the position on war and women's relation to it is ambiguous. The document states that 'the Arab World receives 50 per cent of the third world share from arms trade' and that these 'huge expenses on armament [sic] are being done without any role for women to play. They do not participate in the decision-making on the purchase of arms and their use' (p. 19). And: 'the rate of women involvement in armed forces is very poor [sic]. The nature of this involvement does not go beyond office and administrative works in addition to the medical services. She did not share as a fighter [sic]. This may indicate that the wars and armed conflicts are some male issues [sic]' (p. 21). A paragraph calls for governments to reduce their military budgets '*after* reaching the just and comprehensive settlement of the Arab Israeli conflict and the Palestinian cause' (italics mine), and then notes the importance of funds for economic development, 'which our area needs badly'. The influence of the Palestinian delegates at the NGO conference is unmistakeable.

On Women's Human Rights and Political Participation

The section on violence against women is frank, and reflects growing concern in the Arab region. It should be noted that the Beirut-based magazine *Al-Raida* devoted an entire issue in 1994 to a candid discussion of family violence, especially wife battering, with a focus on Lebanon. The NGO document states that 'some of the Arab societies still exercise violence against women', which continues partly because of women's lack of awareness of their rights and 'submission to traditions and customs' (p. 18). The paragraph also refers to honour killings, and notes that 'women are being killed whilst men are left alone although they are partners in crimes of honour' (p. 19). The formulation of this sentence is perhaps unfortunate, but the intention is doubtlessly to underscore the asymmetry of punishment for illicit sex. Later in the document a section on the elimination of all forms of violence against women contains ten specific recommendations, many having to do with legal literacy and services for battered women, training for police and medical personnel, legislation against honour killings, cooperation of schools and mass media in this effort.

In the chapter on Strategic Objectives there are thirteen recommendations to strengthen women's participation in political structures and decision-making positions. These include the demand for quotas to speed up participation at the village, municipal, parliamentary, and diplomatic corps levels; for political parties to recruit women and offer them training in political functions; for the local media to cooperate in the 'formulation of the new woman image'; for support services to facilitate women's public roles and family responsibilities; legal literacy and training in political rights. This is followed by nine recommendations regarding implementation and enforcement of rules and international standards to guarantee women's human rights, including: ratification of the Women's Convention and what appears to be a sentence asking governments to reassess their reservations to clauses they have found to be contrary to 'Islam and other divine religions' (p. 25);[17] legal services for poor women, offered by male and female lawyers; promotion of a marriage contract 'to include stipulations guaranteeing the wife's rights especially after separation' (p. 26); 'the revision and modernization' of family laws; promotion of women judges; and the amendment of nationality laws so that children may acquire their mother's nationality.

On Economic Liberalization and Women's Economic Participation

Early in the document criticism of economic liberalization includes the fact that women are being forced to shift towards the private sector, but that this sector is unfriendly to women workers in that it does not provide social security, health insurance, or unionization (p. 7). Elsewhere, the document notes that in the context of high rates of poverty and large numbers of unemployed males, women's employment prospects are dim (p. 15). One suggested solution to the economic crisis is 'achieving Arab integration and supporting Arab identity and Arab economic integration . . . and the Middle East market' (pp. 9–10). The NGO document does not show evidence of a firm grasp of economic issues, nor does it discuss the main features of the current economic context, the factors behind stagnation and crisis, and alternative development strategies. It is similarly very weak on recommendations pertaining to enhancing women's economic participation. Although it contains some refreshingly radical insights, most of the statements are rather conventional. It notes that women face obstacles in the areas of ownership rights, rent, credits and loans, labour laws, and 'civil planning'. There follow some abstract statements on helping women in the informal sector, training for women, inclusion of women in the national plans, expanding the female labour force, supporting women-owned businesses, supporting women in untraditional occupations, motivating women to become involved in the agricultural cooperatives. (The latter is followed by the interesting rationale that women in producer cooperatives are able to receive their rightful share, 'away from the abuse of employers and parents'.) This is followed by a section on the elimination of poverty, which begins by noting the role played by external debt. It is suggested that removal of indebtedness would free Arab countries from the adverse effects of adjustment policies (p. 28). There are paragraphs calling for: training for poor women to enable them to seek productive employment and acquire social security coverage; priority to health and educational services for 'all social classes' as a way of tackling poverty and its effects; academic institutions and NGOs to carry out analyses of poverty and its causes; governments to disburse funds for women maintaining households alone. The last paragraph then calls for 'some amounts of money' to be reallocated from military to development projects that generate employment, provide welfare, or alleviate poverty (p. 29).

The seven recommendations on financial arrangements are formulated in ways that are general, or unclear, or repetitive. There is nothing more specific than: 'Governments must be requested to adopt a certain policy to provide financing within their budgets of development projects that help the development of women' (p. 35). Similarly, the final chapter on institutional arrangements merely calls on governments to establish bureaux of women's affairs, to support women's national and regional NGOs, to allocate a third of all seats in agencies and councils, and to cooperate with NGOs in the preparation of national plans.

Women's Health and Education
Fourteen detailed recommendations on enhancing women's access to health services throughout the life-course make these among the strongest sections in the NGO document. Priority is given to health education, family planning, studies and data on women's health status, support for NGOs working in the health field, education of midwives, attention to rural areas and refugee women, and a paragraph on requiring a health certificate before marriage. The document also calls for free and

compulsory education, programmes to prevent girls from dropping out, state support for NGOs dealing with rural and refugee education, and curriculum development to include the following: 'family education, human rights, and environment preservation' as well as 'the responsibilities of enhancing the national spirit and loyalty in addition to freedom of opinion and speech', and 'the importance of peace' (p. 29).

Silences: Islamic Fundamentalism and the Question of Algeria

The NGO document contains not a single word on the spread of Islamic fundamentalism and its implications for women. This deserved to be mentioned in the sections on the regional context, on the human rights of women, on violence against women, and on the effects of armed conflicts, among others. As mentioned above, there are many references to the suffering of the women of Palestine, Lebanon, and Iraq, but no reference to the conflict in Algeria and the suffering of women there. Apparently, Algerian participants sought to include some mention of fundamentalism and/or the plight of women who have been bullied, threatened, attacked, and killed by Islamist terrorists. But the NGO grouping could not agree on the formulation. However, when the matter came up at the official, inter-governmental conference, the Algerian delegate made an emotional speech and was given a standing ovation by the participants. A resolution was drafted expressing sympathy and solidarity with Algerian women and, moreover, the governmental delegates condemned terrorism in all its forms, including religious (although the Sudanese delegation objected). The final document does not mention religious terrorism or fundamentalist movements, but it contains a reference to civil wars and armed internal conflicts.

It seems clear that the Arab women's NGOs wished to avoid tackling a controversial and potentially contentious issue. As such, they evinced a circumspection at odds with the real risks that women face and one that contrasts starkly with the bold positions taken by North African feminist groupings. It is possible that there were fewer delegates from the feminist organizations of Tunisia, Algeria, Morocco, and Egypt, and that delegates from the more conservative Gulf states, Syria, Jordan, and Lebanon succeeded in framing the issues in such a way that women's health and education were prioritized – although women's political participation is also given some prominence in the document. The NGO document is furthermore infused with nationalist sentiments, and contains little or no identification or criticism of the legal constraints, misguided economic policies, and political-cultural backlashes that women face. By March 1995, however, the women's NGOs had clarified their views on issues either missing or ambiguously stated in the regional NGO document. At the final preparatory conference in New York, the following priorities were added:

> To strengthen the basis of the democratic process in both the political and social realms; to ensure the sanctity of human rights and the amendments of legislation that target the elimination of all forms of discrimination and violence against women, in particular, family laws. To condemn fundamentalism and cultural extremism, which can lead to terrorism and violence against women. To promote social development to counteract the negative impact of applied structural adjustment programs and to ensure the basic human needs of women.[18]

Conclusion

During the past decade, and especially during the 1990s, not only have NGOs proliferated, but women's NGOs have grown exponentially and are taking on increasingly important responsibilities in the context of state withdrawal from the provision of social services and in the context of a global trend in the expansion of civil society. This paper has identified demographic, economic, political, and international factors behind the growth of NGOs in the Middle East and North Africa. Women's NGOs encompass the full range of women's practical needs and strategic gender interests, and include service-oriented organizations, professional associations, research institutes, women's rights organizations, development-oriented NGOs, women's organizations affiliated to political parties, and worker-based or grassroots women's organizations.

It is still early days in the development of non-governmental organizations in the MENA region. Issues of organizational sustainability, internal structure, and efficacy of project implementation will require further research. With respect to the latter issue, studies have shown NGOs to be flexible and innovative in some contexts, but ill prepared or ineffective in others. An evaluation of NGO-implemented projects in the MENA region would be helpful, particularly in terms of their role in facilitating 'bottom-up' development. Another useful study would be a comparative assessment of different types of women's NGOs in terms of their ability to attract funding for project implementation and in terms of their commitment to women's empowerment. Research is needed on the internal dynamics of NGOs, their ability to recruit volunteers and members, their managerial approaches, and their commitment to democratic procedures. Finally, research is needed to determine whether NGOs are contingent upon external funding and international conferences, or whether they are of a more embedded and enduring nature. Because the emergence of NGOs is tied to changes in development policy and in the political environment, it will be important to observe the extent to which they become institutionalized, as part of the slow process of democratization and participatory development in the region. In particular, it will be useful to follow the progress of the women's rights organizations and of those WID-oriented NGOs that seek to empower women in the development process. These could play a central role in organizing women for collective action, with a view towards bringing pressure to bear on the state to include women and women's concerns in economic and political decision-making.

Appendix

Palestinian Women's NGOs

A recent UNDP-funded survey of women's organizations showed that there were 174 in the Occupied Territory in 1993. Of these, only 34 were in the Gaza Strip and 60 were in the Jerusalem and Ramallah area. Like other NGOs, they represent a multitude of factional political divisions. The umbrella General Union of Palestinian Women is composed of the membership of 55 women's societies. Women's NGOs have been the major channel for disbursing technical assistance to meet the needs of Palestinian women, mostly through income-generating activities.

Some of the ongoing activities funded and implemented by women's organizations are: agricultural cooperatives, artificial limb factories, brass production, cancer screening centres, care for orphans, carpentry, centres for the disabled, ceramics projects, chicken farms, children's clothing factories, cooperatives, copper production and marketing, daycare centres, dental clinics, diabetes clinics, dormitories for college students, educational training, education programmes for the disabled, embroidery, elementary schools (including those for orphan girls), family planning education, family sponsorship programmes, fashion exhibits, film festivals, financial aid to students, folklore exhibits, food production (including baby food), girl scouts, gynaecological clinics, hairdressing, handicrafts, health care, health education, health insurance for the blind, home economics programmes, homes for the elderly, hospitals, hotels, kindergartens (including boarding), knitting, laboratory services, legal counselling, libraries, maternity hospitals, MCH clinics, medical care and treatment services, museums, nursing and midwifery schools, orphanages, physiotherapy, physiotherapy clinics, pre-schools, primary health care centres, production of educational toys, rehabilitation programmes for the handicapped (including the mentally disabled), relief to needy families, religious activities, research on women, restaurants, scholarship programmes, secondary schools, services for the elderly, sewing, speech therapy (including training of therapists and mothers), social and psychological counselling, sports programmes, summer camps and clubs, training courses (Arabic language, ceramics, painting on cloth, computer literacy, counselling, English language, flower arrangements, French language, fundraising, graphic design, hairdressing, health, Hebrew language, home economics, human rights, karate, kindergarten management, lectures, literacy, management, political leadership, sewing, typing and weaving), under-garment factories, women's employment centres, vocational training schools and programmes, and painting on wood.

The capacities of the women's NGOs vary in technical know-how and organizational and financial sustainability. The fact that the NGOs have shouldered many developmental responsibilities normally delivered by the public sector has left them with a wealth of experience. Their outreach role at the grass-roots level cannot be underestimated. Since it is expected that many of the activities performed by these NGOs will be assumed by the emerging Palestinian administrative authority, this creates some ambiguity regarding the future role of women's NGOs. There may also be pressure to incorporate some of these NGOs into the administrative structure of the future government.

At this historical juncture, there is a need to carry out an in-depth analysis and assessment of the women's NGOs. An inventory of their present capacities should provide information on their capacity-building needs in important areas, such as economic and financial management, negotiating skills, participatory planning and evaluation of their programmes. Focusing on these areas would assist these women's organizations in determining how they make their eventual transition from substituting for government activities to complementing the future public-sector activities. . . .

Source: UNDP, *At the Crossroads: Challenges and Choices for Palestinian Women in the West Bank and the Gaza Strip*, New York: Gender-in-Development Programme, UNDP, 1994, pp.100–103.

Notes

1. The Palestinian NGO position paper is reprinted in *Civil Society*, III, 33, Cairo: Ibn Khaldoun Centre, September 1994, pp.10–11.
2. The document was prepared at the Non-Government Organizations Conference, which took place just before the official, inter-governmental Arab Regional Preparatory Meeting for the Fourth World Conference on Women Amman, November 1994. I attended the latter meeting, and there I was able to obtain the NGO document in an (unedited) English translation.
3. According to Nabil Samuel of CEOSS, 'Upon examining the nascent Egyptian experiment of shifting towards market economy and democratization, we realize that a kind of transformation is beginning to take shape in society. The state can no longer struggle under the burden of production and welfare for the citizens, and is beginning to open up vistas for the private and community sectors to assume their roles in building civil society, participating in production, and shouldering the efforts to offset the negative side-effects of economic restructuring' (Samuel 1995: 26).
4. *Zakat* committees operate under *al-waqf*, or the jurisdiction of Islamic trusts. Under Islamic law, the income from these trusts is used for welfare activities, which also include community health-care services.
5. According to Kandil, religiously-oriented NGOs are 'very prominent in Egypt as well as in the Gulf States and in Lebanon'. In Egypt, Islamic organizations accounted for 35 per cent and Christian organizations 9 per cent of the total number of NGOs/PVOs in 1991 (1995: 69).
6. Information from a diskette with a complete list of the NGOs registered as participants in the NGO Forum '95, Copenhagen, March 1995, kindly provided by the organizers.
7. Information on the organizations themselves comes from a variety of sources, including lists of NGOs provided by ESCWA; I am grateful to Fatima Sbaity Kassem for her kind assistance. Much of the information on North African human rights and women's rights organizations comes from Touria Hadraoui and Myriam Monkachi (1991) *Etudes Feminines: Repertoire et Bibliographie*, Casablanca: Editions le fennec and The United Nations University.
8. WEDO is an international women's NGO based in New York that has been active since the Earth Summit (Rio, 1993).
9. I am grateful to Dr Lisa Taraki, of the Women's Studies Programme of Birzeit University, for this information (personal communication, 14 November 1995).
10. During the Madrid Peace Conference, all the committees were dissolved and became part of the Palestinian Authority structure. The Women's Affairs Technical Committee was formed as an advocacy, lobby, and training group. According to Lisa Taraki, it 'has sought, unsuccessfully, to become something like a women's commission in the framework of the Palestine Authority' (personal communication, 14 November 1995).

11. Author's interview with Hussein Hassan, International Labour Relations Department, ETUF – Egyptian Trade Union Federation, Cairo, 9 February 1995.
12. For example, at the Institute of National Planning, a government agency in Cairo, a gender unit was established in the Department of Regional Planning, and headed by Dr Azza Soliman. Funding for gender training and other purposes, however, was not forthcoming from the INP, which led the gender unit to turn to UNICEF-Egypt for support (personal communication from Dr Azza Soliman, in an interview in Cairo, January 1995).
13. CAWTAR has been plagued by organizational and leadership problems. Its first director resigned in protest, while the second director was forced out.
14. Dwyer (1995: ch 11). In Egypt, there is also resentment on the part of some, regarding the ability of other women's NGOs to garner funds. When I was in Egypt during January/February 1995, I was told that a certain women's NGO was considered to be the 'darling of the Americans'.
15. Personal communication from Lisa Taraki, Birzeit University, 14 November 1995.
16. It should be noted that the Arab NGOs received guidelines, as did women's NGOs everywhere, in the preparation of the document and its organization around specific chapters.
17. The meaning may be the exact opposite, and the poor nature of the translation makes it difficult to discern. The sentence reads: 'Countries signing it with some reservations must review these reservations especially that the items related to equality do not contradict with Islam and other divine religions.' In the governmental document (E/CN.6/1995/5/Add.5, dated 23 February 1995) the language is as follows: 'All legislation related to women should be reviewed in order to develop and amend it to bring it into line with the rapidly changing economic, social and cultural conditions in Arab societies, and in such a way that it does not contradict to original religious values' (p. 7).
18. The list of new demands was reprinted in the Lebanese journal *Al-Raida*, XII, 69, Spring 1995.

References

Abdo, N. (1994), 'Nationalism and Feminism: Palestinian Women and the Intifada – No Going Back?,' in V. M. Moghadam, ed., *Gender and National Identity: Women and Politics in Muslim Societies*, London: Zed Books.
Badran, M. (1994), 'Gender Activism: Feminists and Islamists in Egypt,' in V. M. Moghadam, ed., *Identity Politics and Women: Cultural Reassertions and Feminisms in International Perspective*, Boulder, CO: Westview Press.

Bouatta, C. (1995), 'Evolution of the Women's Movement in Contemporary Algeria: Organization, Objectives, and Prospects,' paper prepared under external contract for UNU/WIDER, Helsinki, 1995.

Chafetz, J. S. & Dworkin, G. (1986), *Female Revolt: Women's Movements in World and Historical Perspective*, Totowa, NJ: Rowman and Allanheld.

Cherifati-Merabtine, D. (1995), 'Evolution of Women's Employment in Algeria,' paper prepared under external contract for UNU/WIDER, Helsinki, 1995.

Dwyer, K. (1991), *Arab Voices: The Human Rights Debate in the Middle East*, Berkeley: University of California Press.

Edwards, M. & Hulme, D., eds (1992), *Making a Difference: NGOs and Development in a Changing World*, London: Earthscan Publications.

Hadraoui, T. & Monkachi. M. (1991), *Etudes Feminines: Repertoire et Bibliographie*, Casablanca: Editions le fennec and The United Nations University.

Hiltermann, J. R. (1991), *Behind the Intifada: Labour and Women's Movements in the Occupied Territories*, Princeton, NJ: Princeton University Press.

Ibrahim, S. E. (1993) 'Crises, Elites, and Democratization in the Arab World,' in *The Middle East Journal*, 47, 2: 292–305.

Kandil, A. (1995), *Civil Society in the Arab World*, Washington DC: Civicus.

El-Messiri, S. (1994), 'Women and the Law in the Near East: Legal and Regulatory Constraints to Women's Participation in Development. Research on Women, Law and Development in Egypt,' mimeo, Cairo.

Mir-Hosseini, Z. (1996), 'Stretching the Limits: A Feminist Reading of the Shari'a in Post-Khomeini Iran,' in M. Yamani, ed., *Islamic Law and Feminism*, London: Ithaca Press.

Moghadam, V. M. (1993), *Modernizing Women: Gender and Social Change in the Middle East*, Boulder, CO: Lynne Rienner Publishers.

——, ed. (1994), *Identity Politics and Women: Cultural Reassertions and Feminisms in International Perspective*, Boulder, CO: Westview Press.

Moser, C. (1993), *Gender Planning and Development: Theory, Practice, and Training*, London: Routledge.

Norton, R. A. (1993), 'The Future of Civil Society in the Middle East,' in *The Middle East Journal*, 47, 2 (Spring 1993): 205–16.

Peteet, J. (1991), *Gender in Crisis: Women and the Palestinian Resistance Movement*, New York: Columbia University Press.

Samuel, N. (1995), 'Egyptian NGOs and Civil Society,' in *Ru'ya*, Cairo: Institute of Cultural Affairs, 6 (Winter 1995).

Al-Sayyid, M. K. (1993), 'A Civil Society in Egypt?,' in *The Middle East Journal*, 47, 2 (Spring 1993): 228–42.

Sen, G. & Grown, C. (1987), *Development, Crises, and Alternative Visions: Third World Women's Perspective*, New York: Monthly Review Press.

Sood, K. (1995), 'Trends in International Cooperation and Net Resource Transfers to Developing Countries,' Helsinki: UNU/WIDER Research for Action Publication Series.

UNIFEM (1995), *Arab Women Towards Beijing 1995*, Monthly Newsletter published by UNIFEM Western Asia, 1, 1, (March 1995).

UNIDO (1993), 'Women in Industry: Tunisia,' Vienna.

WEDO (1995), *Women's Environment & Development Organization News & Views*, 8, 1–2, (June 1995).

Yamani M., ed. (1996), *Islamic Law and Feminism*, London: Ithaca Press.

Zulfikar, M. (n.d.), 'The Egyptian Woman in a Changing World,' Cairo: The New Civic Forum.

3

The Reproduction of Political Process Among Women Activists in Lebanon: 'Shopkeepers' and Feminists

Suad Joseph

Women and Shops

The fact of women's organizations in and of itself is a positive indication of women's mobilization into civil society. Women working on behalf of women represents an achievement of a degree of socio-political participation in public spheres (see Moghadam, this volume). Yet, since women's organizations can reinforce inequality based on class, race, religion, ethnicity, or gender (Al-Mughni, Chatty and Rabo, this volume), they need to be scrutinized for their reproduction of social systems of domination. Analysing women's organizations in terms of their paradoxes and contradictions entails a recognition that they can reproduce domination even though they work for, and at times succeed in, improving women's status and conditions. I argue in this chapter that women's organizations can reproduce hierarchical patron/client patterns of leadership such as those found in men's organizations of their society, culture and class – even though their work may contribute to the improvement of women's situations in some ways.

I investigate leadership patterns in women's organizations by focusing on a case study of one organization in Lebanon. Like the men of their society, culture and class, women often set up *dakakeen* (little shops). The identifying characteristic of these shops is their highly personalistic organizational dynamics.

I use the term 'shop' because the Lebanese themselves refer to organizations so identified with their leaders as *dikkan* (pl., *dakakeen*) and refer to the organizational leader as *dikkanji* (shopkeeper).[1] These *dakakeen* are based on patron-client models of organization in which the leader is at once head of the organization, benefactor, often sole or main decision-maker, and frequently the founder of the organization. Patron-client models of organization, as will be discussed below, are perhaps the most common organizational form found in Lebanese civil society. Indeed, patron-client organizational models are found not only in the non-governmental sphere, but also within government bureaucracies and between government officials and non-governmental personnel (Joseph 1990, Huxley 1978).

The shop (*dikkan*) is often founded by the same person who continues to lead it so that it comes to be publicly linked with the identity and personhood of the leader (shopkeeper). In organizations that outlive their founders, leaders tend to stay with the organization in leadership positions for long durations (10–50 years) also establishing a close identification between the leader and the organization. Often the leader is succeeded by a relative (especially a son or daughter) or a personally chosen successor. The successes of the organization (and failures) are directly linked to the abilities and character of the leader, who is usually a member of the upper or upper-middle class with access to material resources, services and sites of social and political decision-making. Organizational achievements are closely linked to the class privileges, personal networks, and specific skills of the leader.

At times an organization sustains more than one leader. In *dakakeen* with more than one leader, each will often set up his or her own 'shop' within the organization. These leaders compete with each other for control of the organization and its personnel and clientele. In the process they often violate the organizational chart (if there is one), cross the boundaries of their job description (if there is one) and inspire loyalty of staff and members to their person by manipulating organizational resources and services for distribution as gifts to their clients. The result of such intra-organizational competition for leadership status is often confusion, conflict, stalemate and personal animosities.

Decision-making in these shops is top heavy. Leaders tend to make decisions unilaterally, even when the structures for more participatory decision-making are formally recognized. In addition, leaders often recruit members in a highly personalized manner, recruiting from their families, villages, neighbourhoods, religious sects or other such networks. Relationships between leaders and members are also person-alized. Members are encouraged to create and feel personal bonds, obligations and loyalties to the leader. The leader in such shops is frequently personally involved with the members, evoking responsibility on the part of the leader toward the members, even in their private lives.

The successes of these organizations are closely linked with the personas, power, and class position of the leaders, and often to the women leaders' effective manipulation and reproduction of male processes of political action and domination. These patterns of behaviour and belief are available to the women leaders, in part, because they are members of privileged classes. They learn the skills from men and other women of their class and when they put them into practice, they have the weight of class privilege to undergird their actions.

The women's organizations, I argue, do not offer structural alternatives to men's patron-client based organizations. In fact they tend to reproduce, in feminine circles, the structures of domination current in masculine arenas. I suggest that these organizations, while adding a female component to civil society, do not offer a basis for an autonomous, liberatory women's movement. The patron-client structure of organizational relations makes it difficult for their founders and members to transcend the particularities of their interests to form coalitions with broad-based membership and interests. The organizations tend to be committed to gaining access to political processes and power for the leaders rather than for women in general.

While it is not the focus of this chapter and I cannot here document the assertion, nevertheless I would argue that many of these women's organizations have achieved important benefits for women. At times the benefits are highly specific, such as the delivery of social services or charity to particular women. At other times, the benefits are more generalizable, as when these groups succeed in affecting changes in legislation. The long-term impact of women working in such organizations may paradoxically improve the situation of some (even many) women, while reproducing relatively hierarchical and authoritarian political processes commonly found in male-run organizations.

To develop my argument, I will first depict the background to patron-client relationships in Lebanon. I will then discuss the patterns of leadership in one women's organization as an ethnographic example of this phenomenon of women reproducing men's organizational patterns. The case study will be discussed through extended interviews with a number of women who have been involved with the organization from three to fifty years.

Patronage, Class and Patriarchy

From the beginnings of the modern period in the eighteenth century, if not much earlier, patron-client relationships have been central to political organizations and processes in much of the Mediterranean (Gellner and Waterbury 1977). The interventions of regional and international actors which affected political communities (Polk 1963) often were organized through patron-client relationships based among one or more of what later became the seventeen formally recognized religious sects of Lebanon.

A part of the Ottoman Empire from the fifteenth century, the region of contemporary Lebanon did not have a single name until the eighteenth century (Harik 1968: 13). During the nineteenth century, its political boundaries and the communities contained within those boundaries changed numerous times as France, England and Russia competed for regional footholds by aligning themselves with and becoming the patrons of the leaders of different religious and ethnic communities.

After the First World War, France (the widely perceived patron of the Maronites) became the mandatory power over the region today called Lebanon and Syria. France continued to shift Lebanon's boundaries and change its political membership (including admitting thousands of Armenians as citizens into Lebanon shortly after the Second World War). The political boundaries and composition of Lebanon were finalized with independence in 1943 – but were disrupted in 1948 by the influx of thousands of Palestinians (some of whom became Lebanese citizens), the creation of an informal Palestinian state within Lebanon and the influx of thousands of Syrians in the period of the 1950s to 70s.

Each ethnosectarian group developed its own organizations; also organizations crossing ethno-sectarian boundaries developed in the non-governmental sphere. Both kinds of organization tended in large part, however, toward patron-client leadership dynamics, focusing on highly personalized leader/follower hierarchical relations.

By the outbreak of the civil war in 1975, Lebanon had a population of 3 million. Half a million Syrian citizens and 300,000 Palestinians lived in the country just prior to the war, but soon after it started many Syrians left. Under current Syrian control of central Lebanon, however, the country is being repopulated with Syrians. Now Lebanese leaders seek out the patronage of Syrian officials if they intend to engage in politics, except in southern Lebanon which Israel occupies and controls through its client, the Southern Lebanese Army. For some Lebanese leaders, France remains an active patron.

Lebanon inherited from the French mandate a political system representing citizens on the basis of their membership in one of the seventeen legally recognized ethnosects (Joseph 1978). Lebanese citizens have been required to carry identity cards which name their ethnosectarian membership. Government positions, from top to bottom, have been filled on the basis of proportional representation of ethnosects. Government allocations and projects have been monitored for proportional ethnosectarian distributions (Hudson 1968). Thus, Lebanese nationhood has been formally fractured from its modern beginnings on the basis of ethnosects (Salibi 1988). Membership in the ethnosectarian communities has been felt more strongly than membership in the nation (Meo 1965).

Leadership in these communities has been most frequently organized on the basis of patron-client relationships. Political leaders (*zua'ama'*) from key families have tended to represent 'their' communities for generations with sons replacing their fathers as heads of the communities. Followers of specific leaders have tended and are encouraged to feel personal bonds, obligations and loyalties to them and to their families. Leaders often have taken a personal interest in their followers, offering services, protection and access to material resources to those followers in a personalized manner (Huxley 1978). The members of the political elite have used their positions in the state and other public institutions to funnel favours to their personal following. Since access to such public services and resources has been often channelled through personalized networks, citizens often have felt that their rights are a result of personalized relationships rather than generically assumed and given in the fact of citizenship (Joseph 1978, 1993).

Lebanon was a weak state prior to the civil war of 1975–91 (Hudson 1968). One of the reasons for this weakness was that political leaders decentred the state by using their position to extract resources from the state to redistribute to their clients (Khalaf 1968, 1977; Johnson 1977). Citizens made themselves clients in order to gain access to public resources. One lived through brokerage, webs of relationships centered in kinship and ethnosectarian ties (Barakat 1977, 1985; Khalaf 1968; Huxley 1978). In this political system, citizens have experienced their citizenship as a matter of having access to the appropriately situated people through ties of patronage often rooted in family or family like relationships (Joseph 1983).

Women's Organizations and Civil Society

Few would argue that there is much in the way of a women's movement in Lebanon. Yet there is considerable and often effective action on behalf of women led by numerous women and women's organizations. Nevertheless, such organizations in Lebanon, to a large extent, reproduce the political processes of men's hierarchical patron-client socio-political organizations. Women in their groups, like men in their groups, often set up shops, which share with the men's shops several critical patterns (Gellner and Waterbury 1977; Sharabi 1988; Khalaf 1977).

First, they are run characteristically by a single woman or a small clique of women who retain control of the organization for their lifetime or for the duration of their involvement in the organization. As a result, the organization becomes significantly identified with the persona of its leader(s). Its potentials and achievements come to be regarded as aspects of the will of the leader(s). The leader is the personification of the organization and the organization is embodied in the personhood of the leader(s).

Second, succession to leadership is usually controlled by the current leadership. At times the organization is entirely synonymous with its founder and disintegrates at the death or retirement of that person. At times, the founder or current organizational elite will pass control to their daughters or chosen followers. New leadership may gain power through other means, but the new elite often also attempts to maintain control for long durations. As a result, there tends to be certain kinds of routinizations and reproduction of organizational patterns. The organizational culture becomes closely tied to the specific culture of the leaders.

Third, the organizational structure of women's groups (like that of their male counterparts), is usually hierarchical with members in a subordinate position to the leader(s). Idea generation is top-down with relatively little room for bottom-up innovation. Decision-making is top down. Subordinates rarely feel empowered to challenge their leaders' decisions or innovate new philosophies or practices.

Fourth, the staff and members of the organization, in relational terms, are more often treated as clients and followers of the leader than as equal partners. Rights and benefits of group membership are often seen as gifts from the leader or extensions of the leader's generosity (or lack thereof), rather than being inherent in the person's membership. As a result members often are keenly aware that remaining in the grace of the leader is crucial for them to enjoy the rights and benefits of membership.

Fifth, the fact that members of *dakakeen* often feel indebted to specific leaders for their jobs, access to services, resources, benefits and perks is rooted in the family-like relationships often encouraged and subsidized in these shops. Familial relationality results in part from the fact that members often recruit other members from their own families, villages, neighbourhoods, religious sects, and friendship networks. In part familiality results from the expectation that members will become like family to each other, taking care of each other with the kind of loyalty, concern and reciprocity expected in family relationships. Given that family structures in Lebanon are generally patriarchal (gender and age hierarchical, privileging males and seniors), the reproduction of familial moralities in *dakakeen* further reinforces the reproduction of the type of hierarchical structures of leadership found in the male patron-client based socio-political organizations. In the women's organizations, this supports the privilege of seniors and the indirect forms of communication often found in families, especially among subordinates.

As a result of these patterns, women's organizations tend to take conservative to moderate approaches to solving women's problems. They either see themselves as subsidiaries of men's organizations and activities or they agitate to give women access to the structures and organizations dominated by men. They tend not to take the radical position of arguing for structural change in governmental, market, or domestic arenas which would result in structural changes in gender relations.

Case Study: The Women's League

The specifics of these organizational processes can be analysed using an ethnographic case of one organization with which I have had contact since 1968. For the purposes of this paper, I will call this organization the Women's League. The League was started in Lebanon in the early part of the twentieth century.[2] Like many organizations of long standing, it has a number of branches around the country. While it has been primarily a Christian organization in membership, leadership and clientele, it has also served Muslims. Its members and staff have included Lebanese Protestants, Greek Orthodox, Maronites, Catholics, and Quakers. A few of its employees have been Muslim. A majority of the League's staff and members have been Lebanese, but a number have been Palestinian and Syrian. Its staff has included men and its services have extended to men.

The data for the case is based on extensive observations since 1968 and discussions with many members and staff. Some of the interviewees, such as Ms Badi'a Raji, Ms Mazbut, Ms René Aswad and Ms Lillian 'Ameed[3] worked for the organization in several branches and capacities over a span of 40–50 years each. Others, such as Ms Dunya, Ms Jean Dawwoud, and Mr 'Adel 'Abdullah were relatively new when I met them in 1968, but continued to work with and for the League for many years. While I have noticed differences among staff and members and some changes over the years, the specific organizational patterns that I focus on below were in place by 1968 and for the most part continued to be reproduced in various ways.

Leadership for Life

Etel Adnan has observed that leaders in the Arab world often feel they are born into their chairs. 'Our leaders live sitting. When they arrive in power they grow into their chairs, until they, body and chair, become inseparable' (Adnan 1982: 76). The sense that leadership is for life pervades *dakakeen* in Lebanon (Barakat 1988; Sharabi 1988).

Many women's organizations follow the *dakakeen* pattern in this regard. The Red Cross and the YWCA each had, at one point, one president for about thirty years. In the case of the YWCA, that president was succeeded by another president who served for seventeen years. The Children's Foundation was headed by the same president for between fifteen and twenty years. The Women's Rights Organization has had the same president, its founder, for a period of 20–25 years. The Muslim Youth Organization's president has been in office for fifteen years. The president of the Chain of Friends has served for over five years. The Human Rights Organization has had one president, its founder, for between fifteen and twenty years.

When I first met League members and staff in 1968, some of the founding figures were still active. A number of the leaders had already served between twenty-five and forty years in the organization. Several were so publicly and self-identified with the League that they were considered its 'trademarks' by staff and members. Most of the seventeen members of the Board of Directors of the largest branch in 1968 were in their 50s and 60s. Most had worked in multiple capacities, serving on a number of different committees, heading up a series of different projects and rotating as League officers. For example, by the late 1960s, Ms Mazbut, a member of the largest regional board who was in her early 50s, had already served six or seven two-year terms on the Board of Directors, including rotating off after each consecutive two terms. Ms Aswad had begun serving in various volunteer capacities in the League in the 1920s and was still volunteering in the late 1960s.

In 1968, almost all the Board of Directors and higher level staff members of the largest branch were of upper or upper-middle class origins. Few Board members were gainfully employed. All had relatively wealthy husbands and came from relatively wealthy and educated family backgrounds. Almost all had come from the class of families which expected women to serve society through charitable work. A few of the Board members had been staff members at one point. In 1995 this pattern had not only not changed, but had intensified. While part of the reason for the repetitive recycling of the same personnel through different offices and capacities was the difficulties of recruitment during the civil war of 1975–91, that pattern had been set even before the war broke out. When I asked one long-term staffer what changes she would like to make in the major branches of the League, she said, 'I would move them from their seats. I would let others take over. I would have a whole new board.'

My Organization, My Self

Their longevity of service inspired some staff and members to feel that the organization belonged to them. Ms Dunya, a director of the Beirut branch pointed out to me in 1968 that some staff and leaders had made the League their life. She, wanting to focus on her family more, thought it was unnatural. 'I don't like that someone has only one thing in her life,' she complained, giving as an example the head of the League's national office, Badi'a Raji. 'She wants everyone else to become like her,' Ms Dunya protested. Despite her desire for a family life apart from the League, she found herself often taking work home or waking at 5 in the morning to start work.

For Ms Dunya, Badi'a Raji's identification with the League led her to micromanage all the affairs of the organization, even those not in the domain of her office. She complained that Ms Raji, who had headed a regional branch office before she became the national director, continued to intervene at the branch level, even though Ms Dunya was responsible for some of those matters. Ms Raji recruited personnel for branch offices, took personnel from branch offices for national projects and intervened in events organized by branches, even though that was not part of her job, according to Ms Dunya.

The identification of the League with particular leaders and the identification of particular leaders with the League, as in most patron-client based organizations (Suleiman 1965), was often the result of who founded the organization. 'It all depends on who organizes a group. I started this branch of the League, so it sticks to me. If it fails or succeeds, the failure or success is mine. The one who starts the group does all the contacts, the building, etc. The volunteers come and go, but the staff person stays, so it becomes hers,' Lillian 'Ameed observed to me. 'This branch sticks to me now. But I don't dare leave yet because it is not in their soul yet. I tried to keep the League from belonging to anyone. I heard one woman say, "I want to do this." I talked to her to omit the "I".'

One staff member noted that in the largest branch, 'The leaders feel the League is theirs. They have been working so long. They are old. They pass it from one generation to another.' She continued,

> One woman was in the League as a staff, then on the board. So the League is in them. In the largest and oldest branch, for so many years, the same members were elected and reelected on the board again and again. It is against the constitution. Many people left during the war so they feel they have to use the same people again. Even before the war, they used the same people over and again.

In a newer branch founded in the late 1970s, she observed that members were not identified with the League to the same extent. Members rotated on and off the board, taking only two consecutive terms, therefore allowing for 'new blood'.

Several staff members felt that changes were needed, particularly in the national office and the largest branch. One staff member explained:

> I would give the leadership to the young. I would involve the young more, especially in those things that pertain to their lives. Let them decide their plans. I would change some of the old programmes, reevaluate and cancel them if they are not working. I would give a chance for people to progress. I would not just focus on the good leaders and congratulate them on being good leaders.

This life commitment and identification with an organization was characteristic not only of leaders, however, but also of members and lower level staff. One young man whom I met in 1968, a Muslim, worked as a driver for the organization for over twenty-five years. Years after the organization could no longer support his salary and he had found work elsewhere, he continued to help the organization whenever need presented itself. He had a highly developed sense of personal loyalty to the organization in general, but especially to particular staff within it. During the civil war, on a number of occasions, he had acted to ensure the safety of those staff. Similarly Ms Hadi, a staffer, had worked, by 1995, for over a quarter of a century for the organization in different branches and capacities. A low key functionary, she knew the organization by heart. Dutifully she went to work, even during the war when getting to work was hazardous. Lillian 'Ameed spent almost all of her adult life with the League, logging in about fifty years of service. Working through wars and national crises she knew everybody in the organization, their families, their histories, their activities. The League was her family.

My Organization, My Family

That so many staff and members made long-term (and life) commitments to the League was an expression of the way that it was, for many, like a family. Repeatedly in interviews, the reference to family came up. Family became a model of relationships both because of the dedication of people to the organization and each other and because many in the League were in fact relatives.

In 1968, the head of the national office, one staff in the national office and one staff in the largest regional office were related to each other. Two sisters were on a regional board. Two other regional board members were sisters-in-law. Two others were related through more distant marital relations. Another board member recruited her aunt who eventually became an active board member. Ms Aswad, a regional board member active in the organization for forty to fifty years, had a daughter in a high position in a transnational League branch and a second daughter and a granddaughter involved in other capacities. An engineer contracted to build a new branch office was related to a board member. Members therefore often recruited each other, using personal networks based in kinship, friendship, and village of origin. A significant concentration of staff and members in some of the branches or the national office were related to each other, came from the same village and/or were parts of the same friendship networks.

In addition to actual kinship relations, members often felt and acted like kin. Almost all members and staff with long years of service not only knew each other well, but knew each other's families and friends. They visited each other on occasions of births, deaths, weddings and other significant familial events. They substituted and stood in for each other in times of personal crisis; they lent each other money; helped each other prepare for significant events or acted as brokers on each other's behalf when needed. In one of many such instances, for example, the son of one League member wanted to change his major at the American University of Beirut but was having difficulty doing so. Lillian 'Ameed intervened on his behalf by speaking to the husband of one of the League board members who was a faculty member at the American University of Beirut. Delicately introducing the subject, she repeatedly apologized for bringing it up, pleading her own ignorance in the matter and appealing to the expertise and knowledge of the faculty member. She managed to win his sympathies and the change of major of the student was achieved. In addition, League members helped each other find jobs for family members, intervened with government ministries to complete paperwork, made connections for medical care and assistance and so forth. In an endless array of matters, League members turned to each other for help.

As a result, they often demanded family-like service and loyalty on the job as well. Working unpaid overtime and carrying out tasks outside their job description was an on-going organizational dynamic. In fact, many did not know their job descriptions (if they existed) and therefore had no formal grounds on which to limit or bound the claims on their services. In addition members bore the emotional eruptions of those senior to them. I once asked Lillian 'Ameed why she tolerated the humiliations she sometimes suffered during emotional outbursts by Ms Dunya and Ms Raji and why Ms Dunya and Ms Raji (among others) tolerated each other's emotional outbursts. She shrugged her shoulders. Giving a long explanation of the lives and times of each of the women I named, she indicated they were all like family (real or imagined) and had to bear each other.

My Organization, My Interests

That many thought of the League as family did not mean that they all put it ahead of themselves, as one would be expected to with family in Lebanon. Rather, as some staffers pointed out, many used the League for their own self-interest and self-promotion. Ms Mazbut, for example, had a reputation as being driven by the need for status and putting herself at the centre of events. One staff member reported to me that Ms Mazbut had been in charge of a fundraising event for the League one year. The following year, someone else was responsible. When the newspaper article covering the event did not mention Ms Mazbut's name (since she had not been involved), she scolded Ms Raji in front of several board members and staff. She accused Ms Raji of not giving credit to other people, of not sharing decisions, of keeping everything to herself. Even Ms Mazbut's husband became angry and complained that his wife had not been mentioned in the newspaper article. Ms Raji was reduced to tears. This was particularly vexing to Ms Raji and some staff who knew her well because she had invested considerable energy in recruiting Ms Mazbut and creating her position in the League. The view of these staffers was that Ms Mazbut always needed to be at the centre, and did 'things for show'. Ms Aswad, another long-time volunteer, was also seen as 'dedicated to herself' rather than the League. She was not alone in this conceit. As a staff member remarked of many of the board and senior staff, 'All people have a feeling of *farju*, showing themselves off.'

Another staff member noted that the women who worked very hard for the League had a more difficult time accepting new ideas.

The ideas have to come from them to be accepted. I would throw out ideas and pretend that they did it. I'd go to their homes and convince them quietly, individually – not in groups. I still do this. If you have progressive ideas, they say it is not in the League spirit.

The harder a member or staff works for the League, the more they identify with it and the more they are inclined to impose their will on it. It appears that their sense of self comes to be linked with the organization so that ideas, events, changes become personalized.

Succession of Leadership: Like Mother like Daughter

Some women's organizations – such as the Lioness, the Women's Council of Lebanon, the Women's Guild of AUB, and the YWCA – have had a practice of electing board members and senior leadership. In other organizations the succession of leadership has been more informal, often by designation of previous leaders. At times succession fails and the organization dies with the leader/founder. Not infrequently, leaders have been succeeded by their children. In typical patronage based male organizations, the leader/founder's son succeeds his father in a leadership position (Suleiman 1965). Pierre Gamayel, founder of the Maronite-based Lebanese Kata'ib Party was succeeded by his sons Bashir (who was assassinated shortly after being elected president of Lebanon) and Ameen (who succeeded his brother Bashir as president). Kamal Jumblat, founder of the Druze-based Progressive Socialist Party was succeeded by his son Walid Jumblat. Camille Chamoun, former president of Lebanon and founder of the National Liberal Party, was succeeded by his two sons, Dory and Danny Chamoun. Suleiman Frangieh (former president of Lebanon) was to be succeeded by his son Tony, but Tony was killed during the war. This is a pattern found not only in male political organizations in Lebanon, but in much of the Arab world and in the Mediterranean (Gellner and Waterbury 1977; Giacomo 1990).

When I first shared with Lillian 'Ameed in 1968 my observations on the succession to leadership patterns in the League, it was the first time she had thought about kinship connections in the organization. It had seemed natural and unnoteworthy to her until then. In 1994, she pointed out to me, 'The mothers train the daughters to take over.' Three of the board members of the largest regional office had their daughters on the board. One member had her sister representing the League in trans-national meetings. She noted that she was allowed to go to the transnational meetings, a perceived perk, only once after almost fifty years of service in the League. Yet, one woman with much fewer years of service was president, one of her daughters was on the board and another daughter on the board of the transnational League. Lillian called them 'the father, son, and Holy Ghost'. Lillian commented, 'They feel it is theirs,' an observation I heard repeated by a number of middle range staff.

This mother to daughter succession, however, appeared to be much more prominent in the oldest branch of the League. In some of the newer branches, mother to daughter succession was more class-based – middle-class daughters appeared to be more inclined than upper-class daughters to succeed their mothers. In the oldest branch, upper- and middle-class daughters both often succeeded their mothers in membership and leadership of the League. This difference could have been a result of a tradition not yet having been established in the newer branches. 'It is not yet in them,' a director of one of the newer branches observed.

Typical of organizations where succession is highly personalized and kin-based, I observed in the late 1960s that the League did not have systematic procedures for replacing senior staff. 'The hiring board just looks around until they find someone who tickles them,' one staff member reported, chuckling. Several staff told me that they did not know their own titles. They could list the different things they did, but did not know how that would fit into an organizational chart. One staff member claimed that most staff and board members were not familiar with the organizational chart.

In the 1960s and 1970s, the staff at the national office and largest branch had never been gathered together to discuss their job descriptions, responsibilities, lines of authority or rights. When Ms Raji moved from the regional office to the national office, it took six months to replace her because the Board did not know what they were looking for. When Ms Dunya was hired, no clearly articulated job description was used for recruiting.

This difficulty in recruiting replacements for top leaders appeared to be continuing in 1996. One regional director had indicated to me for several years that she wanted to step down from her position but had not been able to find a replacement for herself. She had begged the regional board a number of times to find a replacement. None had been willing to take an initiative in recruiting. No advertisements were placed. The director was left to network on her own to find her replacement. This was particularly difficult because of the low pay associated with the position of director (in 1996, less than $500 a month). A salary double that amount would have been needed to recruit someone at that level in the city where the branch was located. When I asked why the director was willing to work for so little pay, she replied that the League was her family, her life.

Decision-Making

> Members in the largest regional branch listen to each other, but you feel that the decisions are made outside the meetings. There is a clique. They meet outside the meetings to make decisions. In the meetings there are motions, seconding, voting. It feels democratic, but it is not. There are 5–6 women who are in charge. They control everything so they can go to the transnational meetings.

Thus, Lillian 'Ameed reported her observations about the appearance of democracy and the reality of a ruling clique in the largest branch of the League. Part of the autocracy came from a highly personalized style of decision-making.

Many of the staff and members felt that the key to the decision-making process was the personality of the leader. Lillian 'Ameed contrasted her approach to that of Ms Raji as follows:

> Ms Raji had a *dikkan*. She had a *shakhsiyyi* (strong character). She imposed what she thought was right. People say that if Lillian (I) leave this branch of the League, it will fall apart. I would hate this because all my work would be gone. I involve people, let them make decisions, let them plan. I give them a free hand as much as I can trust them. Ms Raji used to be our hands. She wanted to do everything. She'd meet with all the committees and it would be her work. I did not dare to do any programme without consulting Ms Raji. She controlled everything. We in our branch have an anti-drug group. They work on their own. I support them in doing their own work.

Ms Dunya was proud of her highly organized approach to work. As I came to meet her for our luncheon appointment on an August morning in 1968, she opened her appointment book and checked me off her list. 'I had such a bureaucratic feeling as she checked me off her morning list,' I wrote in my fieldnotes that day. While I waited, Ms Badi'a Raji called to tell Ms Dunya to take a visiting student to lunch with us. Ms Dunya protested that she did not know where this student was. She made an effort to find her. Later, Ms Dunya's daughter told me that they had not wanted to take this student to lunch and that Ms Raji always intervened in Ms Dunya's plans. For Ms Dunya to work with Ms Raji, noted for a dedicated but less than organized approach to work, led to daily conflict.

An example of this conflict occurred in my presence in 1968. As I was preparing for my doctoral fieldwork, Ms Raji became interested in my carrying out a survey that she could use as the basis for future planning. To carry this out, I needed the assistance of Lillian 'Ameed, a staff member working under the direction of Ms Dunya. Ms Raji informed me and Lillian that Lillian could accompany me and assist me for a short period in the project. Ms Dunya, who had not been consulted in advance, refused permission arguing that Lillian was already committed to other work slated for that period. Ms Raji found someone to replace Lillian on a volunteer basis, a person who was willing to work unpaid on her vacation to free Lillian. Despite the provision of a replacement who was experienced and capable of carrying out the work, Ms Dunya continued to resist. Ms Raji, for her part, argued that Lillian needed a break, that her work was too exhausting, that this would give her an opportunity to learn different tools and that furthermore the replacement was not only skilled but also free of charge. Ms Dunya relented only after days of negotiating that climaxed in a meeting that included Ms Raji, Lillian and myself. But she made it clear to me that this was yet another example of Ms Raji's high-handed intervention in a part of the organization's affairs that did not belong to her domain and of her inability to separate herself from the organization.

For her part, Lillian 'Ameed felt that her ability to take advantage of this opportunity was due only to Ms Raji's intervention. She therefore left personally indebted to Ms Raji. Her indebtedness had a long history since it was Ms Raji, a relative, who had brought her into the organization in the first place and had helped her move up through it. Yet this personal obligation had its down side. Lillian thought that Ms Raji had also held her back from promotions that she deserved and prohibited her from gaining important experiences that would have advanced her career.

Often staff and members in patron-client based organizations like the Women's League feel that their benefits, opportunities and access to resources and services are personal gifts from specific patrons (Joseph 1994). The lack of organizational charts, the vagueness of job descriptions and the unarticulated lines of authority leave staff and members vulnerable to the manipulations and behind-the-scenes operations of strong personalities. Indeed, without the patronage of such people, subordinates in these organizations may lose out on perks and benefits.

The highly personalized and at times chaotic nature of decision-making was more characteristic of the League than the apparent bureaucratic style of Ms Dunya. In the late 1960s, the League had decided to make a film about itself for publicity purposes. I happened to be around when parts of the film were made and when the finished product was shown. The project had been in the planning stages for four to six months, yet the film-maker apparently received no direction as to budget, what to film, how to film, or how the film was to be used. I watched him film scenes that struck his interest with no thematic connection to each other. The final product, a failure in the eyes of most of the League members with whom I talked, displayed long shots of signs and buildings of no particular interest or sequencing, long sessions in meetings with old ladies who appeared motionless, repetitive scenes of people dancing in different branches with no connection to each other, shots of fundraisers with no transitional moments.

Parts of the film were shot at activities without advance notice to the staff in charge. Jean Dawwoud, one of the staff treated in this manner, pointed out that the leaders showed no respect for the staff. They came with the photographer, shot the film and did not even say 'hello' to her. 'Never mind me as a person,' she said, 'They should consider my position as a staff of the League.' She added that the 'whole League has no understanding of how to handle workers' and that she herself had no respect for Ms Raji and Ms Dunya.

The disrespect shown to staff during the filming was only part of her complaints. She contended that the League leaders did not know how to lead because each board member and senior staff wanted to be the leader. 'There are too many heads,' she pointed out with frustration. 'Every board member and senior staff think they have authority to do whatever they want. There is no line of authority'. She had been asked to work on a project, then told that she was not needed in the position she had been originally assigned. She told Ms Dunya that she would not come, but Ms Dunya insisted that she must. Resentfully, Jean Dawwoud complied.

Lillian 'Ameed, a highly organized and professional member of the League, repeatedly experienced the chaotic interventions of senior staff and League leaders. In charge of a large summer event which convened hundreds of people, Lillian had a reputation as hard-working and charismatic. She worked for months ahead of time to plan and organize for the summer projects. With no advance warning, Ms Raji imposed upon her two visiting staff whom Lillian would have to train and incorporate into the summer events. She was not told they would be coming, what they would do, how to incorporate them or what their responsibilities would be. Nor was she put in touch with the visiting staff ahead of time. One of them was later told by Ms Raji to take over as programme director. Lillian told me there already was a director for the summer events. The previously assigned programme director was not given advance notice of the change. 'They don't look to see what they have and what they need before they jump into a project. There is no planning,' Lillian woefully pointed out to me repeatedly in the 1960s and 1970s. Jean Dawwoud, the displaced programme director angrily concurred.

According to Lillian 'Ameed, this was an example of the lack of definition of lines of authority in the League. I saw it as the result of the highly personalized decision-making process in a patron-client based organizational form. Lillian observed that hardly anyone knew the organizational chart except herself, and those who did ignored it. They carved out roles for themselves based on their personas, not on their formal roles. As a result, when two or more strong women found themselves in the same activity, there was conflict over who was to do what. This led to staff being asked to do work not in their description and rarely rewarded for going above and beyond. Lillian frequently worked long hours, evenings and weekends, on projects which were not formally a part of her position and yet was rarely recognized for it. In one fundraising activity, which was not part of her job, Lillian did most of the work preparing for the event. When the press came to cover it, Ms Dunya referred to Lillian (a professional woman) as 'the secretary' and directed the press away from her. Neither Lillian's picture nor her name appeared in any of the coverage of the event.

I experienced the 'spontaneous' character of activities when I agreed to carry out the survey for the League. Ms Raji decided it would be a good thing to do. I was given little direction and yet expected to complete it in short order. Discussions with Ms Raji and Ms Dunya revealed that they had different conceptions of what I was to do and that their ideas changed from one discussion to another. At one point it appeared as if this minor survey had taken on monumental significance in the 'future' planning of the League. A graduate student at the time, I was anxious that the expectations, unformed yet inflated, would be impossible to meet. When the survey was completed, none of the leaders knew what to do with it or how to evaluate it. While this may have arisen from the nature of the research, I suspect it had more to do with the fact that (like the film project), they did not know exactly what they wanted from it to begin with. This lack of vision, goals and planning in advance was characteristic of the decision-making process.

Decision-making was charged with the personal connections among board members, staff and the people they served. In one event I observed in 1968, Ms René Aswad, a long-time board member of the largest regional branch, intervened to try to have a relative receive an award for the outstanding achievement in one of the branch's activities. In another event, a person related to Lillian 'Ameed cried and threatened to leave a project if she were not allowed to have her choice of activities. League members who happened to be visiting intervened and pressed Lillian to let the person have her way. Lillian relented.

Branch Differences

While the general patterns of leadership and organizational behaviour were quite similar throughout the League, there were important differences among the branches. Since the League, like many national women's organizations, had offices throughout Lebanon, these regional differences must also be considered in understanding women's organiz-ations. Some of the differences among the branches were connected to larger national and transnational cultural differences.

The oldest League branch is almost 75 years old. Members have felt it is rooted in their region. Since the early founders were mainly Protestant and remain involved, this branch has had a reputation of being Protestant and perhaps more American/English oriented. Some staff felt that the minority status of the Protestants made them socially minded. Staff members with experience in this branch, the national office and other regional offices observed style differences in the mode of operation that they attributed to these cultural roots. 'The Protestants are more diplomatic. They are more orderly. Their meetings are efficient, orderly and parliamentary. They get what they want behind the scenes,' one staff reported.

In this branch, there has been a greater pattern of daughters following their mothers into the League. Nevertheless, some staff felt that women in other branches were more cooperative. They commented that compared to some branches, the members of the oldest branch did not socialize much with each other, organize outings together or become friends. One reason suggested was that members 'are saturated'. Staff in other branches also thought that the staff and volunteers in the oldest branch were not as qualified as in others.

One of the regional branches, in contrast, was associated, with French culture. Since Lebanon was a French mandate from the First World War to independence in 1943, much of the country – particularly Christian Lebanon – has been influenced by French culture. 'French culture is more self-centred,' one League staff observed. 'They don't care about what is going on outside their circle. One board member tried to get her daughter to go to conferences outside Lebanon, but the daughter would not go.' In this regional branch, the leading group has been Greek Orthodox and Maronite. No Protestants have been involved. 'Maronites are more direct, more disorderly. I had a hard time because they are French culture. It was a different mentality,' a regional League staffer explained. She noted that in this branch, members tended to be disorderly in meetings, which she thought was a cultural phenomenon. 'I want them to be more quiet in meetings. Listening is hard for them. They all talk at once. It's like a race. They are not orderly. They don't know when to talk, to listen or to ask permission to talk.'

However, a staff member noted that the women in this branch were very cooperative and friendly with each other. They socialized and organized outings together. She observed that, 'Whatever programmes we put on, they like it. They want to do it again. They are enthusiastic. They are new. They race to do work. They are responsible. You can rely on them. The current president is creative, a good listener.' The regional branch director complained that this sociability had a down side. Members of the regional board came to her office 'as if I were here for *subhiyyi* (morning coffee). But I need to work.'

Despite their friendly and cooperative spirit, this regional branch witnessed conflicts among the Greek Orthodox and the Maronites. 'They are both large members and both know how to do things. They are two forces competing for power. But I stand like a sword between them,' the regional branch director explained. 'I don't let them fight. I won't let there be two groups. Each member can be active without groups and regardless of whether she is Greek Orthodox or Maronite. There are trouble makers in each group and you have to stop them.'

Relations Between Women's Organizations

Typically *dakakeen* are singular in their activities. Organizationally, there is little capacity for sustained coalition building, collaborative efforts or working collectively with other organizations. This has been relatively true of men's patron-client based *dakakeen* in Lebanon and elsewhere in the Mediterranean. Similarly, I found among the women's service organizations that there was little in the way of inter-organizational efforts. Each organization in service to women has worked on its own. Even within the League, there have been few collaborative efforts between branches; most activities have been carried out by a branch on its own. Some staffers pointed out that there has been considerable jealousy between some branches of the League. One staff even felt that another branch would have liked to destroy her branch because it has been successful.

Shopkeepers and Feminists

The organizational patterns observed in the Women's League resonate with my observations of many women's organizations and find parallels in men's patron-client based organizations in Lebanon. These patterns are not exclusively Lebanese, however. I have found them in many other Middle Eastern as well as Western countries. A number of characteristics are particularly striking.

1. The domination of the League by a few people came up repeatedly. One or a handful of women controlled the organization, passed on control to their daughters or chosen followers, controlled idea generation, and were identified, like glue, as trademarks of the organization. Despite the appearance of democracy at times, the League was undemocratic. The clique came to own the organization, the ideas were their ideas, the success and failures of the organization belonged to them personally.

   The size and structure of the League allowed for numerous leaders, who tended to be competitive with each other. Each vied for control over clients, manipulating access to services, resources, perks and benefits. They distributed these benefits to their subordinates in a highly personalized manner which led to the benefit being regarded as a personal gift of the patron. The effect was to create a series of personalized debts which the client had to repay with loyalty and service.

2. There was a strong sense that the League had to be 'in you'. For some the League was a movement; it had to continue to grow, to bring in new blood, to claim loyalties. There was a sense that a woman must identify with the organization and commit to it.

3. I also observed class differences. The oldest League branch has been more upper class, with other regional branches more mixed in class terms. The upper-class daughters of some regional offices did not follow their mothers into the organization, but the middle-class daughters did.

4. The competition and jealousy between organizations, between branches of an organization and between members of an organization has been a continuity in my observations. This seems to be related to the need that people have to show themselves, *farju*, as one staffer called it.

5. The League has been a service organization, but for the elite women who are members, it has also been a social organization. It has given them something to do. It has been a social activity. Because of this, the members in some branches have felt they could visit and socialize with staff, even though staff had work to do.

6. The battle over cultures has also been important. Organizations inherit, as well as create their cultures. How an organization is founded, who

founds it, who funds it, and who remains identified with it significantly affect its culture. The differences between the American/English culture and the French culture in the different branches of the League have created an ongoing struggle. While these cultures are local, they have been linked to global cultures of the metropolitan colonial and neocolonial centres as well as being linked through the transnational structures of the organizations.

In addition, I found differences between local ethnic/sectarian cultures such as the Lebanese Protestants versus the Lebanese Greek Orthodox and Maronites. Local ethnosectarian cultures, linked sometimes to international ones, have created different values and orientations that impinge on organizational behaviour – such as the greater orderliness League members observed among the Protestants, and the greater disorderliness of the Maronites and Greek Orthodox. Such local cultures and global cultures, whether channelled through international organizations or colonial and neocolonial agencies, have a significant impact on women's organizations.

The problems and limitations of women's organizations which share organizational patterns with men's hierarchical patron-client based organizations are crucial to the development of a liberatory women's movement in Lebanon. These organizations have had successes in offering services to women and in making legislative, social, or economic inroads for women. Yet they have not offered structural alternatives to the men's patron-client organizations. Some of their success has been purchased at the expense of democratizing their organizational structure and their decision-making process. Their contribution in transforming gender relations has been constrained by the organizational dynamics that they manipulate for their successes.

Notes

1. The term *dikkan* was especially used during the Lebanese civil war 1975–90 to refer to the many small militias and political organizations that sprung up during the war.
2. I write the case study in the past tense to avoid a-historicizing. The data gathering covered relatively regular contact with staff and members of the organization between 1968 and 1996.
3. Names of all persons interviewed and referred to have been changed.

References

Adnan, E. (1982), *Sitt Marie Rose*, Sausalito, CA: The Post-Apollo Press.

Barakat, H. (1977), *Lebanon in Strife. Student Preludes to the Civil War*, Austin: University of Texas Press.

—— ed. (1988), *Toward a Viable Lebanon*, London: Croom Helm.

Gellner, E. and Waterbury, J., eds (1977), *Patrons and Clients in Mediterranean Societies*, London: Duckworth.

Harik, I. F. (1968), *Politics and Change in a Traditional Society. Lebanon 1711–1845*, Princeton: Princeton University Press.

Hudson, M. (1968), *The Precarious Republic. Political Modernization in Lebanon*, New York: Random House.

Huxley, F.C. (1978), *Wasita in a Lebanese Context. Social Exchange Among Villagers and Outsiders*, Ann Arbor: Museum of Anthropology, University of Michigan.

Johnson, M. (1977), 'Political Bosses and Their Gangs: Zu'ama and Qabadayat in the Sunni Muslim Quarters of Beirut,' in E. Gellner and J. Waterbury, eds, *Patrons and Clients in Mediterranean Societies*, London: Duckworth.

Joseph, S. (1978), 'Muslim-Christian Conflict in Lebanon: A Perspective on the Evolution of Sectarianism,' in S. Joseph & B.K. Pillsbury, eds, *Muslim-Christian Conflicts:Economic, Political and Social Origins*, Boulder, Co.: Westview Press.

—— (1983), 'Working Class Women's Networks in a Sectarian State: A Political Paradox,' *American Ethnologist*, 10, 1: 1–22.

—— (1990), 'Working the Law: A Lebanese Working Class Case,' in D. Dwyer, ed., *The Politics of Law in the Middle East*, South Hadley, Ma.: J.F. Bergin Publishers: 143–60.

—— (1993), 'Gender and Civil Society. An Interview with Suad Joseph' with Joe Stork, *Middle East Reports*, 183, 23, 4: 22–6.

—— (1994), 'Problematizing Gender and Relational Rights: Experiences from Lebanon,' *Social Politics*, 1, 3: 271–85.

Khalaf, S. (1968), 'Primordial Ties and Politics in Lebanon,' *Middle Eastern Studies*, 4, 3: 243–69.

—— (1977), 'Changing Forms of Political Patronage in Lebanon,' in E. Gellner & J. Waterbury, eds, *Patrons and Clients in Mediterranean Societies*, London: Duckworth.

Luciani, G., ed. (1990), *The Arab State*, Berkeley: University of California Press.

Meo, L. M. (1965), *Lebanon. Improbable Nation. A Study in Political Development*, Bloomington: Indiana University Press.

Polk, W. R. (1963), *The Opening of South Lebanon 1788–1840*, Cambridge: Harvard University Press.

Salibi, K. (1988), *A House of Many Mansions. The History of Lebanon Reconsidered*, Berkeley: University of California Press.

Sharabi, H. (1988), *Neopatriarchy. A Theory of Distorted Change in Arab Society*, New York: Oxford University Press.

Suleiman, M. (1965), *Political Parties in Lebanon. The Challenge of a Fragmented Political Culture*, Ithaca: Cornell University Press.

4

Domesticity Reconfigured: Women in Squatter Areas of Amman

Seteney Shami

Introduction

Describing aspects of the lives and relations of women in two squatter areas of Amman, Jordan, in the context of urban upgrading projects opens up the question of where and how to locate the boundaries of the domestic 'domain'. The squatter areas are here called 'the Wadi' and 'the Jabal'. One lies along the slopes and the bottom of a steep gully, the other on one of the highest hilltops of the city, but both represent some of the most congested and poor areas of central Amman.[1] The families who live in the squatter houses, mostly made of concrete and corrugated metal, are Palestinian refugees from the 1948 and 1967 exoduses from Palestine. The Wadi borders a refugee camp and the Jabal is surrounded by low-income neighbourhoods. However the people do not distinguish clearly between these different types of areas or draw their boundaries according to legal-administrative panoptic definitions of urban space (squatter area, refugee camp, low-income housing). More important for them are the networks of kinship and co-operation that define their identity, give meaning to their social relations and sustain them through difficult and insecure economic circumstances.

On the other hand, public/state definitions of place and space do intrude upon daily life in the Wadi and the Jabal, and such intrusions may become unavoidable or threatening, as in the case of the possible demolition of the site, or inclusion in urban upgrading projects, or the conducting of surveys and research, or NGO activity sponsored from outside the area. For example, the Jabal was one of the four sites selected for an upgrading project funded by the World Bank and implemented, starting in 1980, by the Urban Development Department (UDD), a unit within the Amman Municipality established for this purpose. The Wadi, on the other hand, was part of the base-line survey conducted by the UDD but was then passed over for upgrading.

In this chapter, I explore some of the relations and networks maintained by women in the two areas focusing on the domestic arena and the impact of the upgrading project upon it. This raises the wider issue of the intersections of the private and public domains in the lives of these women, including situations where the public threatens to dominate and appropriate the private. Conversely, it is of particular interest how women deploy the powerful language and symbols of domesticity and femininity in negotiating their encounters with public agencies and personnel.

Domestic Relations and the Spaces of Women's Lives

The house shared by the two households of Um Khalil[2] and Aisha bordered the main road that stretches between the Wadi and the adjacent refugee camp. The dwelling consisted of three main rooms built in concrete with an open courtyard enclosed by a corrugated metal ('zinco') wall. Um Khalil and her six daughters aged three to seventeen lived in one room, her son Khalil and his new bride lived in another and they shared a kitchen and outdoor toilet. Um Khalil's mother-in-law (Um Hasan) lived in another room across the courtyard with her three-times-divorced daughter Aisha, and Aisha's young daughter from her last marriage. They had a separate kitchen but shared the same toilet. The link between the two households was Hasan, Um Khalil's husband and Um Hasan's son. However Hasan lived down the street in another house with his second wife. Another link between the two households was Khalil's wife who is Aisha's eldest daughter from her first marriage.

In spite of these kinship links, the households were economically separate. Although Hasan contributed occasionally towards the expenses of both (while keeping away physically most of the time), Khalil was the main supporter of the first household (from his wages as a mechanic) and Aisha provided the main support for the second one (from her alimony), with some income obtained through Um Hasan's (rapidly decreasing) activities as a midwife and healer. Although Khalil was the wage earner, Um Khalil was clearly the head of her household and took all financial and other decisions. Aisha's household was much poorer than Um Khalil's and a main cause of conflict between the two households was sharing the water tap, which was the only source of water in the house and for which Um Khalil paid the bill. Aisha had to do all the chores of her household since her daughter was small. Um Khalil, on the other hand, maintained a managerial stance. She decided on the daily food to be bought, what cleaning and washing should be done, and when the bread should be baked. Her many daughters did the chores under her direct supervision.

Um Khalil's twelve-year-old daughter, Maryam, usually did the shopping as she was old enough to be responsible but not old enough to arouse criticism for being out in the streets alone. Um Khalil sent out Maryam an average of six or seven times a day, to check the prices and the availability of the foodstuffs before finally sending her out to buy the items one by one. Maryam often grew impatient with this system and would ask her mother to just tell her everything she needed at one time. She also was anxious to do well in school and wanted more time to study. Her requests were ignored, but Maryam had the compensation of buying a little item for herself with every shopping trip like a bag of chips or an ice-cream which she sometimes shared with her younger sisters.

The two older daughters were in charge of the more complicated tasks of baking bread and cooking. They also spent a lot of time wondering about love and having giggly conversations with Khalil's wife in her room with the door closed. At times one of Aisha's older daughters from a previous marriage would come to visit her mother for a few days. Invited by her sister (Khalil's wife), and much to Um Khalil's disapproval, she would cross the courtyard and join the secret conversations of the young girls, but would not help with their chores. Instead, she would help her own mother with that household's tasks.

The ambiguity of these relationships was constantly being played out in the four square metres of the courtyard. The doors of the two sets of rooms did not face one another and there was an invisible line drawn across the courtyard that only the younger children would cross with impunity. The adults kept to their side of the courtyard except when entering or leaving the house. When the adults quarrelled, the children were forbidden to cross the line, or crossed at the risk of being hit and taunted by the children of the other side – behaviour which was encouraged and even instigated by the adults. Sometimes Khalil's wife was said to be 'visiting her mother' – an action which only entailed crossing the courtyard and yet was conducted with formality and during which Khalil's wife locked up her room as she always did when she left the house to go to the market or to visit her sisters in another area of Amman. Um Hasan once gave a lunch party for her daughters and invited her grand-daughter (Khalil's wife) but not her daughter-in-law, Um Khalil. The parallel activities of washing clothes, washing cutlery, putting herbs and bread out to dry in the sun were done separately and in that part of the courtyard particular to each household. Aisha, not normally of a diffident nature, always came and went to the water tap with an averted head and look, but still could not avoid audible comments by Um Khalil about her wasteful use of water.

In this way the courtyard and the dwelling were 'shared' and yet not 'shared' by the two households who related to one another simultaneously as kin and non-kin, and simultaneously through descent and marriage. On the rare occasions when visitors common to both came to visit, the two households would sit together. One such occasion was a visit by Hasan's second wife who is Um Khalil's co-wife and Um Hasan's daughter-in-law (previously her sister-in-law because Hasan married his uncle's widow as his second wife), and the tensions of the complicated relationships involved were clearly expressed in the seating arrangements. When individual members of the two households wanted to socialize with each other they chose to do so outside, in an open space overlooking the main street a short distance from the house, rather than in the courtyard. In that neutral public space they would sit in a close circle and be joined by other neighbours and kin.

Um Khalil's house and household was not a particularly extreme case of shared space in the Wadi. There were a number of such multiple-household-dwellings (MHD) in the area with similarly complex relationships. However, the complexity of spatial divisions and social relations existed even in the more common situation of multiple-family-households (MFH) where a household consists of a conjugal couple plus a married son or more and their respective families.[3] Although the dwelling space that such households occupy may be considered to be both private and domestic, yet within it there are divisions and boundaries structured intimately by household relations. These divisions are not, as may be expected from the literature on the Middle East, divisions into male and female space. Rather each conjugal family unit within the multiple-family-household has its own space, and whenever possible they have their own room. In the case of Um Khalil's household, it was obvious that when Khalil was at home, he and his wife would usually remain inside their room. If they ate separately from the rest of the household, which happened on occasion when his wife would prepare something special for him, then they would sit at the very corner of the courtyard nearest to their own room. This corner was an incipient private area for the potentially new household.

The demarcation of space for the use of each family unit is clearly demonstrated when families which form part of a household are away on extended visits, or are working abroad. Their rooms are always kept locked till their return even if the extra space is needed badly by the crowded household. A situation which illustrates a similar point involved one of Um Khalil's married daughters who lived across the main road bifurcating the Wadi. The young woman had quarrelled with her in-laws and had returned 'in anger' to her mother's house. She was waiting for her in-laws to send intermediaries to effect a reconciliation according to accepted practice. When more than the normal time elapsed and no intermediaries came, she grew anxious that the in-laws would not take her back. Her main question to any person who knew her in-laws was whether or not they were using the room that had been hers and her husband's. If they were, that would be substantial proof that her conjugal family no longer existed and that a divorce would ensue.

Revisiting the Private and the Public

To understand how Um Khalil structured her time and space daily through and across the relationships in which she was involved raises questions concerning analytical categories such as 'household', 'family', 'private/public' and 'group'. An extensive literature and numerous debates in feminist writings and gender studies during the 1970s and 1980s may seem to have exhausted the possibilities of reformulating these concepts. Yet, the current interest of social and development studies in women's groups, formal associations and NGOs cannot be addressed without re-opening debates on the relationship between the public and private domains in social life.

As Nelson (1974) pointed out in an early seminal review, the analysis of public and private domains in Middle Eastern societies was long structured around an uncritical assumption of the 'dual and separate worlds of men and women' (1974: 551). These worlds were seen as demarcated by gender segregation and spatial/physical divisions and units in addition to types of relationships, activities and meanings. This was also presented as reflecting the indigenous point of view. Thus Rosen, describing a small city in Morocco, says:

> It is often remarked that women's lives are largely restricted to the private realm of household, family, and kin group while men lead public lives in the workplace, the market, and the sphere of political relations. Women, as we shall see, are viewed by men as naturally weak and unreliable, and the differentiation of spheres is directly related to this view (1984: 34).

These dichotomous notions perpetuated the assumption that the presence of females established space and domain as private and their absence as public. Gender segregation, associated with female seclusion, became an organizing principle for understanding Middle Eastern societies. Space itself was seen in terms of an opposition between inside, enclosed space (house, courtyard) as opposed to outside, open space (market, coffeehouse, mosque). This type of argumentation gathered strength from early feminist writings which posited a congruence between private/public, female/male, nature/culture dichotomies, and decried the ensuing 'natural' and 'universal' inequality (Rosaldo 1974). Others disputed, or at least modified, these dichotomies and criticized assumptions which justified restricting research and analysis to one domain to the exclusion of the other (Reiter 1975; Rosaldo 1980; Sciama 1981). The domestic domain was seen as particularly under-analysed and under-theorized cross-culturally (Yanagisako 1979).

Inspired by such debates, ethnography began to reveal the cross-cultural variations and intricacies of the relationships between private and public domains on the one hand, and gender on the other. Few anthropologists disputed that notions of the private and public exist in every culture, with the possible exception of the simplest small-scale societies where the residential community is at the same time a kin or fictive-kin group.[4] What activities and social relationships characterized each domain, and the nature and meanings of the boundaries between them however, were seen as empirical questions. This led to a focus on such issues as the gender division of labour, the practice of political power and the multiple meanings of kinship.

Less explicitly explored was the issue of space and the way spatial boundaries intersected with social ones in different settings. An early and powerful exception was Ardener (1981). The various essays explored the patterning and perception of space, and the complex ways in which it articulates with social action and relationships in specific contexts. These illustrated that 'societies have generated their own rules, culturally determined, for making boundaries on the ground, and have divided the social into spheres, levels and territories' (Ardener 1981: 11–12).

The notion of space itself also needed to be reinterpreted. As Gupta and Ferguson pointed out, 'Representations of space in the social sciences are remarkably dependent on images of break, rupture and disjunction' (1992: 6). This is particularly true in the literature on Middle Eastern societies, where the distinction between the private and the public, was applied 'isomorphically' to space, gender roles, politics and economics. Although person-centred ethnographies and their critique of structuralist approaches, most notably from urban North Africa (Eickelman 1974), effectively helped break down monolithic and static concepts of social groups such as family, kinship, city quarter, and ethnic group, powerful representations based on notions of disjuncture and opposition persistently, though often implicitly, continued to inform ethnography and theory.

As Nelson (1974) and Joseph (1986) argued, the fact that women do participate in political life in spite of varying degrees of segregation in different contexts should lead us not only to re-examine assumptions about the status of women in the Middle East, but also to re-examine definitions of politics and political participation. Thus the domestic may become political as in the case of Palestinian camp women in Lebanon (Peteet 1986). Conversely, as shown by Tucker's (1986) work on nineteenth-century Egyptian women, over time the state may appropriate public roles which had been within the domain of women leading to their subsequent encapsulation and subjugation within the domestic sphere. Even where strict segregation is maintained, as in urban elite Saudi households, Altorki (1986) argued that women's control over marriage, which has widespread economic and political repercussions, makes the distinction between private and public a tenuous one. Another study of a different setting in Saudi Arabia clearly showed women's economic and public roles (Altorki and Cole 1989). Women's participation in agricultural labour and the role of household production and family labour in wider economies cast doubts on the validity of excluding the 'private' household from productive processes of the market (Keddie 1979; Khafagy 1984; Myntti 1984; Taylor 1984).

Similarly, physical boundaries of the built environment do not demarcate divisions between the private and the public spheres in any direct manner. This is especially, though not exclusively, true in a situation of high population density and scarcity of space. Women's lives in the squatter areas of Amman show that private is not 'inside' and public 'outside' the dwelling. Social divisions do not translate neatly into spatial divisions and the walls that surround a dwelling do not delineate the main social group to which its inhabitants belong. Furthermore, precisely because there is a high degree of sexual segregation, the same spaces transform themselves into male and female space depending upon the time of day, the people using the space and the type of activity performed in it. This is true whether the space is enclosed space or open space. There can be no total separation of space into female/male, private/public and family/non-family. Rather, the use of space is characterized by fluidity and adaptability, both inside the dwelling and outside. In situations when the 'public' threatens to take over the 'private', however, struggles over the space of the domestic domain become evident. From this perspective, rather than a 'culturalist' approach seeking to delimit the boundaries between private and public domains in an 'essentially' Middle Eastern, Arab or Muslim fashion, the relations and boundaries between the two domains could be seen as emerging and re-emerging out of the articulation of the socially and culturally constructed strategies of various actors in a specific setting, including states, families, individuals, collectivities and communities.

Domesticity Reconfigured: Women and the State

According to the Urban Development Department's 1980 baseline survey of the two research areas, a 'typical' family in the 'Wadi' and the 'Jabal' lived in 1–2 room houses with courtyards, made of concrete and a corrugated metal roof, with water and electricity connections (though often illegally and sometimes through sharing with a neighbour) but no sewerage. The average size of household was 6.58 and density per room was 3.54 persons. The average income for the household was 90 JD/month earned by one or possibly two members of the household.[5] Males worked mostly in small-scale workshops, the construction industry and low-level government employment and most families had at least one member working in the Arab Gulf. Women's work concentrated on domestic labour, peddling and home industries (sewing, embroidery, food preparation for selling) as well as running micro-groceries from the home. Distribution according to household composition showed 69.7 per cent single-family households, 10.2 per cent extended family households and 8.8 per cent multiple-family households.

Yet this representation of the 'average' squatter household does little to help us understand the social circumstances and arrangements in which people such as Um Khalil live. Classifying households into three types (single, extended and multiple), although an improvement over the two classic types of nuclear vs. extended which is the norm in survey research, obscures rather than edifies. When the survey data on household composition are listed in terms of the different relationships existing within a household instead of grouped into types, 75 different kinds can be seen in this small number of overall households.[6] The example of Um Khalil's living space gives an indication of the complicated situations that poverty creates in a dwelling, even when almost all its occupants are female and of one kin group. Furthermore, even though the survey took into account the fact that a dwelling (however small) may contain more than one household, it did not take into account the fact that a household may stretch over several dwellings.

In the 'Jabal', the families of the squatter area have been part of an urban upgrading project since 1980, along with three other sites in Amman. The project has been implemented by the Urban Development Department (the UDD), then an ad hoc agency created for the purpose at the Municipality and now part of the Ministry of Housing. The aim of the upgrading project was to extend basic services to the squatter areas and to enable its inhabitants to acquire legal tenure to their land and houses. The major part of the upgrading was carried out in 1980–81. It involved buying the land where the squatters had built their houses from the legal owners, extending water, electricity and sewerage services, paving the paths and alleys, and, finally, making available long-term loans to enable families to pay for the land and the cost of the services and thus to acquire legal title. Furthermore loans were made available to build new houses.

The incentives for building a new house or upgrading an existing one were many. A house would be a more viable economic proposition with the acquisition of tenure, but also the municipality refused actually to connect any of the new services to a house that did not meet the legal building codes. Most important among these was that the house had to be built of 'permanent materials' e.g. concrete or stone. In addition, there were regulations concerning the degree of set-back, the percentage of built-up and roofed areas of the plot and the number of floors which could not exceed two storeys. These physical changes meant that the spatial and social arrangements within and between dwellings were disrupted.

The project also planned the space in the areas as a whole, creating minuscule 'green' spaces. These new 'public' spaces, which were assigned to the responsibility of the 'community', overrode the spaces in which women of different households used to gather for socializing. Women continued trying to use the areas in front of the house as an extension of their private space, sitting on the front stoop to sew, prepare vegetables for cooking or to chat with neighbours. But this was made awkward by the fact that the areas were being invaded constantly by outsiders: the engineers of the project, the social workers, the constant surveys that were being carried out, the visitors from the government and from the World Bank.

The role of the upgrading project in restructuring the lives of the women and the families went beyond the physical aspect. The change in the structuring of space was related to the project's definition of not only how a family 'should' live, but also what a family 'is'. Thus married sons were eligible for separate plots and housing loans. Since each household sought to maximize its ownership of plots, this meant that extended households tended to split up with each conjugal family moving into a separate plot.

The project also defined what a 'community' comprised and how it should organize its activities. Firstly, the project had to impose the idea of the use of the community centre which it built as a space for activities and decision-making. Thus all public meetings with the inhabitants began to be held in the community centre instead of the houses of local leaders. Secondly, a committee for organizing sport and cultural activities was formed, composed of younger, educated young men who immediately came into conflict with the elders over the establishment of a soccer team. As one woman explained:

> The people don't want mixing (of men and women) – forming the football team means the mixing of boys and girls because the centre will be used for literacy classes and sewing classes as well – the centre should not be treated as a University.

The uneasiness concerning the centre was partly due to the fact that it represented a space that would not be controlled by the people themselves – just like a university, it is a public space controlled by the state. The activities of the centre (literacy classes, sewing workshops) were to be decided by outside authorities. Not only was the space not controlled by the people but also the use of it was undetermined – whether it was for women or for men or when it would be used by one or the other.

Resistance to the UDD project in the Jabal was strong. There were many reasons for this, the most important of which was that the Jabal had been settled mainly in 1948 and had by 1980 developed into an established area. The inhabitants generally felt secure from eviction and most houses already had connections to services. This was in contrast to many other squatter areas established later or which were more peripheral to the city. At first glance it would appear that the resistance was mostly carried out by men. Community elders refused to cooperate with the UDD and refused to attend meetings organized by its staff. After a series of negotiations, confrontations and intercessions by government officials and the mayor, the project went ahead but with significant changes and a substantial reduction of its cost to the inhabitants.

Interspersed with these public confrontations were other strategies for contesting the terms of the project. It was the women in this, and other squatter areas, who interacted on a daily basis with the UDD staff, who argued with them, expressed dissatisfaction with the project and tried to negotiate better terms. In many ways this was unavoidable due to the heavy presence of the UDD staff in the area throughout the major phase of project implementation. It was the women who were at home to answer the questions of the successive surveys and to interact with the various personnel of the project.

What all this points to, is that as a result of the project, the whole area and its inhabitants became a public space. For the first time since the squatter settlement had been established, the area came under the direct jurisdiction of a public governmental agency that took responsibility for every aspect of life, from health to family relationships to community activities. What started as urban upgrading by the World Bank project, ended up including community services, community centres, vocational training and income-generating projects for women. In this way, the UDD project took upon itself the restructuring of life and social relations in the community. Having provided the area with so much, it then felt unable to leave and turn it over to its inhabitants. Partly this was motivated by a feeling that they knew the people best and could run these services better than the different government agencies that should be in charge of them, and partly out of a feeling that the people would destroy what had been set up if left to their own devices.

If we define the 'private', following Barrington Moore (1984), as the arena which people try to keep immune from intrusion by public authority, then we can say that even the domain formally acknowledged by the upgrading project as private, had also become public. For the household and family was being targeted for 'upgrading' as well: lectures, censuses, surveys, child-rearing classes, nutrition classes, income-generating projects and so on were directed at them. Every aspect of family life from habits of toilet use to household budgets became the object of enumeration, classification and analysis – and the family became part of the public domain. Beyond that, the individual body of each woman also became public, or at least public knowledge, through surveys of fertility and reproductive behaviour and family planning interventions. In this way, the domestic domain became a contested arena of the interpenetration of private and public domains, with the public authority trying to impose its own definitions and women trying to maximize their autonomy and interests.

Housework and Network

The Saadis were one of the largest kinship groups in the Wadi. Originally from a small village near Jaffa, in 1948 they immigrated to three different places: Amman and two towns in the West Bank. The Ammani Saadis settled in a refugee camp and were later joined by their relatives from one of the West Bank towns. Since there was no room in the camp, the newcomers had no choice but to squat on the vacant land adjacent to the camp, the Wadi. In time the camp grew so dense that newly married couples and families, including some Saadis, left the camp and squatted in the Wadi. After the 1967 war and the Israeli occupation of the West Bank and Gaza Strip, the third group of Saadis joined their relatives in Amman and preferred to live in the Wadi rather than in any of the refugee camps.

Most of the Saadis now lived in the Wadi, concentrated in one part of it. The rest lived in the somewhat better-off surrounding areas. Later two or three families managed to obtain flats in one of the low-income housing projects on the outskirts of Amman, which is quite a distance from the Wadi. Though they retained strong ties with their relatives, their departure was considered a sad event and a loss. The Wadi thus constituted a point of aggregation and dispersal for the Saadi kin-group.

The Saadis felt quite distinctive in the Wadi, and had a strong sense of common identity. But they were also divided between the Ammani Saadis and the West Bank/Gaza Saadis, meaning the third group which were the last to arrive in Amman. Despite the fact that the two groups were related by a common great-grandfather, relations between them were formal and not very friendly. They visited and helped each other but not as much as they did within each group. Even intermarriages between the two groups were few.

There were constant flows of reciprocity and mutual aid among the women within the Saadi kin-group. Um Hassan, forty-five years old, rotund, the mother of twelve children, was a focal point of these flows. She readily spared her many daughters to help relatives in housework or child-care. She could also leave her daughters in charge of the house and so had the time to visit and strengthen her relations with others. Thus, Um Farid, the mother of four little boys aged between a few months and four years, sought to establish a close reciprocity with Um Hassan, who was her husband's sister and not with Um Bilal who was also closely related. This was in spite of the fact that her husband, Abu Farid, had a better relationship with Abu Bilal than with his sister.

Um Farid's mother-in-law had recently died very suddenly. Um Farid had found herself in a situation of decision-making that she had not experienced before. She worried that she could not run her house or take care of her children by herself. Her husband was not sympathetic, he always reminded her of his mother's efficiency in running the house.

Um Farid sought recourse with Um Hassan. She exchanged food with her and Um Hassan's daughters helped Um Farid with the housework. They did the shopping for her and looked after her children. Farid, who was four years old, would spend most of the day at Um Hassan's playing with her daughter Ahlam and other children in the alleys. Sometimes the two of them would come to Um Farid and eat, sleep, play and go to the shop to buy sweets together. Once when Farid had a sore throat Um Farid sent him to Um Hassan to have this throat massaged with olive oil. Instead Alia, Um Hassan's ten-year-old daughter, took Farid to the traditional healer.

No matter what the relationship between the women, the relationship among their younger children was not affected. When Um Farid and Um Hassan were no longer on good terms with each other, Ahlam spent her time at Um Farid's just the same. Um Farid would seize the opportunity to question her about her mother's activities, visitors and who had said what. However, after her dispute with Um Hassan, Um Farid no longer received the help of Um Hassan's older daughters. She therefore sought the help of Karima and her sister, eleven- and twelve-year-old girls living next door, unrelated to Um Farid by kinship. They ran her errands and she gave them a little money, explaining that she felt sorry for them since their parents were divorced and they were motherless and very poor.

The relationship between Um Farid and Um Hassan suffered when Um Farid tried to build a friendship with Asma (Um Hassan's daughter-in-law), separate from her relationship with Um Hassan. Asma was living in the same household as her mother-in-law and had no say in matters related to her child or her daily life. She found in Um Farid a sympathetic listener to her complaints. This infuriated Um Hassan and she accused Um Farid of encouraging Asma to rebel against her. Soon Asma herself was accusing Um Farid of interference and her relationship with her mother-in-law improved as soon as Um Farid was excluded. Unable to compete otherwise, Um Farid tried to regain status by persuading her husband to buy a video machine. Soon her house became a gathering place for women eager to watch Egyptian movies.

The example of the relationships within the Saadi kin-group shows that one of the most sensitive ways to explore relationships in the domestic domain is through women's work, both in terms of child-care and daily chores as well as income-generating activities. The intensely social nature of housework in these areas becomes clear when looking at how women organize their day and their obligations. The scope and weight of women's responsibilities and decision-making is observed in the fact that most men in the Wadi and the Jabal (and all of those who are considered to be 'good' men) turn over their entire wages, other than a small amount of 'cigarette money' to their wives or to their mothers. This money is an indication of a woman's authority in the household and the measure of her control over it. It also means that it is up to her to make the money last the month and to provide for the food, the necessities and the emergencies.

Running a large household on a small amount of money is a time-consuming and difficult matter. To make it possible, women in different households have to rely upon each other for help in housework, shopping and child-care; for aid in financial emergencies; and for information on where the cheapest vegetables or the cheapest doctors are to be found. Shopping, or rather the search for affordable foodstuffs, is a constant occupation and preoccupation.

Households that reciprocate daily in such matters may be said to form 'mutual aid units'. Although such units are generally based on kinship, yet they are formed selectively. That is, not all households related by kinship will form one unit. Rather, from all the possible combinations, one or two units will emerge. The prevalent pattern is that units tend to be formed between sisters-in-law; between husband's sister/brother's wife as with Um Hassan and Um Farid.

The same relationship may also form between two or three households that are not related by kinship, and in this case propinquity is the major factor in the choice of households. Sometimes these non-kin units form because of the absence of other households related by kinship in the community, or because of conflict among kinsfolk. However, sometimes non-kin units are not just a substitute for kin-based units but exist alongside them.

In addition to these units characterized by multiplex relations, there also exist what may be called 'special-purpose units', that is those formed around a single task. The best example of this is the cooperation and collaboration between women in embroidering Palestinian dresses. The cloth, thread and panels of the dress circulate among women according to their expertise. A woman who is particularly good at the difficult embroidery of the neckline may not be as skilled as another at a particular stitch, or in cutting out the dress. A particularly admired dress may circulate in different households for the design to be copied or adapted. A great deal more can be said on the activity of embroidery which acts as a condensed symbol of Palestinian identity, as a marker of femininity and its accompanying skills, and as economic capital for women.

These mutual aid units are formed and maintained by women,

irrespective of the quality of the relationship between the male heads of the households. The units have some continuity over time but they are not permanent and subside and re-form according to the relationships of the women involved, although in the case of kin-based units a complete severance of ties rarely occurs. Reciprocity within these units flows on two levels: women to women; and children to children. In addition there are adult/child relations as in child-care and vice versa in the services that children perform for women, such as shopping and running errands and taking messages back and forth. Children play as important a role in the maintenance and perpetuation of these units as do the women.

Constant visiting and a flow of food and children connect these households, which may be at different ends of the residential area or in 'other' neighbourhoods according to urban administrative definitions. This means that a household actually has, in addition to its own private space in a dwelling, the use of the private space of the various households in their units. Going to and fro between these houses is not regarded as 'visiting', nor as 'going out' into the public sphere – even if it entails crossing the main street or the market area. Where houses bound by reciprocity are clustered closely together, this creates a bounded 'private' space which includes the dwellings and the alleys in one unit. More often, however, the houses are quite distant from one another since the different families of the same kin-group settled in these areas at various times and did not build their houses next to one another. With other households united by kinship, but not by intensive reciprocity between women, relations are more formal, visits are announced and prepared for, best clothes are worn, and visits are mostly restricted to formal occasions such as the birth of a child, a wedding and so on.

The Boundaries of the Domestic

Focusing on the kinds of networks that women in squatter areas create, negotiate, sustain and contest, may seem to be begging the question of just what constitutes a 'group' and a 'women's group'. On the other hand, this focus could open up the question of where the boundaries lie between individual strategies, and collective action and meaning. Women's relationships with one another within the dwelling unit raise the question of what constitutes the 'household' and the 'domestic group'; and their strategies vis-à-vis the state and its agencies raise the question of the boundaries between the public and the private.

The domestic domain cannot be delimited in terms of the physical boundaries of space. Rather it is inscribed in space through repetitive visiting, the paths trodden by women and children, exchange and other activities that sustain the family. It extends well beyond the space of the family dwelling. On the other hand, the example of the courtyard shared by Um Khalil and Aisha shows the centre of the dwelling to be ambiguously both a private and a public space: shared but also divided, used for mundane household activities but imposing certain proprieties and formalities.

The state, through its public and municipal authorities, draws spatial boundaries and delimits them as house/private and street/public. In addition to fixing fluidity in the use of space, the state attempts to assert its control through extending the public reach into the most intimate realms of the private. In return, the women of the squatter areas retaliated by continuously trying to negotiate the changing conditions to their, and their family's, benefit. The interaction with project personnel in their homes, alleys and 'community centres' caused their private, communal, domestic spaces to become arenas of public negotiation and contestation.

Women further achieved their ends by carrying the domestic domain into the corridors of the public, that is by constant visiting of the UDD and other offices. A visit to the UDD offices usually would find the corridors full of women in their Palestinian embroidered dress, sitting, standing, arguing and always trying to see the *mudir*, the director, to negotiate the way the project regulations were being applied to their particular case. If they did not achieve what they needed on the first visit, they repeated and repeated the visit until some compromise was achieved. The presumed ideal of female seclusion was flaunted nonchalantly in these most public of spaces, but in their negotiations women appealed to public officials as women, in their roles as mothers, wives and guardians of the domestic domain. On the other hand they did so by physically transcending community and neighbourhood boundaries and emerging into the full gaze of the public.

Despite the appearance of more critical and sensitive understandings of Middle Eastern women's lives, NGO and other formal organizational activities in these countries are often predicated on the assumption that women need to be 'brought out' from the household (with its corollary slogan of 'integrating them into the development process'). Household relations are presumed to be confining for women by limiting their interactions to immediate family members. This chapter has not dealt with formal groups and yet shows that there are a variety of ways in which women organize their activities and lives in relation to other women. It is when dealing with public authority that women act as individuals, although at that point they invoke collective cultural categories of womanhood and the domestic. In this way the most public of activities may take place under the guise and symbolism of the domestic and the private. It appears, in practice, that the domestic is not synonymous with the private at all.

Our understanding of society and the state has undergone revision in recent years and we have become more aware not only of 'informal structures' and 'influence versus authority' but also of the 'technologies of power', the 'tactics of resistance', the 'power of negotiation' and 'the subversion of dominant categories'. Recognizing that women engage in these latter types of relations and practices does not (as early feminists feared) cast them out of the formal arena, or even necessarily into the category of the powerless. The formal arena is now shown to be as vague and ambiguous and ill-defined as the private, or perhaps even more so. The construction of the category of 'woman' is one that takes place at all levels of practice and discourse in society and the category contains within it the space to encompass both private and public domains. To assign only certain kinds of activities and organization to one domain or the other appears to be gratuitous and not very useful. Nelson's (1974) objection to the extension of such notions into presuming a separate 'social life' for each gender, with different cultural symbols and expressions, still holds. Segregation, seclusion, and the domestic are not synonymous and are in constant transformation in Middle Eastern societies.

Notes

1. The data upon which this chapter is based were collected during eighteen months of fieldwork, during 1984–6. The research was part of a wider study on the impact of a World Bank funded upgrading project, focusing especially on household relations and child health. The study was directed by Dr Leila Bisharat under the auspices of the Urban Development Department, then a unit within the Amman Municipality (see Bisharat and Zagha 1986; Population Council 1982).
2. Um Khalil, i.e. 'the mother of Khalil' is the most common way of referring to married women in these areas. Khalil's father would be similarly referred to as 'the father of Khalil' or Abu Khalil.

3. The terms 'simple-, extended-, and multiple-family household' and 'conjugal family unit' are used here according to the definitions by Laslett (1978). However, in this context, I prefer the term 'multiple-household dwelling' to his 'houseful' in order to place the emphasis upon the fact that the components represent households and not other types of units or individuals. Also the term 'dwelling' here is not used according to Laslett's definition but refers to a structure surrounded by a perimeter wall, which makes it parallel to his use of the term 'premises'.
4. For a study that seeks to find the distinction even in simple societies, see Barrington Moore Jr. (1984) for an extended discussion.
5. At the time of the research 1 Jordan Dinar equalled approximately $US 3. Now it equals approximately $US 1.4.
6. The two areas consisted of 224 and 335 households respectively according to the 1980 baseline survey.

References

Altorki, S. (1986), *Women in Saudi Arabia*, New York: Columbia University Press.

Altorki, S. and Cole, D.P. (1989), *Arabian Oasis City: The Transformation of 'Unayzah*, Austin: University of Texas Press.

Ardener, S. (1981), 'Ground Rules and Social Maps for Women: An Introduction,' in S. Ardener, ed., *Women and Space: Ground Rules and Social Maps*, London: Croom Helm.

Bisharat, L. and Hisham, Z. (1986), *Health and Population in Squatter Areas of Amman: A Reassessment After Four Years of Upgrading*, Amman: Urban Development Department.

Eickelman, D. (1974), 'Is There an Islamic City? The Making of a Quarter in a Moroccan Town,' *International Journal of Middle East Studies*, 5, 3: 274–8.

Gupta, A. and Ferguson, J. (1992), 'Beyond "Culture": Space, Identity, and the Politics of Difference,' *Cultural Anthropology*, 7, 1 (February): 6–23.

Joseph, S. (1986), 'Women and Politics in the Middle East,' *MERIP*, 138: 3–7.

Keddie, N. (1979), 'Problems in the Study of Middle Eastern Women,' *International Journal of Middle Eastern Studies*, 10: 225–40.

Khafagy, F. (1984), 'One Village in Egypt,' *MERIP*, 124: 17–21.

Laslett, P. (1978), *Household and Family in Past Time*, London: Cambridge University Press.

Moore Jr., B. (1984), *Privacy: Studies in Social and Cultural History*, N.Y.: M.E. Sharpe, Inc.

Myntti, C. (1984), 'Yemeni Workers Abroad: The Impact on Women,' *MERIP*, 124: 11–16.

Nelson, C. (1974) 'Public and Private Politics: Women in the Middle Eastern World,' *American Ethnologist,* 1, 3: 551–63.

Peteet, J. (1986) 'No Going Back: Women and the Palestinian Movement,' *MERIP*, 138: 20–24.

Population Council (1982), *A Baseline Health and Population Assessment for the Upgrading Areas of Amman*. Population Council Regional Papers. Cairo.

Reiter, R. R. (1975), 'Men and Women in the South of France: Public and Private Domains' in R. R. Reiter, ed., *Toward an Anthropology of Women*, N.Y. and London: Monthly Review Press.

Rosaldo, M. Z. (1974), 'Woman, Culture and Society: A Theoretical Overview,' in M. Z. Rosaldo and L. Lamphere, eds, *Woman, Culture and Society*, Stanford, CA: Stanford University Press.

—— (1980), 'The Uses and Abuses of Anthropology: Reflections on Feminism and Cross-Cultural Understanding,' *Signs*, 5, 3: 389–417.

Rosen, L. (1984), *Bargaining for Reality: The Construction of Social Relations in a Muslim Community*, Chicago: University of Chicago Press.

Sciama, L. (1981), 'The Problem of Privacy in Mediterranean Anthropology,' in S. Ardener, ed., *Women and Space: Ground Rules and Social Maps*, London: Croom Helm.

Taylor. E. (1984), 'Egyptian Migration and Peasant Wives,' *MERIP*, 124: 3–10.

Tucker, J. (1986), *Women in Nineteenth-Century Egypt*, Cairo: American University of Cairo Press.

UDD (Urban Development Department) (1981), *Summary Tables of Comprehensive Social-Physical Survey*, Amman: Urban Development Department.

Yanagisako, S. J. (1979) 'Family and Household: the Analysis of Domestic Groups,' *Annual Review of Anthropology*, 8: 161–205.

5

Women in Groups in Africa: Female Associational Patterns in Senegal and Morocco[1]

Eva Evers Rosander

Background

Compared with Morocco, the number and multiple forms of female groups or associations found in Senegal are overwhelming.[2] This difference between North and West Africa intrigued me when I changed the geographical area of my anthropological fieldwork from northern Morocco to central Senegal. It started a process of thinking and comparing field data along the lines described below. That is why this chapter deals with material not only from Morocco – which we generally include in the Middle East – but also from a sub-Saharan country such as Senegal, whose usual fate is to be excluded from all kinds of social science-related activities with a connection to the so-called Middle Eastern region. Still Senegal offers many cultural similarities to Morocco: it is deeply influenced by Arabo-Islamic culture and traditions and the Senegalese people often go to Morocco to study Arabic or religion. As an example it is worth mentioning the greatest Sufi brotherhood (*tariqa*) in Senegal, the Tijaniyya, which originates from the Maghreb. The founder's mosque in Fez is frequently visited by Senegalese Tijanis. Dress, music and food dishes are other vital examples of popular Arabic influences on Senegalese life style.

In this chapter I mention women and associating in *Africa*, without further distinctions. Following the general tradition in social science I then primarily think of sub-Saharan Africa. However, there are certain structuring principles for social life which are strikingly similar in North and West Africa, to which I will draw attention in my presentation of female associations in the two regions. Thus, even if women's associating and networking take partly different forms due to varying cultural, social and economic backgrounds, basic values such as honour and shame, which often relate back to descent, do affect women's groups in Morocco as well as in Senegal. So do the individual female careers in terms of status and prestige, which are connected to the values mentioned. Through the study of women's organizational forms in these countries, key issues in the formation and maintenance of social structure, its ideology and social content, become visible. It also reveals to us how women's groups cope with social and economic change. The associations, networks and so on could be seen as reflecting basic structures of power and hierarchy, deeply rooted in people's minds, expressed in their rituals and in their daily interaction.

This chapter is based on social anthropological fieldwork in northern Morocco (Qbila Anyera in Yebala, and among Moroccan immigrants in Ceuta, a Spanish enclave on the North African coast, opposite Gibraltar), and in the town Mbacké with the surrounding countryside, situated 180 km. east of Dakar. My Moroccan field data were collected in periods of various lengths from 1976 to 1987, while my Senegalese fieldwork has been divided into annual short stays in Mbacké with visits to the adjacent rural villages in the period 1993–6.

The aim of this chapter is, thus, to compare female organizing in groups in Senegal and Morocco. I am here not referring to formal associations; 'formal' used in the sense of having links with the state or with state-related regional institutions. Rather, I refer to traditional and informal female associations or networks which are activated in connection with weddings and name-giving rituals and parties held by the members, and the 'habits' or 'conventions' which guide female network members' behaviour. An important part of the aim and direction of the associational activities is related to the collection of money; the economic motivation for the running of the association or network being crucial as a female way of realizing one's ambition in life outside as well as inside the household.

I will start with an overview of the ethnography of women's associations in Senegal. I will then proceed to a description and analysis of Moroccan women's associational patterns through their networks and how these are manifested in different social activities in relation to the great rites de passage such as the marriage and name-giving parties. Women's relations to and dependence on men ideologically (expressed in ideas about honour and shame, morality and religion) and economically (manifested in the household composition and marriage structures) will be mentioned in relation to current social and economic changes of the employment situation. By looking at society in Senegal and Morocco from the point of view of female organizing in groups, one may be able to formulate tentative ideas about women's position in general in societies like the Moroccan and Senegalese ones, which are permeated by a male Islam-dominated ideology. The moral codes for the women are hard to cope with and contribute to keeping women within the family and in the often polygynous household. In Senegal, for the rich 'upper-class' or caste-less women or for women with a maraboutic descent, the main forum for realizing themselves may be inside the house in close relation to the family and the relatives. A woman without a big family, without many relatives, is perhaps in greater need of linking herself to other people – be it a marabout, a president of an association or to a distant powerful classificatory 'cousin'. This coincides with the Moroccan case, in which only low-status and poor women would work outside the home leaving temporarily the more prestigious female home sphere and female family-, kinship- and neighbour-based networks. The field data and arguments presented below point in that direction.

Networks, Associations and Organizations: Some Conceptual Clarifications

A clarification is needed with reference to the different categories of 'group patterns' with which we are dealing. While *networks* are mostly informal, channelling both material and immaterial resources along lines of kinship, propinquity, patron-clienthood and so on, and sharing belongings or interests of different kinds, *associations* are more acknowledged as entities or groups with a certain organizational structure and a certain constellation of people as participants or members who perceive of themselves as such. The associations may be informal or formal, private or public.

Thus, 'associations' are groups of people organized around certain activities and with some form of internal hierarchy in terms of a 'leader' and 'followers' or 'members'. 'Association' so defined is often undifferentially used in parallel with 'organization'. However, in this chapter I would like to indicate by 'organization' something wider and more general, namely 'structures of recognized and accepted roles' (Uphoff 1986: 8), which may not necessarily be institutionalized, although this is often the case. 'Organization' is seen as a generic term, pointing out capacity to accomplish goals through collective action within a structure (cf. Bryant 1985: 21–3).

Africa is considered by some social scientists to be the continent with the greatest number of women's associations. Research on formalized women's organizations has yielded valuable information on the ways in which such collectivities are used by women to acquire greater economic control over the products of their own labour, or to affirm established female rights. However, much less is known about non-formalized or semi-formalized female collectivities, and for both categories little insight has been gained concerning motivational factors and the nature of the linkages and sentiments between the women concerned. Such networks or collectivities include, as mentioned above, relations based on kinship, neighbourhood, friendship, patron-client relations or special interest groups of a more or less temporary or sporadic character. It is necessary to understand the potential or actual role of such collectivities as gender-political mechanisms and the individual's role in such collectivities including their function as economic coping and corrective measures (cf. Woodford-Berger 1997).

Global economic forces of capitalization and market integration have in many cases transformed former types of social formation (household/compound/family structure) away from collectivity, extended families and complementarity between men and women towards individualism, nuclear families and dependent wives. Christianity as well as Islam has long worked to legitimize and reinforce these processes. Effects for women have been social isolation, increased differentiation between women and loss of social networks. From this perspective women's associating in different forms becomes all the more important and necessary (cf. ibid 1997). On the other hand, economic development has affected the increase in number of the polygynous households and the number of wives (above all in Senegal) that a man can afford to have. Co-wives often need the female associations as an economic and moral support in their daily struggle to please the husband and provide for their children.

Self and Others – Individuality and Collectivity

Individuality and collectivity should be investigated both in relation to one another and at different levels. At the subjective level individuality concerns people's inner and political selves. Collectivity may in this case be seen as the culmination and embodiment of individual needs organized on different levels, forms and spaces. At the social level the individual and the collectivity are both crucial features of social organization, and their interrelationship essential to social dynamics. The combination of these two levels of analysis constitutes a rich field of investigation, which appears fully evident in the organization of women's activities within the framework of their associations (cf. Ardener 1995: 7; Bortei-Doku and Aryeetey 1995: 90; Bülow et al 1994).

The study of African organizations seen from the overall perspective of individuality and collectivity cannot avoid focusing on social identity, including ethnic, religious, gender and kinship identity. For the sake of simplicity 'identity' will here be considered as a process of naming: naming of self, naming of others, naming by others (cf. Brenner 1993: 59). In the group under study people will define themselves and others in accordance with the criteria of sameness and otherness. Mapping these emic categories will be of interest for the understanding of the more complex social and discursive processes. The use of 'mother' as a denomination of the woman 'presidente' of an association reflects the cultural importance of motherhood in the society in question. In addition it ranks the speaker hierarchically in a subordinated role or position within the association under study.

Another important variable for identification of self and others in Africa is religion. Religious beliefs provide the means whereby people negotiate the personal, social and political conditions they experience and through which they may be empowered (cf. Roberts and Seddon 1991). The great dividing line is between Christians and Muslims (the so-called Animists constituting a very small minority), although micro studies may reveal a wide repertoire of culturally important subcategories even in a religiously homogeneous region ('good' Muslim, 'bad' Muslim, 'more' Muslim, 'less Muslim' or 'not a real Muslim'). These are just a few examples of identity-creating, -maintaining and -reproducing concepts, which ought to be linked into the study of women's strategies and life careers in relation to the current African organizational structures (Bülow et al 1994).[3]

According to Paul Riesman, one's identity is initially entirely constructed by *others*. Identity, he argues, is the single most important component of the sense of *self*. Yet he insists that one's sense of self is subjective to each individual. It is the fact that it is built out of a shared system of meanings which implies that other people's thoughts in fact are major constituents of a person's sense of self (Riesman 1992: 186). These statements lead us into the central and yet complicated issue concerning people's perceptions of self and others. In this chapter, I use 'people' to refer to women in northern Morocco and Ceuta and in the town of Mbacké, Diourbel region, in central Senegal. The interactional framework is, as always, female associating.

Crucial for the understanding of the women's view of themselves in relation to the collective or the group is the sense of *connectedness* that they as individuals come to have from others, especially relatives (Riesman 1992: 10). For many of the Moroccan and Senegalese women *society* constitutes, as far as I can understand, the people one lives with or is surrounded by, and the people who may live elsewhere but with whom one is related. The creation and maintenance of a family is seen as a main goal in life and the expression of success for both Moroccan and Senegalese people. This is possible through having many children. The women's role as reproducers and mothers is highly valued by men and women alike. The presence of many people, being more or less dependent on one's favours, is a goal to which most people aspire. It is not wealth itself which proves success but rather the collection of dependents one has. What counts is the size of the entourage that wealth and moral reputation enable one to attract and support (ibid: 42). Thus, principles for female associating are to lead a group or to adhere to a leader of a group or a social network, be it a family, an association or a religious group, centred around a marabout or his mother, sister or wife.

Senegalese Women's Associating

Senegalese women's perception of self and others and of individuality and collectivity is worth considering before trying to grasp something of the meaning of their rich associational life. In northern Morocco, according to my findings after having done extensive fieldwork there, women fear *other women*, i.e. women who are outside their intimate social circle and who do not form part of their 'moral community', whose members are 'prepared to make moral judgements about each other' (cf. Bailey 1971: 7) and who are engaged in a constant competition for respectability (cf. Evers Rosander 1991: 182ff). The family women are the only ones that could be trusted and that should be trusted. Besides, too much associating with 'other women' outside the family gives a woman a reputation for being excessively devoted/prone to gossip and outdoor activities.

For the Senegalese women, maintaining relations with other people can be seen as a way of reminding themselves of who they actually are. I have arrived at this standpoint through conversations with people in Mbacké and with Senegalese researchers in Dakar as well as through my comparative reading of Riesman. Added to this of course are the periods of time I spent observing the women, in their associations.

In a hierarchical social structure like that of Senegal, where ideas are still strong about a non-caste superior group of people (*geer*) acting as an upper class in relation to the 'caste' groups, based on traditional professions, with the lowest rank ascribed to the *griot* (bard, praise-singer), the stress on dependency relations to others is important for the balancing of the power structure. This is particularly the case for women, who ideologically should be industrious, devoted and obedient to their husbands and outstanding moral examples for their children. The mother's good or bad moral behaviour is reflected in the success or misfortune of her children; accordingly she is held responsible for the well-being of her children not only when they are small but also when they have left the home.

Women's associations are fora for work (party preparations) and for social, economic and religious activities. The associations are organized in a top-down way with a president, a vice president, a treasurer, a number of secretaries (general secretary, social secretary, secretary of conflicts and so on) and the members. The president is always a *geer*, a non-castée. She is usually an influential woman with many connections in society, not the least with powerful male relatives and marabouts. She has a few chosen 'assistants' whom she calls on, for example, to run errands or convoke the meetings. They are *griot*s, who occasionally get paid for their services. In the villages, all women participate in the female associations; those few who do not will be considered socially non-existent and completely isolated by the others. In the cities the social control is less strong, and women may be less strictly integrated into female associational networks. Still, all my data point in the same direction: women need their associations to be able to realize themselves as social persons and to finance their ritual and party activities in relation to rites de passage. Their position in the husband's household, both in relation to other households outside their own and in relation to their co-wives within the house or compound where they live, makes access to large sums of money for investment in presents and ritual passage parties necessary. Thus, as individuals they need the benefits which the collective activities of the associations can offer.

They also need the group of women to legitimize these activities; a woman alone is regarded as morally weak and exposed to all kinds of temptations and evil powers; as if she would occupy herself with witchcraft or illicit love affairs. Again, transparency (*leer*) and honesty are key concepts in all female activities. Being in a group together with others, what one does is clear and evident to all the members.

Regarding the boys, they are also expected to develop their associating spirit, although not to the same extent. Both young boys and young girls become socialized into the patterns of organizing themselves in associations by their membership in *maas* (Wolof), the age group association, in which all Senegalese children and youngsters are members, at least in the countryside.[4] These are social fora, in the girls' case under the formal leadership of the president of the married women's association called *mbotaye* (see below) but organized by a young *geer* girl or boy (the *maas* being sexually separated, but with many common activities). The girls pay small weekly or monthly membership fees and organize parties or dances ('tam tam') where they sell snacks and soft drinks. The money they earn is invested in party equipment like kettles, bowls and so forth for the grown up and married women to hire/use on the great party occasions like weddings and name-giving parties.

Senegalese Family Ceremonies or 'Events' (Wolof: xew)

The Senegalese family ceremonies (*xew*) constitute a series of rites de passage which form an important part of people's social as well as religious life. Socially, particularly marriages and name-giving rituals and parties are the foremost markers of status and prestige for the involved families, not to forget funerals. Also more religious rituals such as male circumcision, *la Korité* (Arabic: *Aid es Seguir*) and *Tabaski* (Arabic: *Aid el Kebir*) are socially important, as they reflect and reveal ranking through the way the rituals and parties are performed. The giving and receiving of gifts according to complicated reciprocity rules is the most eminent characteristic of the ceremonies. Historically, the general pattern of change for these rituals has been from 'la prestation de service jusqu'à la prestations de biens, pour arriver maintenant à la prestation d'argent' (from doing favours to giving property to the current situation when one gives money) (Mottin-Sylla 1988: 4). By this Marie-Hélène Mottin-Sylla refers to the rural traditions which originally contained an element of symbolic favours like washing one's laundry or a person's body (purity symbols) mediated by the ritual access to material resources – such as giving four kinds of grain to the young recently married girl – and later to gifts of money (Mottin-Sylla ibid). According to my informants, the raison d'être for women's associations like *mbotaye* is as a female way of financing these expensive and yet socially absolutely crucial family ceremonies.

Mbotaye[5]

The word *mbotaye* has motherhood connotations. It is associated with the burden the mother carries on her back, i.e. her baby, who leans towards the back and neck of his/her mother, wrapped up in a cloth and closely pressed against her body. In this association, the women carry each other's economic burdens, one might say. The president is the 'social mother', often called mother (*ndey*) by the members. She is also the super president for the young girls' association (*maas*). Once married, the girl/woman leaves the *maas* to become a member of a *mbotaye*, a kind of social and economic association for married women of child-producing age. Each newcomer has to pay a high entrance fee, which is used for buying the party equipment that every *mbotaye* is proud to dispose of. The old women, who no longer give birth and whose children are already married, may cease to participate, as the association is based on a reciprocal giving and taking of money and presents for the marriage and name-giving parties. Membership in the *mbotaye* also offers the possibility to use the common party equipment and to get help from the members with the preparation of the big meals.

Each time a member is going to celebrate one of these expensive ceremonies, the women unite to give her a stipulated sum of money, the same for everyone, and some soap and cloth. This sum of money could be used for buying food and drinks or to pay back debts for purchases already made. The presents are to be given away in the ritual exchange of gifts which is integrated into the marriage and name-giving ceremonies. Even if a member has more than one party of this kind within a short period of time, she will not get another joint sum of money or any goods from the *mbotaye* until all the members have had their share. The meetings have a strong social character: soft drinks are served, the women dance, chat and laugh together. The sum to be paid varies according to the women's means: in the rural villages, all the women of a village usually participate, the fee being not higher than a dollar each or less. In the town of Mbacké, I participated in the meeting of a *mbotaye* for women school teachers (first grade level), who paid a ten times higher fee. Neighbours of a certain urban area may have formed a *mbotaye* together, which they run. One woman may be a member of several *mbotayes*, if she can afford it. That gives her greater possibilities to be able to meet all the costs in connection with her own or her children's ceremonies. Thus, while the *nat* (rotating savings associations, see below) members meet at regular intervals, when the sums of money are distributed to the members in turn without consideration taken to special needs and in accordance with drawing lots among the participants, the *mbotaye* group meets whenever one of its members needs material help and support to be able to arrange a family ceremony (generally a marriage or a name-giving ritual).

Ndeye Dické

The *ndeye dické* is a dyadic relation between two women in or outside the *mbotaye* group formed in order to support each other in a more unlimited and generous way than the one stipulated by the *mbotaye* rules. The procedure for this particular constellation is, that one partner of such a dyadic relation has to give twice as much or more compared to what she got herself from her partner when she held her own rite de passage party. In this way, a woman member of a *mbotaye* could count on the joint sum of money of all the members plus one considerably larger sum from her *ndeye dické* partner, when she calculates her economic resources for her marriage or name-giving party. However, there are far more and varied nuances in the formation and maintenance of these dyadic relations than is to be read from my rudimentary description above. These subtle variations reveal other important structuring traits in female social life than the mother image mentioned and its symbolic relevance for female associating.

Ndey, mother, and *dick* (verb: come, arrive, manifest oneself) mean in this expression probably something like 'the mother has come to manifest herself' (Mottin-Sylla 1987: 9). This custom among married women aims at choosing one's favourite among a group of clients (if one is a seller, seamstress, president and so on) or among a number of members of an association. The relation does not necessarily have to be reciprocal and the one who takes the initiative to create the special link is often more of a patron than a client (a '*ndey*' in one sense or another). It is rather within the *mboteye* setting that the *ndey dické* relation has the more 'democratic' or 'equal' forms accounted for above. It has also more of the character of a 'relation de copinage' (Mottin-Sylla 1987: 10), i.e. a relation between friends, in combination with its economic orientation. Sometimes the financial aspect will be the dominating content of the *ndey dické* relation. I quote from Mottin-Sylla's information which stems from a questionnaire:

> We are 15 women who are organized in a *ndey dické*. The day that the association was created everybody placed her arm rings in a bag and a child was asked to take out two bracelets at a time from the bag. The two women whose arm rings were taken up together formed a *ndey dické* between them. Then the group of women meets each other every fortnight in one of the

members' homes. All the participants contribute with 100 Fr CFA and a kilo of soap and a bottle of milk and a litre of javel (water), or sugar, or nescafé. The woman who has a *ndey dické* relation to the hostess of the day brings more things to the hostess than the others: a basin, glasses and things like that. We have decided to limit the amount of such things that should be brought by the *ndey dické* partner. The one who receives all this has prepared donuts and bissap (syrup) for the friends who have come to see her. We chat a while together and then we go home. The hostess who has got all these things has to write everything down, in detail, what she has got and from whom, so that she can give exactly the same thing to the other people when their time comes (Mottin-Sylla ibid: 11; my translation from French).

Sanni jamra

The name refers to one of the rites that the pilgrims carry out in the neighbourhood of Mecca during their *hajj*. At a certain point during their walk, they have to collect seven pebbles and throw (*sanni*) them away as a symbolic act, actually as a stoning of Satan. These seven stones are called *jamra*. Maybe the Senegalese women traders who have been on *hajj* in Mecca have picked up the name there and transferred it to their country and to another context. In Dakar as well as in Touba Corniche (a village outside the city of Touba, 8 km. from Mbacké) I have seen a group of women assemble around a piece of cloth which they have laid out on the ground. Each woman present throws something on the cloth as a gift for the group member whose turn it is to receive it all. The presents vary; they are given according to what the individual considers she can afford: a soap, a few kilos of rice, a bottle of eau-de-cologne, some money. The 'harvest' of this particular turn is given to the woman who has won (the names are drawn by lots) this time. The great advantage for a woman is to get all these items at the same time; it may even help her to 'régler un problème' (fix some financial problem) which she has.

Nat

Nat (*nat* in Wolof; *susu* in Anglophone West Africa; *tontine* in French), is a form of rotating savings and credit association.[6] Such associations are defined in general terms as 'an association formed upon a core of participants who make regular contributions to a fund which is given in whole or in part to each contributor in turn' (Ardener 1995: 1). This means in its simplified form that a group of, let us say, ten women meet regularly, with each member each time contributing for example 100 fr CFA. This fund (1000 fr CFA) is straightaway handed over to one person at each meeting. At the end of ten meetings, everybody will have put in 1000 fr CFA and received the same sum. The first member to receive the fund has thus become a debtor to all the other members and remains one until the last contribution has been made. The last member becomes a creditor to all the other members throughout. The success and sustainability of each *nat* depends on the members' reliability. For the system to work it is necessary that all members continue to pay their fee to the cashbox until all members have had their share. Therefore, the advantages to all the members are far from equal and the social and moral dimensions of this form of savings and credit association are strong (cf. Ardener 1995 in Appendix p. 211). Social solidarity and mutual aid obligations must have a high priority, for this system to work. In spite of many conflicts between women in different *nats* and cases of rupture and lack of solidarity, the female cultural emphasis on collective activities, including savings, does strengthen the survival of the rotating savings associations as well as the other associations with a somewhat similar content (see above). According to the women members in *nats*, the benefit consists in receiving a large sum of money on one certain occasion. This offers otherwise non-existent capital for repaying loans or investing in merchandise to be sold in one's petty-trading activities.

The Senegalese *nat* is more frequent in the urban than in the rural areas. In the villages lack of cash is always the problem. While *mbotaye* and *ndeye dické* are forms of female associating only, *nat* could just as well have male as female members. The reason it is considered particularly well suited as a saving form for women is that small sums can also be saved. Banks often demand relatively big sums – too big for most women – before permission is given to open a bank account. The *nat* exists in many forms and variables. The members of the association could meet once a month or once a week and even – in cases where people need small amounts of cash to be distributed often – once a day, paying a fixed sum of money to the cashbox. According to the rules of the particular *nat*, the total sum of money in the box will be distributed to one member at a time, but *who* will be the lucky one is mostly decided by drawing lots. Each *nat* decides how often the sum will be distributed, according to the opinions of the members.

The meetings of the female saving associations that I have attended, have all been linked to social activities of one kind or another. Even if the drinks offered may consist of only a glass of water with ice, the women participants have stayed for more than one hour in the house of the president, chatting, trying to sell cloth to each other or discussing prices, and even dancing and drumming a little. Most urban women take part in many different *nats*; membership may be based on sharing the same profession, on sharing a neighbourhood, or suffering from the same physical handicap, or even coming from the same geographical region outside the town or city. The women I met preferred this system to saving their money in the bank for many reasons. One reason was, that by 'giving' money away to the different *nats*, it was out of reach and could not be claimed by a husband or relatives or anybody else, whom it would otherwise have been very difficult to deny money.

Daira

The *daira* is a religious association, in which the disciples of a certain great Sufi leader (Arabic: *sheikh;* French: *marabut;* Wolof: *Serigne*/title) assemble regularly to sing religious songs and to organize religious activities. The members are mostly adult men and women and also young people, although they are often divided into age groups, so that older people and youngsters have meetings on different evenings of the week. Even if men and women have their meeting together, they usually sit separately and have their own male and female presidents and secretaries of the *daira*. All the members collect money (Wolof: *addiyya*) to give to the marabout on the yearly pilgrimage (*magal*) to his house, but again there are differences in the size of the stipulated sum according to the members' sex and age. Adult men pay the biggest amount. Women are often very active in these associations. Even if in some of the *dairas* women are not allowed to sing the religious songs aloud, they are there listening, they pay the weekly or monthly fees and they prepare themselves for the annual pilgrimage. The female workload is temporarily heavy when it comes to the preparation of food in relation to different religious feasts. All of these activities, as well as the excursion itself to the tombs of the great marabouts and the visit to the living marabout's house, are considered by the women as religious activities of great importance for their experience of themselves as *daira* members and as members of their particular Sufi *tariqa* (Arabic: 'way', 'order' or religious brotherhood). My informants are mostly from the Muridiyya order, which is the dominant one in Mbacké and the adjacent city of Touba.[7]

The only women who do not participate in secular or religious associations of any kind are the *sokhnas*, i.e. the women of maraboutic descent or women married to a marabout. They are considered to stand above any female associating and have no need to get support and esteem outside the limits of the family. It is below their dignity to ask women in non-descent groups for help for the fulfilment of certain demands, in order to obtain access to material and immaterial resources. The young *sokhnas* are supposed to get financial support for their weddings from their fathers, so they and their mothers do not need the contribution of the *mbotaye*. The weddings are never lavish but rather modest, as there is no need felt to manifest the marabout's wealth and power through potlatch-like offerings of gifts to the in-marrying family. A great Sufi leader's authority is uncontested and confirmed by God's blessing (Wolof: *barke*).

Compared with the ordinary female *daira*-members, the *soknas'* position and relation to the marabout are different. While the 'ordinary' *daira*-members are disciples of the marabout, the *sokhnas* occupy the roles of daughters, mothers or wives. In a way these women see their position as a superior form of 'disciplehood'. Their arena is the maraboutic polygynous household and their duties in the first place are to organize the reception of the marabout's disciples at the important annual religious event, i.e. the pilgrimage (*magal*), taking place in his house. On this occasion the marabout will bless all his present disciples. Food and accommodation for one or several days will be provided for the guests/disciples. All practicalities in relation to this big event will be in the hands of the women of the maraboutic family. Their role as highly prestigious hostesses in this social and religious context certainly distinguishes them from 'ordinary' women/disciples.

The *geer* ('non-castées', aristocratic) women of non-maraboutic lineages often play leading roles in the female religious and secular associations. They constitute board members with a considerable power and influence. In particular, the president and the treasurer, who have control over the collected sum of money kept in a secret place, are important persons in the women-members' lives. The *njenjo* ('femmes castées', who are of lower status) become supporters of the leaders' ideas. The relation between the president and her members is often referred to in terms of the mother with her daughters. The more 'daughters' that adhere to the president, who is their social mother, the more powerful she becomes.

Men appreciate women's financial investments in the *mbotaye* and the *nat* as these activities alleviate the burden of providing their wives and female relatives with economic means for the ritual passage parties and for the yearly pilgrimages to the marabout. Concerning women's participation in the *dairas* men cannot oppose it, as ideally everybody ought to be a disciple of a marabout to be a proper Muslim and Senegalese. Ideally, the wife should have her husband as her marabout, serving him in total obedience and subordination just as he treats his own *sheikh*. 'The one who has no marabout has the devil as his master'; so the saying goes. The male disciple is connected with his religious leader through a vow of obedience, something which most women have not been allowed to promise anyone else but the husband. Many exceptions to this rule do exist, however. As mentioned, all women members in *dairas* see themselves as disciples of a certain marabout, even if they may not have pronounced the vow of obedience to him. They also obey his order (*ndigeul*) whenever he gives one for the men and women disciples to join him in harvesting his fields or to vote according to his will. Most women are petty traders and earn small amounts of money, which they partly use for paying the different fees of the associations. Very few women are too poor to be able to fulfil the demands of at least one association – the monthly payment of the *dairas*, for example, is usually very low, especially for women.

Moroccan Women's Arenas and Networks[8]

Moroccan women in groups will be found mainly in two female 'arenas': the house among trusted relatives and 'close' (*qriba*) people, i.e. neighbours, and the ritual passage feasts, with large numbers of variously connected women, mostly close and distant relatives.[9] Particularly for the married women it is important to build up and consolidate their positions in the local arena – both inside the houses at the women's daily encounters with their close-knit conversational circles and in the yards and houses at the women's rites de passage parties.

Exchange of information is one of the main purposes of creating and maintaining social networks. Entertainment is another. Both are connected with the fact that the women's lives are anchored in and oriented towards their immediate surroundings. They display an intense interest in other people and in their own position in relation to the others in terms of respectability. Concern about things going on at a distance and among unknown people is minimal. Another purpose for married women's talk in their networks is connected with their role in society as testers and reproducers of norms and traditions. In this endeavour much time is spent on gossiping about other women's moral reputations. Gaining supporters for their interpretations of reality is an important goal and a requirement for their female prestige careers. One key to ascendancy is a close-knit and reliable network of allies who will hide a woman's disgraces and advertise her successes. Her allies would willingly collect and communicate as much information as possible about people outside her own group. Such a broad, close-knit network is a great resource – a threat and a source of power that the other village women cannot ignore. A mother and her married daughters can form such a constellation, as a woman's female kindred are her most reliable allies. This presupposes that they live relatively near to each other, at least in the same village. Not only daughters and female relatives but also more recently settled neighbours may join a powerful woman, being brought in under her 'umbrella' of respectability and esteem in exchange for support for her versions of reality and moral judgement. Such a group can build up an information pool of considerable significance.

To exemplify with a case from a border village in Qbila Anyera, close to the Ceuta enclave, I will mention *haja* Rahma (her name fictive), who in 1987 was a woman in her mid sixties, and her network. She had two married sons and three married daughters in the same village as herself, something which gave her an unusually strong position among the other village women. Age, being a *haja* (having done the *hajj* to Mecca), successful sons and many grandchildren added to her status. The kinship network was dense, especially due to the solidarity of her daughters, who supported her, surrounding her in the afternoon during long seances of talk and tea drinking. Non-related neighbours with few kinship ties in the village wanted to become her allies and supporters to be protected by her in relation to other women, outside *haja* Rahma's network. These women confirmed by small gifts of food or other gifts and by daily visits to the *haja's* home that they wanted to be her 'clients' having her as their 'patron'. Thus, she could be seen as a kind of 'social mother' or 'presidente' for these women, in some aspects similar to the Senegalese counterparts described above. The weak links in *haja* Rahma's network were her two daughters-in-law, living in her house as potential traitors. Much time and energy was spent on manipulating these links and building up strategies to dominate the situation. The solution was to split up the extended household so that the sons moved into houses of their own with their wives and children. This was however not a very positive arrangement from the *haja's* point of view, as she then lost the control of her sons' families and had to watch silently as other women, non-members of her network, visited her daughters-in-law.

But even if in smaller circles, like inside the household of *haja* Rahma, a daughter-in-law may have different strategies and loyalties than her husband's female kin, in the greater arena like the wedding and name-giving parties, women perform mainly as representatives of their husbands and in-laws. They are also individual actors with the other women as their audience. The party hostess, her female family members and her guests constitute a group which serves as an example of female networking with characteristic structuring aspects. The segregation of sexes (no men among the party guests) and the separation of kin and affines (the two mothers of bride and bridegroom have separate parties for their respective relatives and neighbours) are very crucial aspects. The competition for prestige between the party guests is apparent in garments and jewellery.

Yet the giving of money *(grama)* to the hostess is balanced by reciprocity. The same sum that is given by each guest to the hostess as a contribution to the financing of the party will be received from today's hostess the day that each particular guest has her own party – be it a wedding or a name-giving party. As the female married participants/ donors are seen as representatives of their husband's family and household, it would be shameful for the women and dishonourable for the men if their wives failed to fulfil their obligations by not paying or paying less money than they themselves have received (Evers Rosander 1991: 189f). Poor women, whose husbands or close relatives lack the economic means, cannot give them the sums needed. These women remain outside this reciprocal party financing system. Consequently they do not form part of the party networks, a factor which contributes to their marginalization in the society.

Just like in Senegal the Moroccan wedding and name-giving rituals and parties are great occasions for the families involved to show off their wealth, status and prestige. This is achieved through the women's whole-hearted engagement. Different forms of traditional associations in Senegal aimed at facilitating the female part of the financing and arrang-ing of these parties have been described above. In northern Morocco, where such associations are non-existent, the kinship and neighbour networks could be said to serve as a kind of equivalent or substitute. In the case of a *seba*, a name-giving feast, the idea is that the hostess will be able to count on certain women with whom she maintains reciprocal party relations, for help with the party preparations, and on the invited guests' financial contributions to the party costs. Also these contributions are based on a reciprocal system, where all women pay the same 'party fee' when visiting each other's *sebas*. This makes it possible for the hostess to pay the bills for the food, drinks and so on to her debtors after the party has been arranged. In Senegal, the members of the same *mbotaye, ndey dické* and *nat* will contribute to the collection of this capital.

The Moroccan name-giving feast begins in the afternoon. All the women of the hostess's 'inner circle' or her close network have been preparing the party since early afternoon. They contribute to the preparation of the food. Their kitchen yards are used for fires to cook the meat stew in big pans. If more space is needed the women offer their homes and front yards to seat the guests. Some women lend their tables, glasses, teapots and other items so that the hostess does not have to hire the equipment. In Senegal the *mbotaye* associations have their own equipment for members to use, as mentioned. The tasks are distributed rapidly and smoothly among the Moroccan hostess's 'party helpers'. Two dishes will be prepared and served at a name-giving party: intestines (Arabic: *kershi*) and a meat stew. In good time before the arrival of the first guest the mother adorns herself. She puts on heavy make-up and a beautiful dress and lies with her baby on the matrimonial bed. The guests enter the bedroom to congratulate the mother on her birth. On the bed they leave the current sum of money (1985: 10 dirhams) for attending the name-giving party and a little present for the baby. While the money is obligatory and reciprocal, the same fixed sum for everybody, the gifts for the baby are voluntary and differ in shape and value depending on the relationship in terms of kinship and neighbourhood. The main object is to repay the mother for her party expenses. If any money is left after all the bills have been paid, the mother will keep the rest for her own purposes (cf. ibid 1991: 113–14).

Wives and husbands are dependent on each other for the realization of their female and male selves. This is expressed in an idiom of shame (*hashuma*) for women and honour (*erd*) for men. Woman's sexual behaviour is closely linked to her moral reputation and that of her family. Thus, as we all know from studies in other places in the Middle East, control of female sexuality is considered a male duty. These ideological concepts are linked to economic well-being and descent. Wealthy men from well-reputed families or *shorfa* families (Arabic: *sherif*, descendant from the Prophet Muhammad) manifest their superior position by keeping their women more secluded than poorer women, who may have to work outside their homes to support the family or to contribute to their provision. Yet, the ideal for all women remains to situate one's activities as much as possible within one's own home or close to it. The alternative would be inside another woman's home or house yard, the condition being that this other woman forms part of one's own social network. Strange women who are not relatives and come from other places are often experienced as dangerous; there is a fear of 'others' as being the potential source of evil, sorcery and misfortunes beyond control. That is probably one of the reasons why the female Senegalese ideas and practice of associating and linkage based on other criteria than kinship and neighbourhood are not to be found in rural, northern Morocco.

Summing Up: Female Senegalese and Moroccan Associating Patterns

The investigation of female associating patterns in Morocco and Senegal has thrown light on the fact that women's lives in both countries are guided by very similar moral and religious ideals in combination with financial needs and demands in order to cope with moral and economic female obligations. Female prestige structures are integrated into the wider setting of the family and household. The frames vary according to local and cultural habits, but the main conditions under which women live and create their life strategies are surprisingly similar.

Without having gone into any details, I have shown that women both in Morocco and Senegal form groups of different kinds for the financing and preparation of the great ritual passage parties – and, in the Senegalese case, also for religious purposes in connection with their Sufi assoc-iations. While in Morocco membership in these networks is based on kinship and neighbourhood, and the financing is made by the women participants of the parties, in Senegal, the members of the *mbotaye* associations could be women who have many other things in common. The *mbotaye* members are offering party help without themselves being invited guests to the marriage and name-giving parties. The financing is made partly through this association, not by the party members only, as in Morocco.

Women are dependent on men as husbands and fathers for their realization of self in both Morocco and Senegal. However, while ideas about male honour and female shame knit men and women closely together in Morocco, in Senegal the stress is much more on women's shame, endurance of sufferings and ability to keep secrets about the husband and his family (Wolof: *soutoura*), than on men's honour. In both countries the cultural ideal is to restrict women's activities to the house or the compound, especially among urban Arabs in Morocco and to a lesser extent among the Wolof (Muslim) people I have studied in Senegal. This is a sign of wealth but also of moral superiority, which only high status families can offer their women. Thus, the *sokhnas'* life in the maraboutic houses displays great similarities with those of certain urban middle-class and upper middle-class Moroccan women. Also their networking patterns are similar; i.e. limited to family members and close relatives.

The traditional matrifocus that we still find in West Africa, where the social role of the mother is much more widely acknowledged, women's participation in the informal labour market much greater and the sexual segregation is less rigid than in North Africa, is contraworked by the ideas about female behaviour presented above. The current situation of the Senegalese woman, both from an ideological and practical point of view, is characterized by more contradictions and more aggressive gender relations than is the case in Morocco.

The Senegalese female associations are not solving these problems but underlining them and maintaining the present hierarchical caste and gender structure. The same is the case with the Moroccan networks, which conserve prestige structures based on ideas of women as respectable housewives and mothers only. So even if in Senegal women often are comparatively independent economically in relation to their husbands, they are ideologically not free from men's demands on them to be pleasant, understanding and obedient to their husbands. That is why the polygynous households are so often tough arenas for competition: the wives compete between themselves to win the husband's favours. They try to serve the best food, to be the most seductive and beautiful and to have the greatest number of children. These are individual battles, which could be of benefit for the husband, but which put great strain on the women in the household collectives.

In Morocco, where women's economic dependence on men is much more accentuated and sexual segregation is more practised, the ideological system is under severe strain because of the changing realities of everyday life. Current male unemployment has increased women's necessity to support themselves and their children by accepting remunerated work outside the home, without giving them any moral credit for it at all – but rather the opposite. The Moroccan society is permeated by a patrilineal and patriarchal spirit to a much greater extent than in Senegal. That is probably a contributing factor to the resistance towards creating groups or associations of women outside the family unit. In Qbila Anyera, a decent, married woman should not associate with 'other people'. Female 'friends' (*sahabta*) seemed to be a concept reserved for a woman's 'patrons'; i.e. people with whom a woman had some kind of financially or religiously beneficial relation. The rare occasions when I heard the word 'friend' used by the women in Qbila Anyera referred to the older and experienced female Mecca pilgrims, who took care of the female novices on their first or second pilgrimage.

This leads us into the religious domain in which both Senegalese and Moroccan women can meet in spontaneously formed groups without being morally questioned. The Moroccan women who visit the famous saints' tombs to express their wishes, to ask for help and give vows, do so in groups consisting of women from their own village and from the adjacent region (cf. Mernissi 1977). They meet other pious women there and share each others' sufferings, listening patiently to the stories told by other female visitors. The big pilgrimage to Mecca has already been mentioned as constituting an acknowledged and prestigious religious arena for women as well as men. The Senegalese *dairas*, Sufi associations for both men and women, offer religious space and activities also for women. Within the framework of the *dairas* the members work, sing, pray and give money to their marabout or religious leader, receiving his blessing (Wolof: *barke*) and the hope of entering Paradise after death as a result of their endeavours. Senegalese and Moroccan women have a common interest in religious and economic activities, which sometimes coincide and sometimes need the one to be a precondition of the other. Religious rituals during a pilgrimage can very well be combined with the purchase of goods in the large market-places which are usually found close to the holy places. Trading this merchandise can be one way of financing coming pilgrimages. The importance of religious practice as an organizing principle for women's social, economic and emotional life is worth reflecting on when dealing with both Senegal and Morocco.

Notes

1. This paper was presented in a first version at the Third Nordic Middle East Conference in Joensuu, Finland, 19 June 1995 and later thoroughly revised for the Workshop on Women Organized in Groups in the Middle East: Issues and Constraints.
2. I think here of a 'group' in the sense of an organized group, be it formal or informal, with some kind of a board, which is acknowledged by its members, and belonging to a certain type or category of group, which carries a certain name, such as *daira* (religious group), *mbotaye* (social and economic group) and so on. See below for further clarifications of the content and meaning of these groups.
3. The text above is extracted from a larger paper called 'The Africa Gender Group', and somewhat revised. The paper was presented to the Center for Development Research, Copenhagen, in October 1994.
4. The *maas* institution is gradually being abandoned in the big cities of today.
5. Another similar form of association is *mbaxal*.
6. Rotating savings and credit associations can be found in Asia, Africa, Europe, the West Indies and the Americas. In Europe, they were found in the seven-

teenth century. Their European origin (in 1653) is attributed to a banker from Naples called Lorenzo Tontin (Desroche 1990). Shirley Ardener states that in West Africa, the term *(e)susu* was already found in the Yoruba vocabulary in 1843 (Ardner 1995 in her Appendix, p.204). Membership criteria may be sex, kinship, ethnic affiliation, locality, religion and so on. The number of members may range from just a few to several hundred. The individual contributions are collected and handed over to members in rotation. Regularity in payment of contributions is one of the criteria distinguishing rotating credit from other institutions. The fact that it is rotating is the other.

7. In Senegal most people are members of a Sufi order (Arabic pl. *turuq*, sing. *tariqa*). The largest order is the *Tijaniyya,* followed by *Muridiyya*, *Quadiriyya* and the *Layennes.*

8. 'Moroccan women' indicates those women I met and studied during my fieldwork in Qbila Anyera, Yebala, northwestern Morocco and in Ceuta.

9. An 'arena' is a stage for women's oral communication and the display of affluence. It is a space for parading clothes and jewellery, for performance, for the presentation of self to others and for each other. It is more than a stage, however, more than a space for performing social roles; 'arenas' are also niches, institutions, customs. While the concept of 'arena' can be used abstractly, as when referring to a woman's network, it evokes the idea of many people coming together on purpose for the performance of a particular social activity (Evers Rosander 1991: 12).

References

Ardener, S. (1995), 'Women Making Money Go Round: ROSCAS Revisited,' in S. Ardener and S. Burman, eds, *Money-Go-Rounds: The Importance of Rotating Savings and Credit Associations for Women*, Oxford: Berg.

Bailey, F.G. (1971), 'Gifts and Poison. Public and Private Interests,' in F. G. Bailey, ed., *Gifts and Poison: The Politics of Reputation*, Oxford: Blackwell.

Bortei-Doku, E. and Aryeetey, E. (1995) 'Mobilizing Cash for Business: Women in Rotating *Susu* Clubs in Ghana,' in S. Ardener and S. Burman, eds, *Money-Go-Rounds*, Oxford: Berg.

Brenner, L. (1993), 'Constructing Muslim Identities in Mali,' in L. Brenner, ed., *Muslim Identity and Social Change in Sub-Saharan Africa*, London: Hurst & Co.

Bryant, C. (1985), 'Development Management and Institutional Development: Implications of their Relationship,' Mimeo for International Development Programme and Overseas Development.

Bülow von, D., Evers Rosander, E. and Nautrup, B. (1994), 'The Africa Gender Group,' Unpublished paper, Copenhagen: Center for Development Research.

Desroche, H. (1990), 'Des tontines nord aux tontines sud,' in M. Lelart, ed., *La tontine pratique informelle d'épargne et de crédit dans les pays en voie de développement*, London/Paris: John Libbey Eurotext.

Evers Rosander, E. (1991), *Women in a Borderland: Managing Muslim Identity where Morocco meets Spain*, Stockholm: Stockholm Studies in Social Anthropology.

Mernissi, F. (1977), 'Women, saints and sanctuaries,' *Signs*, 3: 101–12.

Mottin-Sylla, M-H. (1987), *L'argent et l'intérêt. Tontines et autres pratiques féminines de mobilisation de moyens à Dakar*, Dakar: ENDA-GRAf-ARGENT 11.

—— (1988), *Les céremonies familiales à Dakar. La participation en action*, Dakar: ENDA.

Riesman, P. (1986), 'The Person and the Life Cycle in African Social Life and Thought,' *African Studies Review*, 29, 2, June.

—— (1992), *First Find your Child a Good Mother. The Construction of Self in Two African Societies*, New Brunswick: Rutger University Press.

Roberts, P. and Seddon, D. (1991), 'Fundamentalism in Africa: Religion and Politics,' *Review of African Political Economy*, 52: 3–8.

Uphoff, N. (1986), *Local Institutional Development: An Analytical Sourcebook with Cases.* Connecticut: Kumarian Press.

Woodford-Berger, P. (1997), 'Associating Women: Female Linkages, Collective Identities and Political Ideologies in Ghana,' in E. Evers Rosander, ed., *Female Fora for Organizing. Women's Associations in West Africa*. Uppsala: Scandinavian Institute of African Studies. Forthcoming 1997.

6

Bahraini Women in Formal and Informal Groups: The Politics of Identification[1]

May Seikaly

At the beginning of April 1995, 310 Bahraini women signed and circulated a petition presented to the ruler of Bahrain, Shaikh Isa Bin Salman al-Khalifah, expressing their concern with the mounting wave of riots that had engulfed the country, and had left deep rifts in its society, grief at the number of deaths and strong bitterness and frustration at official handling of the crisis. Since December 1994, an uprising had erupted from among the less favoured strata of society demanding employment, better opportunities and justice. This was the tip of the iceberg and the circle of opposition, anger and accumulated bitterness acquired momentum and adherents in spiralling speed and vociferous activities. In addition to the class dimension of the conflict it also expressed sectarian and ethnic differences and animosities, and one common demand from all elements was the return of the short-lived democratic process that had been scrapped by the ruling family in 1975. Strife conditions created a network of common grounds between various currents, elements, groups and strata of the Bahraini society, Shiis and Sunnis, liberals, leftists and Islamists, workers, professionals and intellectuals, men and women. As a result contacts, relationships and exchanges between them were activated, thus clarifying and exposing ideological differences and channels of cooperation.

In this particular petition, the women of Bahrain, citizens and mothers addressed the grievances of the nation and its fears and demanded in clear and concrete terms redress of the deteriorating conditions through grass-root reforms of the political system. A return to a constitutional democracy was advocated as the channel in which women are to be involved in the process of political decision-making and sharing in national development. In the statement, this group of Bahraini women were attempting to achieve two goals in one battle – national and social liberation. While their national commitment is clear, non-sectarian, in favour of social equality and participation, they were also proposing a gender agenda of equality and social justice. They were striking while the iron was hot. It is clear that they refused to mask their gender requests in the fervour of nationalist demands; demands that incorporated and masked the wide spectrum of societal categories of class, sectarian and ethnic groups, but not women. In view of the highly volatile and politically dangerous conditions that the country was passing through, such a challenging act, similar to the case of women driving in Saudi Arabia, is an expression of the autonomous, courageous, and unde-featable spirit of women even under excruciatingly trying conditions. It is also an act which bespeaks of an underlying array of developments that Bahraini women as a group, and in groups have undergone and found now an opportunity to express. It is indicative and cynical that the reaction to their petition from the authorities in Bahrain was again in the same spirit of backlash that the Saudi women received – intimidation and unemployment.

Involvement of Middle Eastern women in the struggle for national liberation and reform is not new and Arab history is dotted with many examples, not the least of which are Algeria and the on-going struggle of Palestinian women. The struggle of Kuwaiti women for democratic rights and participation is a model often cited, and their achievements, however minimal applauded (Ghassoub 1987: 11; Ghabra 1993). These are issues of which Bahraini women are aware and bring up constantly. It was enlightening to relocate Bahraini activists who had experienced and lived through the anti-colonial demonstrations of the 60s and the 1971–5 Parliamentary protest movement in Bahrain. These secular nationalists were trained in the school of liberal nationalism of the 60s and 70s of the Nasserite era. During the peak of their activism, this brand of nationalists had fought for equal participation and a role in national development but were disillusioned. Today it is in the same spirit that Bahraini secular nationalists have petitioned for parliamentary part-icipation again after twenty years.

Theoretical and Methodological Considerations

In order to understand the full significance of women's participation in this popular protest experience it is essential first to situate it within the broader historical and theoretical context. It is under extenuating conditions that Bahraini women, their voice, role and contribution have had the opportunity to be heard and viewed. In this situation, the political context has provided the framework whereby Bahrain's social and economic structures are exposed as well as the crisis of confidence between its government and people. Economic and social categories defining the problems of society are contested and redefined in terms of gender as an index of development, again highlighting the role women have achieved and reflecting the gendered nature of politics. In researching the identity, role and status of Bahraini women, before and during the crisis, the gender system and its socio-cultural underpinnings, class location, state political ideology and its socio-economic development strategy, are categories to be consciously referenced when analysing the dynamics between women's involvement at this juncture (Moghadam 1993: 14–16). Similar to other Third World experiences inequality is the core issue that the nation and women are protesting; economic, social and political inequalities on the national level as expressed in class, sectarian and ethnic differences. However another perspective to be kept in mind is that women as a subaltern within an oppressed social system, when caught up in a crisis situation, could find their causes and rights used as a battle field between the subordinating authorities and suppressed male society bargaining for agendas of their own (Mallon 1994).

The aim of this chapter is to investigate the evolution of women's role, defined and focused as a result of socio-economic changes and particularly highlighted in unfolding crisis conditions. Women's identity as defined by religious, social and cultural parameters is being challenged to new levels of expression. To research the changing roles of women as induced by the rapid socio-economic changes in Bahrain and the Gulf region, women belonging to the various ideological currents, the secular liberals, the Islamists both Shii and Sunni have been interviewed during 1982–3 and in the summer of 1984. While the obvious Islamist current and its manifestations on women, society and self identity were the initial direction for the research, political events gave a more poignant dimension to the project when women were catapulted into the centre of the political scene. It was to take into consideration all women's groups from the liberal secularists, to the active Islamists both Shii and Sunni. In addition to the fieldwork, this research has had the strength of my long-lived association with the Bahrainis, friends, students and acquaintances. While living in the country (from 1983 to 1993), the Bahrainis had been generous with their friendship, information and help, which also keeps my interest in their development alive through contact and follow up of events.

However there are many deficiencies in the availability of records as well as difficulties in extricating pertinent and cogent information on women. The focus of Middle East women studies has been confined mainly to Egypt, Iran and Turkey and to a lesser extent some areas of the Levant, notably Lebanon. Parallelling wider trends in history, until the late 1980s, a small amount of research on the history and role of women within Gulf society has entered the field of scholarly consideration. Many publications in the field have given Arabian Gulf women passing attention as part of larger theses on women of the Middle East in general; however it is the work of women of the Gulf themselves, those who identify the dilemmas of their changing status and devise solutions within the reality of their particular socio-political constraints, that has left the strongest impact on the field (Al-Torki; Al-Mannai; Al-Awwadi 1990; Arebi 1994; Fakhro 1990). Nevertheless these are few and face serious limitations not encountered in other regions of Middle East women studies.

In spite of interest in the field by Gulf intellectuals, records are few and whenever recorded, information is often constrained by politics. This constraint is most tangible now when in addition to Bahrain's usual hyper-sensitive security fears, they have escalated into paranoia. Furthermore until very recently there have been deliberate blackouts and cordoning by the international media on information coming out of Bahrain and on Bahrain. When this was slightly loosened up after January 1996, information provided to the US readers reflected concern with US security and barely alluded to the effects of the disturbances on the society itself. It is remarkable that even the most liberal US papers have barely given any coverage for such an inflammable situation.[2] Britain, who has been more closely embroiled in the Bahraini crisis, has more recently, since January '96, published many researched stories on the situation in its major newspapers.[3] Furthermore, formal attention has been awarded the situation by the British Parliamentary Human Rights Group which has deemed Bahrain's situation worthy of its attention (Parliamentary HRG 1996). Although these sources along with the exiled opposition groups, visitors and residents of Bahrain provide information on events and their repercussions, it is still difficult to build a comprehensive picture of the evolving situation there. As a result, this part of the study is necessarily of an exploratory nature, since the succession of events and uncertainty over future developments concerning the political scene and strategies preclude any clear conclusions.

As a historian trained in the conservative school of the Public Records Office and by formal means of historiography, I find research on women – a marginalized and often hidden sector of society – a challenge filled with professional minefields and uncertainties. One of the major difficulties faced is in retrieving the voice or identity of women and other subaltern from records, archives and even from cultural concepts that have been constructed by patriarchal and controlling forces. Written sources do not yield clear pictures of the suppressed and subsumed subaltern voice because these sources are loaded with nuances from various directions. Even women interviewed who are consciously aware of their identity and the role of societal and cultural biases, unconsciously convey their complex view of reality. The difficulty is in extricating a woman's pure voice from the societal web while she remains subordinate within it. It is important to understand these limitations and accept that we are talking about approximations of a reality that cannot be fully confirmed.

Historical Overview

For an understanding of women's participation in the events of the Bahrain political crisis today, it is important to reconstruct the dimension of their role in the nationalist struggle of Bahraini history for the period prior to 1995. It is only by bringing to light the intersection of international, regional and local socio-economic developments that the current events could be properly assessed. Internally the impact of this legacy on the class, sectarian and ethnic make-up of society was tremendous and involved women at every stage and period.

For the last fifteen years, Bahrain's economic and political development had become completely entwined with Gulf regional developments, particularly that of its hegemonic neighbour, Saudi Arabia. The economic and political alignment and subordination of the latter to the world capitalist system and the unchallenged USA has become clear. This has also linked the whole region as well as the Arab world to the same subordination. As a direct result of the Gulf War, Saudi Arabia became deeply indebted to the USA (Aarts 1994: 5). The more integrated the Gulf political-economic structure became in the global economy, the more important it was to the West to maintain its stability even at the price of overlooking its dependency, traditionalism, and authoritarianism.

Development of the economic and social structures of Bahrain, due to oil, experienced two distinctive stages: the first started in the 50s and culminated in the late 70s and the second unfolded in the mid 90s. Both have been prompted by the above mentioned international factor as well as regional and local ones. Even though Bahraini oil was discovered in non-commercial, limited quantities, the country is still dependent on oil production and labour; and because of low production, the state benefits mainly from refining and distribution. Economically, Bahrain is the weakest Gulf state and dependent upon its neighbour Saudi Arabia, which provides it with oil, funds, and investment. By the late 1970s, in an attempt to diversify income and create jobs, it started such industries as aluminium and a dry dock, and in the early 80s it offered Bahrain as an international banking centre. Since the late 1980s these enterprises have visibly weakened and more so after the Gulf War of 1991.

The tremendous growth in oil wealth after 1973, has been successful in building up the infrastructure and other manifestations of the state along modern lines and has provided citizens with a wide range of services such as education, health, social services, even entertainment. These have been central projects by the state, the supreme employer and provider of benefits. Therefore the ruling institution plays the major role in creating and withholding opportunities whether from women or any other subaltern. It has also rationalized its legitimacy through these achievements and by building a network of alliances based on tribal, sometimes religious and/or economic interests (Al-Najjar 1985; Al-Rumaihi 1982). Economic favours in the form of money or land donations, or control of power-generating posts are some of the means by which these alliances were and are cemented.

However this system has created superficially modern looking societies without solving the dilemmas that rapid Western modernization has brought. Change has come into conflict with traditional cultural value systems which control social behaviour that is tied to religion. The policy has always attempted to find a balance between commitment to modernization and economic development and commitment to the internal traditional socio-cultural forces. It has also manipulated both perceptions in order to create allegiance to its continued presence and control (Sharabi 1988; Moghadam 1993: 11). All modernization techniques introduced in Bahrain since the inception of this state were tailored to endorse this relationship and confirm these roles. Modernization also meant the creation of departments and apparatus to ensure control and order.

Bahrain differs from other Gulf states in the make-up and origin of its population. According to a December 1991 census the population of Bahrain was approximately 500,000, with 49.5 per cent women (Bahrain

1991). This population has varied origins: Arabs of tribal extraction, Arabs from the settled communities of the eastern region in the Arabian Peninsula, Arabs from Iraq, Persian/Arab tribes (Hawala) coming from coastal and inland Iran, in addition to a small number of Baluchis, Indians, and Pakistanis who have lived for generations in Bahrain and have become Bahraini. Each of these groups is large enough to leave an ethnic imprint on the fabric of society.

Shiis are a majority (the official estimate is 35 per cent, US estimate is 55 per cent and the Shiis' estimate is 75 per cent) especially in the villages. Shiis are either descendants of the original Arab inhabitants and from the eastern quarter of Saudi Arabia, or Persians who have immigrated in the last fifty years. Sunnis are also either Arab of tribal origin (such as the ruling family), local Arab families of undefined origin, or people from Persian/Arab tribes who settled in Bahrain at different times since the late eighteenth century. These ethnic origins are obvious in linguistic variety, social attitudes and norms, but the people are distributed among most social classes, with the exception of the ruling Sunni family, and the rural villages which are almost exclusively Shii and mostly Arab.

Since early in the century, Shiis of Bahrain representing the majority of the working class have taken part in movements against the established authorities asking for reforms. Such a history and tradition of rebellion is associated with Shii demands for economic equality, union protection and political participation (Khuri 1980; da Lage 1995). Even though Sunnis participated in most of these movements, by the fact that Shiis made up the majority of the economically depressed strata, these activities became associated with them. Whether in the pearl industry or in the oilfields or in government employment, Shiis have felt victimized as the first to lose their means of livelihood. Another historical reason for Shii disaffection is their opposition to the ruling family (the Al Khalifa), a staunch Sunni minority, who are viewed as occupying tribesmen, and have been accused of appropriating and misusing the resources of the country. While the main cause of Shii opposition is economic it also has an ideological base; this has often been fomented by outside inciters, mainly Iran. Sunni and Shii Bahrainis have also had many common causes especially in the nationalist movement against the British in the 50s and 60s and for popular participation in the government in the 40s, the 50s, the 70s and now again in the 90s. It was in the 1950s, that women began to support the male-led demands for reform. A few women are supposed to have unveiled in public in one of the protest demonstrations against the British.

By the 1960s regional Arab development combined with a rapidly growing generation of Bahraini university graduates further developed and politicized this protest current. The influence of liberation movements, Arab nationalism and political confrontations with colonialism in the Arab world in the 1950s, 1960s, and 1970s formed the political orientation of the young Bahraini generation. The tripartite attack on Nasser's Egypt in 1956, the Algerian war of independence, the liberation movement against the British in Yemen in 1963, the Arab defeat of 1967, the Dhofar revolution in 1971 and the Palestinian struggle against Israel all had their immediate reflections locally. Whether the reactions were spontaneous street demonstrations or the growth of underground political organizations or the emergence of civil servants with heightened socio-political consciousness, society changed in unprecedented ways. The unrest culminated in the popular movement for a parliament and political participation following independence from the British in 1971.

Male and female students educated in Beirut and Cairo, Baghdad and Kuwait, influenced by nationalist and radical political currents thriving in these university centres, joined political organizations. Whether left nationalist or pro-communist, the women wanted to take part in changing their society. Since the early 1950s women had organized charitable societies, but in the early 1970s voluntary women's societies sprung up with political orientations. Women of the growing middle class and a few from the working class had benefited from the developing education system, the scholarships to universities in the Arab countries, and the need for Bahrainis in the job market.

Women's earliest political experience was a disappointment when they were excluded from the short-lived liberal experiment with the parliament, partly because the traditional tribal orientation was still very strong in society and among both Sunni and Shii, but mostly because the radical and liberalized men in society did not endorse women's issues. They had encouraged women to support social change and to contribute to political change; but when it came to women's socio-political aims, men turned traditional and conservative. It was unfortunate for males too because the whole project was dissolved by the ruler before it really started.

During the 60s, women made substantial advances in education and employment and these advances gave fruit in the 70s. By the mid 70s women were very visible in Bahraini society. The younger, more educated urban generation discarded the *abaya*, drove cars, took part in political demonstrations, communicated with male colleagues from their student days and from work, were involved in politics, joined the Baathis, nationalists, and radical leftist groups and organized themselves in civil, non-government organizations to further social and political aims. Women's societies, female sections of sport clubs or professional organizations gave them a role. They also aimed at achieving acceptance on an equal footing with men. As the latter accepted changes and the role of women in development, relationship between the sexes became more balanced and involved reciprocal respect and confidence. While the traditional gender values were not openly challenged, women were confident enough to compete with males for jobs and scholarships. With a strong drive to achieve and a nationalist commitment to build, women were active elements in the early years of establishing Bahrain's modern society. The government was also anxious to build the infrastructure of the state and women figured as an important element in the 'Bahrain-ization' (control of the job market by Bahraini nationals rather than employing expatriate workers) of jobs as well as projecting a modern image abroad. This fact legitimized the more liberal behaviour of women in seeking education and socializing outside the home, a behaviour not fully condoned by tradition and the conservative society.

In spite of these many achievements, Bahraini women still had few personal and civil rights, especially in the villages and among the lower classes, which had practically been excluded from what was mainly an urban, middle-class social revolution. In rural areas women were unaware of their personal rights. Lack of, or very minimal education, economic depression, and conservative oppressive socio-religious institutions were the overriding causes of this condition. Even among the new urban middle class, change barely touched on feminism's core issues. The maximum that women acquired was to establish their right to free education and limited participation in the job market. Activities of these women, through societies and personal relations, took a political approach that was often elitist and reflected competition between the different political currents. These modernized young women had unconsciously distanced themselves from the realities of their society and could not reach all strata of women by traditional mechanisms.

Following the 1975 Parliamentary crisis, political activities were banned and women acquiesced. It was a period of economic prosperity during the 70s and early 80s. While the 70s saw the emergence of an urban, largely Sunni middle class, the late 80s saw these developments reach the village, mostly Shii communities. However the difference between the two stages translated itself in economic and social class differentiations, constriction of opportunities and intensification of sectarian conflicts. Educational, health and other services both to rural and urban areas were built along with high-rise office buildings and other modern outlets. The local economic market expanded as various corporations (monopolies by certain families of established status and wealth) were set up and employment in the service sector increased. It was a period of major material expansion which raised the economic and social expectations of people at a time when signs of economic contraction as well as class and sectarian differences were felt.

These local conditions had been exacerbated by international and regional political and economic factors. The decade of the 80s saw the physical sign of Bahrain's incorporation into the Saudi sphere of influence through the 22km. causeway connecting the two countries, the Iraq/Iran war and the Gulf War, both very close to Bahrain and both affecting its population on many and far-reaching levels as well as the final retraction of Arab normalizing policies with Israel. The reversal in the fortunes of the oil-producing nations brought contractions in the liquidity strength of Bahrain and its off-shore operations and banking system, as well as in the available funds for state-sponsored projects. Saudi presence on Bahraini soil, mainly for entertainment, promoted socially and morally laden controversies within Bahrain's conservative, religious society. Government animosity towards Iran and sometimes Iraq hit at a basic chord within the economically depressed strata, mostly the Shiis whose family and religious links with these regions were restricted and monitored. The quiet official endorsement of Western presence and influence in Bahrain deepened both anti-western and anti-government feelings.[4] All these factors contributed to the rise of unemployment and pauperization – street beggars became visible on the streets, and around the mosques of Manama. General social unrest increased also due to the perceived moral degeneration and the social and political inequalities. The government reaction was an iron-fisted policy of repression and control in order to protect Bahrain's projected image of a haven for the business and entertainment industries.

It was in these conditions that religious Islamist movements found adherents and support; feelings of frustration, defeatism, isolation, impotence and discontent had gradually formed pronounced opposition elements in the society which found in the Islamist discourse refuge and response to its outcry against conceived injustices. With the complete absence of all legal or political channels for expressing these grievances, revitalized Islam filled the vacuum. All through the 80s the Islamic idiom was inching in on all levels of life and most particularly among the lower middle classes and the lower strata of society. While the Gulf society generally had always been a more genuinely religious and conservative one, when compared to other parts of the Arab world this modern return to tradition was shocking in its intensity and assertiveness.[5] The religio-political thrust of these movements stimulated a discourse of hope and redemption induced by the modern crisis on the moral, economic and political levels (Ahmad 1984: 25). In view of the previously mentioned transformations in Bahraini society, the social implications of revived Islam should be explicit. An important dimension to this movement is the prominence of the women's issue in its discourse and the creation of a modernized but reinforced traditional definition of the role. While discourses pertaining to gender are clearly used by Islamists as part of their platform and features of self-definition, it is also the discourse used in the cultural project of the leftists and liberal currents.

Anatomy of Women's Activism

Bahraini women underwent the same process of transformation that their country experienced in the 80s and early 90s. In spite of basic improvements in the living conditions, education and politicization of most women, the extent and amount of these improvements were neither uniform nor pervasive. In fact they reflected the socio-cultural differentiations that characterized the society by that date. Women too are stratified by class, religious and ethnic affiliation, education and age, as well as differentiation on ideological and political alliance and orientation. These differences have a bearing on the consciousness and activism of women which has been clearly shown in the latest political events there.

Education and employment have been the main channels that provided women of all classes with mobility and self-awareness, although access to either or both has been constrained by the economic and political system of the country. It is clear that women of the wealthy upper class, similar to women in the same class of other Gulf states and the Arab countries, have utterly different concerns than those of the economically less fortunate classes. While education remains an important index of modernization to them, it is not necessarily for the sake of employment. In Bahrain, similar to Kuwait, a few upper-class women hold high administrative posts, but their limited number makes them symbols rather than the norm. Furthermore it should be noted that the majority of those come from the previous merchant and petty bourgeois class who had benefited from the early economic boom associated with the state. The interest of this stratum is aligned with the establishment and its power base.

The concentration and thrust of this study however, has been primarily on middle-class women and its different layers, especially the lower middle class, as well as those of the lower economic strata. Economic development, state sponsored projects and public work have provided opportunities for mobility, especially for middle-class and upper middle-class women who had taken advantage of the changes during the 70s and 80s. Women in that category have become salaried and professional and, in spite of the constrained economic situation, they still have various options and solutions. It is the lower strata of that class and the lower classes who face restricted opportunities of work and economic advance; while they had expectations of improvement by virtue of education, an achievement that has come one generation too late, and to a subaltern within another less favoured sector of society. This has added to the women's sense of social as well as gender inequality and accentuated their vulnerability.

Interviews with women of these classes have yielded information on their perceptions of themselves and their roles as active participants in the social process. It became clear that whether consciously or unconsciously these women are activists in all the processes of change their country is experiencing. While they all expressed views to the effect that education and employment have strongly influenced their identification, political idiom and activism was the underlying feature of their consciousness. Those who were interviewed in the first weeks of the crisis, in September 1994, clearly projected an identification with the particular political stand of their class, their religious sect and some with their ethnic origin. Political conflicts seem to have a defining impact on the way active and educated women view the world around them and reflect on their role in the process of change.

Nationalism
In spite of the negative experience of women within the movement for national liberation in Bahrain, nationalism still remains an idiom of cohesion and an important category with which to assess women's active participation in the social and political culture of the country. Historically, nationalism should be positioned as one of the central vehicles through which the emancipation of women and their projection into the public arena was initiated (Abdo 1994: 149–52). It has produced a national culture, which even when political nationalism had been dissipated during the late 70s, 80s and further, continued to function as a linkage and cultural affinity among those who had participated in it.

Today, during the crisis, these elements have reformulated and re-expressed demands for a progressive role under nationalist platforms. Nationalism is appropriated by all the parties on the Bahraini scene, liberals, leftists and Islamists, each defining it according to a different agenda. Nationalist liberals, seasoned active women, the first generation of university graduates, mainly from the urban middle class, both Sunni and Shii, who had reaped the advantage of the 60s and 70s period, have shown the continuity of the spirit of activism and its endurance. It is obvious that the goal of these women, like that of all Third World women, remains to end subordination on the international, national and personal levels. In the final analysis active, conscious and politicized women are demanding the repossession of control over their lives and over their ability and power to make life choices. Whether consciously or not this group of activist women in Bahrain have publicized their lack of confidence in the nationalist and the Islamist forces at the realm of the opposition movement and have chosen to define their needs in a feminist paradigm. Nevertheless it is precisely these women who face the most painful dilemmas of deciding on priorities. They are the ones who, for the sake of national unity often pay, forsaking their rights as women.

The Veil

While the agenda, identity and commitment of the above women's groups, having the strength of historical experience behind them, were clear and easy to read, the message of the women identified with the Islamist currents presented a much more complex, diverse and an emerging consciousness. The pervasiveness of the Islamic revivalist movement is more obvious among women because of the dress and behaviour required, and the young generation of women who have joined it see religion as the solution for dealing with modernization without jeopardizing the cultural and religious legacy of a society with such varied ethnic backgrounds and rapid accumulation of socio-economic benefits (Tohidi 1994). Followers of this current are not only from among the economically depressed and youthfully impressed women but it has cultivated women of the liberal eras who had considered themselves politically radical and socially liberal. It is a wave that has swept most of the middle class and practically all of the lower, economically depressed strata. This wave of conservatism and the invoking of tradition and religion affected the view women have of themselves and their role in the social scheme.

Why was the Islamist movement so strong, fast-spreading and so appealing to women? In the Bahrain context the responses should be sought within the socio-economic crisis, the crisis of state legitimacy and the opposition to the political system, selective social justice producing inequalities, and the weakening of traditional structures particularly the extended patriarchal family. Islamists propagate the belief that Islam, tradition and culture are endangered and their salvation is through a reconstruction of authenticity within the religious identity. Gender is politicized and women given the roles of upholders of authenticity, propagators of generations and transmitters of morality and social values. In this active role women are articulating the identity of Muslim women and an Islamic world-view for Bahrainis. Women have an exalted family role, a traditional status and a gender linked to group identity. This should be given priority to all personal inclinations.

The veil and the new Islamic trend in Bahrain are followed mainly by the young educated generation of women who have grown up in the 70s and 80s and saw the economic constraints among the middle and lower classes. Education remains the major inducer for young people, both Sunni and Shii, to join the ranks of the Islamists and it is both in the schools and at the university where conversion takes place. The National University of Bahrain has played a crucial role in this process and has offered conditions where both males and females met and were socially and culturally influenced. The number of women students is much higher than that of men, even though there is a policy of attempting to find a balance between both. Women students are very ambitious and hard working and unlike university male students they are usually chosen from the top performing students of high schools. In the last twelve years the female student body has changed to nearly 95 per cent veiled and strong pressures are continuously exerted on those who are not, to do so.[6] A very large percentage of university students are from traditional and rural backgrounds. For them the university has been a forum of exposure, education and political consciousness. The campus became the arena where Islamists, Sunni and Shii spread their views and demonstrated in support of their convictions facing the bullets of the police.[7] This new university has been the vehicle for popularizing higher education for all Bahrainis and particularly Shiis. Shiis are in the majority among both the faculty and the students by virtue of the same causes of economic, social and political realities and constraints already mentioned. As a result the Campus has become the target of official punitive action against the Shii community who have maintained the more vocal and active opposition to the regime in the uprising, especially in its confrontational stage. Indications are that confessional criteria have been instituted by the administration through which new students could be admitted or turned away from joining the university.

The veil and the Islamic dress are the outward obvious signs of women's adherence to the new Islamic trends. But the veil and the formal compliance with tradition does not necessarily mean commitment to all that its ideologues load it with. In fact all respondents, both Sunni and Shii, conceded that the veil was a source of affiliation and identification, giving them the peace, serenity and security that being in a group affords. Most of them also saw it as an affirmation of ethical and social customs. Both Sunni and Shii Islamic activists stressed that it is different to what their parents understood by veiling and religiosity. To this young generation the reconfirmed faith is due to an awareness, an understanding and an educated comprehension of the written word commanding veiling; the veil has been ordained and prescribes what a proper woman's attire should be. In fact, they insist that this new attire is not the traditional *abaya*, but follows particular Islamic prescriptions. In their view it is a modern, educated Muslim woman's choice. It also signifies a whole spectrum of lifestyle, the understanding of which is also modern in its concern with segregation, education, the family and woman's role.

Islamic activism is very common among the emerging lower middle class and the lower strata of both the Sunni and Shii sects, but it is more obvious and more spread among the Shiis. Both are a young generation who staunchly defend the veil, all stress the family and the role of women in it and her sacred role in creating the society and generations of Muslims, all call for education as being a Muslim duty. In this later issue, some stress it more than others depending on the class and background. They are united in the belief that Islam is the liberator of women and gives her rights and emancipation.

Sunni and Shii Activism

By analysing the positions of both Sunni and Shii women activists concerning a number of vital issues related to their religio-social perceptions – such as the veil, education, work, Sunni-Shii relations and differences, politics and social change – a framework was formed of common identifications and differences. It is clear that the approaches and attitudes of these women have been acquired in a similar process which has its roots in their socio-political background and influenced by what they perceive as Western knowledge. The failure of alternative national solutions has given these Islamization programmes the chance to influence women in different ways. But the obvious difference between Shii and Sunni Islamist orientations is in their structural base and operational philosophy. These in turn are controlled by a political tradition.

Within several of Bahrain's major active Sunni societies, in which Islamic education and socializing are provided, women have established their own branches and sections. Although, at the same time, the participation of women within these organizations' main political and social bodies remains limited and directed by male leaders. As such, the role of the woman projected in these orthodox societies remains fairly strictly bounded by the traditional, non-innovative confines of classical positions. It has been women associated with these currents who have confirmed this impression through the role they assigned to women and themselves.

The Shii Islamist currents, on the other hand, do not have a set structure of religious reference that binds the whole community. Religious referrals are either linked to Iraq, Qum or within Bahrain itself. Many of the religious mullahs have been educated in Iran at the Bahrain Studies Centre in Qum and others have studied in Iraq which remains an important centre of Shii scholarship. Shiis have no formal organizations either to channel the ideological perceptions of an Islamist orientation or to organize on the social level; these are illegal and banned by law.

Therefore Shii women, whether formally or informally grouped in their villages and quarters, through their professional affiliations, in the *Ma'tam/Husayniyya* (religio-social gathering-house similar to a mosque) or even in their extended family settings, express innovative, non-conformist platforms of activism. They view their roles in a wide range of options from the militant to the home-bound traditional position. This diversification and decentralized religious controls are expressed also in more grass-roots manoeuvrability whereby there is an overall cohesive political orientation by Shii women, of all strata, and their difference is in the technique of achieving social justice. While the professionals and middle-class women see their role as catalysts in attaining social cohesion for their community, through education, training programmes and self-help projects such as the charitable funds (*Sanadiq Khairiyya*), the younger generation expresses its identity by participating in opposition and lately in public demonstrations. Today these charitable funds have sprung up as spontaneous projects to help needy families and to support village projects. Again the authorities have cut short their activities by banning them. This is similar to the Palestinian case, during the Intifada, when civilian spontaneous organizations took over from the formal structures to help the civilian population (Dajani 1994: 15). Since the late 70s, Shii women activists had tried to organize women in charitable organizations similar to the urban women's societies but were denied permits to do so. Official women's societies organized since the

50s had lost legitimacy to the Shiis as part of the loss of confidence in the political system with which they were identified. These societies were viewed with suspicion and did not develop a legitimacy separate from the regime, particularly since 1989 when they were all subjected to a new law giving the authorities the right to monitor and scrutinize their activities.

It has been reported by both groups of active Islamist women that feminist issues are under debate, discussion and education; such issues as birth control, the importance of education and the role of women in the family. Among the Sunni women's societies these activities are organized in the form of lectures or internal group meetings with a preference for religious discussions and interpretations of the Quran. As for the Shiis, the *Ma'tam* is a very important venue where formal and informal women's gatherings take place often and where these issues are debated as lived problems and concerns. Furthermore the month of *Muharam* is a period of continuous education for women when teaching is intensified. During that month it is accepted social behaviour for women to congregate, listen to male preachers in the village squares and in front of the mosques and go to the *Ma'tam* for social and religious education.

Conclusion

In a quickly developing society, Bahraini women have experienced tremendous changes in the idiom and form they projected in order to express their particular gender identity, autonomy and subjectivity. While in the 1960s and 70s it was the idiom of national liberation, constitutional democratization, Western dress and political radicalization, in the 1980s and 90s it is the idiom of Islam, activism to fulfil its message for a proper Muslim life and the veil as a symbol of its triumph. In both phases it has been women from within the rapidly changing social classes who have expressed these roles. In the earlier stage it was the urban middle-class women who had travelled, been educated, and broken the barriers of tradition. In this more recent generation it has also been the middle classes, mainly lower, and the lower classes mostly from rural back-grounds and still attached to conservative and traditional ideologies. Islam has found fertile grounds in a class still in transition and vulnerable to the economic and political pressures of the 80s. This explains, in some measure, the division and gaps between these two generations of visible women activists. The liberal, pro-secular first generation also come from conservatively religious backgrounds; however due to various causes they could never break through the class, ethnic or religious barriers to touch the rural, mainly Shii women's sector. That needed another generation and Islam to do it.

Today, nearly four years after the Gulf War, the region as a whole and particularly Saudi Arabia, Kuwait and Bahrain are facing the repercussions of policies binding the region to Western hegemony and economic controls. These states are confronting very serious backlash in the form of opposition/revivalist politics. In Bahrain, this opposition has taken the form of a popular grass-roots uprising which has been going on since the summer of 1994 and accelerated after December 1995 with a clear alliance between the liberal professionals and intellectuals, a wide range of Islamist structures (both Sunni and Shii), the lower middle class and the economically depressed lower stratum of society. In Bahrain as well as Kuwait there are clear indications of women's involvement in these reactions, whether within the organized frames of the Islamist groups or from among the liberal intellectuals and independent elements. The demands of all opposition platforms is for a larger margin of democratization and more equitable share in the wealth distribution of the state. Kuwaiti and Bahraini women have been insisting again on the right to vote and to have a say in the direction of development.

In the latest events, Bahraini women were given exposure through the media due to their contribution in the activities of the opposition, in the negotiations and in giving the crisis a gender dimension. They have taken an active and physical role in demonstrations, particularly those which have been campus-based. Women students at the university have, in some instances, become their families' breadwinners when brothers, fathers or husbands have been arrested. Their academic life and their family life have been disrupted by these disturbances and the reaction of authorities against their villages and communities. Whenever the situation has been reported in the international press or in the underground press of the leftist and Shii Islamist opposition fronts, the issue of women's demand for democracy and their participation within it, are given prominence. Amnesty International has reported cases of young girls and also women having been arrested and whose whereabouts remain unknown, and to cases where women have been detained without access to their families or to medical and legal advice. More recently women have also died as a result of the violence while protecting their children and families. It is clear that women's involvement in the opposition has increased as in the latest reports, together with teenage girls, women professionals, teachers and nurses, are reported to have been arrested and dismissed from their posts. The issue of arrests and long internment with no legal action and no recourse to humanitarian aid has added to the feelings of anger, frustration and bitterness. But of particular impact have been reports of physical and sexual abuse that young women detainees have been subjected to.

The all-women petition discussed earlier stands as a very significant contribution by women to the protest and reform movement in Bahrain. The first popular petition which at least 6000 women signed, many of whom came from Shii villages, is also of great symbolic and political import.

Whether all these activities and events will lead to an immediate change in the condition of women is doubtful, but this is just one more step in the path for women's struggle toward social liberation and to a better awareness of her capabilities, justifiable rights and the potential for a significant role in national development. Similar to Palestinian women during the Intifada, Bahraini women's social and political consciousness has accelerated through political activism. This consciousness is central to their identity. It is clear that at every juncture of radical activism, women in Bahrain were able to extract some openings to improve their conditions then, and thus accumulate status-giving achievements. In the 1960s, women came out in the streets in opposition to Western colonial presence and repression. In the 1990s, they are again demanding constitutional rights and political participation – for society and themselves.

Notes

1. This is a revised version of a chapter by the author which appears in J. Esposito and Y. Haddad, eds, *Islam, Gender and Social Change* (forthcoming).

2. The earliest published analytical articles appeared in *Rose al-Yusif* (16 January 1995); *Le Monde Diplomatique* (March 1995); *Al-Sarq al-Awsat* (25–30 April). In the USA the earliest publications to refer to the situation were: *The Wall Street Journal* (12 June 1995); *The Washington Post* (13 June 1995); *The New York Times* (28 January 1996); *The Financial Times* (30 January 1996); *The LA Times* (3 May 1996). US official concern with the disturbances has remained muted and directed towards the security of US personnel in the region and US interests.

3. The British media had picked up the Bahrain story by early 1995 and by January 1996 all the major publications in Britain carried one or more articles on all aspects of the situation and many gave accounts of the women's role in the crisis. See *The Independent* (all of January 1996); *The Guardian* (January, February and March 1996); *The London Times*, *The Economist*, *The Observer* (February and March); BBC radio programme (March 1996).

4. The fact that the Commander of Police, Ian Henderson, was a British citizen had been a cause of national protest. In the latest disturbances, this was one of the issues that was raised in the petitions to the Emir.

5. From my own personal observation and experience during my stay in Bahrain, the pervasiveness of the movement by women towards the veil as the outward sign of an adherence to Islamic observance was significant. Between 1983 and 1993, the number of my students who joined the ranks of the veiled moved from 5 per cent to 95 per cent.

6. There are no statistics on these facts, however they are common knowledge among those who work at the university. Similar conditions exist in other parts of the Middle East (see Ahmed 1984: 220–2; Moghadam 1993: 122).

7. In the recent confrontations between the student demonstrations asking for political reforms, the police (reported to be mercenary Baluchis, and in another report to be Saudi national guards) shot two students dead. Women students are also reported to have demonstrated and made very incendiary statements.

References

Newspapers and Periodicals:
  Rose al-Yusif, 16 January 1995
  Crescent International, 16–31 January 1995
  Le Monde Diplomatique, March 1995
  The Wall Street Journal, 12 June 1995
  The Washington Post, 13 June 1995
  Al-Sharq al-Awsat, 25–30 April 1995
  The New York Times, 28 January 1996
  The Financial Times, 30 January 1996
  The Los Angeles Times, 3 May 1996
  The Guardian, January, February, March 1996
  The Independent, February 1996
  The London Times, The Economist, The Observer, February–March 1996

Parliamentary Human Rights Group, *Bahrain: A Brick Wall*, House of Lords, London 1996 (correspondence between Lord Avebury and the Foreign and

Commonwealth Office of the British Government on the Human Rights Situation in Bahrain).

Books:

Aarts, P. (1994), 'The New Oil Order: Built on Sand?,' in *Arab Studies Quarterly*, 16, 2, Spring 1994.

Abdo, N. (1994), 'Nationalism and Feminism: Palestinian Women and the Intifada,' in V. Moghadam, ed., *Gender and National Identity*, London: Zed Press.

Ahmad, E. (1984), 'Islam and Politics,' in Y. Haddad, B. Haines & E. Findly, eds, *The Islamic Impact*, Syracuse, NY: Syracuse University Press.

Ahmad, L. (1992), *Women and Gender in Islam*, New Haven: Yale University Press.

Allaghi, F and Almana', A., 'Survey of Research on Women in the Arab Gulf Region,' in *Women*, Paris: UNESCO.

Arebi, S. (1994), *Women and Words in Saudi Arabia*, New York: Columbia University Press.

Al-'Awwadi, B. (1990), *al-Mara'a wa-al-qanum*, Kuwait.

da Lage, O. (1995), 'Bahrain ebranlé par une vague d'émeutes,' in *Le Monde Diplomatique*, March 1995.

Dajani, S. (1994), 'The Struggle of Palestinian Women in the Occupied Territories: Between National and Social Liberation,' in *Arab Studies Quarterly*, 16, 2.

Fakhro, M. (1990), *Women at Work in the Gulf*, London: Kegan Paul International.

—— (1995), 'Al-Mujtama al-Madani wal-Tahawul al-Dimuqrati fil-Bahrain,' (Civil Society and Democratic Transformation in Bahrain), Cairo: Ibn Khaldun Centre for Developmental Studies.

Ghabra, S. (1993), 'Democratization in a Middle Eastern State – Kuwait,' in *Newsletter of the Society for Gulf Arab Studies*, IV, 2.

Ghassoub, M. (1987), 'Feminism – or the Eternal Masculine – in the Arab World,' *New Left Review*, 161.

Khuri, F. (1980), *Tribe and State in Bahrain: the Transformation of Social and Political Authority in an Arab State*, Chicago: University of Chicago Press.

Mallon, F. (1994), 'The Promise and Dilemma of Subaltern Studies: Perspectives from Latin American History,' in *AHR Forum*, December (1510).

Moghadam, V. (1993), *Modernizing Women: Gender and Social Change in the Middle East*, Boulder & London: Lynne Rienner.

Al-Najjar, B. (1985), 'Ma'uqat al-istikhdam al-amthal lil-Qiwa al-'Amila al-wataniyya fi al-Khalij al-Arabi wa-imkaniyat al-Hall' (Drawbacks to the Proper Utilization of National Manpower in the Arabian Gulf and Possible Solutions) in *Conference of Experts on Policies for Arab Labour Mobility and Utilization*, Kuwait: Economic and Social Commission for West Asia [ESCWA] and Kuwait Institute of Planning.

Al-Rumaihi, M. (1982), 'Athar al-naft 'ala wad' al-mar'a al-Arabiyya fi al-Khalij' (The Effect of Oil on the Condition of Arab Women in the Gulf) in *al-Mar'a wa-dawruha fi harakat al-wahda al-Arabiyya* (Woman and her Role in the Arab Unity Movement), Beirut: Institute of Arab Unity Studies.

Sharabi, H. (1988), *Neopatriarchy: A Theory of Distorted Change in the Arab World*, New York: Oxford University Press.

Seikaly, M. (1994), 'Women and Social Change in Bahrain,' *International Journal of Middle East Studies*, 26: 415–26.

State of Bahrain (1991), *Statistical Abstracts, 1990*, Bahrain.

Tohidi, N. (1994), 'Modernity, Islamization and Women in Iran,' in V. Moghadam, ed., *Gender and National Identity*, London: Zed Press.

7

The Impact of Social and Economic Factors on Women's Group Formation in Egypt

Shahida El-Baz

Recent radical political and economic changes in the world have led to the emergence of certain developmental concepts and systems. Among these is the concept of human development which transcends the satisfaction of people's basic material needs and includes other indicators determining the quality of life and widening the range of people's choices. This concept also assumes the full mobilization and effective participation of all the human resources in society including women.

Other parallel concepts were economic, the transformation of all the world economies to the market system; and political, the expansion of the civil society through processes of democratization. The Private Voluntary Organization (PVO) sector was especially encouraged to fill the vacuum resulting from the withdrawal of the state from its welfare functions, of providing social services to its citizens, under the International Monetary Fund (IMF) and the World Bank Structural Adjustment Programmes (SAPs).

Thus, women's organized participation was advocated in such a way that it became the concern of national and international bodies. Further, it became part of women's international documents, such as the Beijing women's document, which affirmed the importance of organizing women, especially at the grass-root level, in order to increase their effective participation in setting the national and international agenda. This issue is specially important in the Egyptian context due to the absence of an organized national women's movement.

In this chapter I assume that women's position, initiatives and abilities to organize themselves for effective participation in social processes are greatly influenced by their economic, social and political status in society. Therefore, the first part of the chapter will present a situation analysis of Egyptian women. In the second part, the impact of this situation on women's abilities to organize themselves or to participate in the already existing PVOs will be examined as well as the impact of their participation on women's status and the changing nature of gender relations in society.

Situation Analysis of Egyptian Women

The position and status of women in Egypt, as everywhere else, are determined, among other things, by the dialectic relationship of their dominant socioeconomic and cultural conditions and the development strategy adopted by the state on one hand, and the women's ability as a pressure group to increase their social opportunities on the other.

After the 1952 Revolution, the state adopted a comprehensive strategy based on social justice and self-reliance for which full mobilization of human resources was a prerequisite. The new Constitution, which adopted a secular approach, granted equal opportunities to all citizens, men and women, regardless of gender, ethnic origin or religion, to participate in realizing the goals of development (El-Baz 1994: 77). The revolutionary government made conscious efforts to promote women's participation on the social, economic and political levels. Although women's position and their perception of themselves were greatly improved, gender equality was not realized. The omission by the state to change the obsolete and oppressive Family Status Law led to the continuing inequality in the private sphere which restrained women's equal participation in the public sphere.

In 1974, four years after coming to power, Sadat adopted the economic 'Open Door Policy' and encouraged the private sector to increase the productive capacity of the economy. This policy resulted mostly in the growth in external commercial activities with no investment in productive sectors, prevailing consumerism, and the emergence of a nouveau riche class which attempted to dominate the political scene after the establishment of the multiparty system. Inflation soared, as did unemployment.

Although Sadat's regime was not against women's equality in principle, the new economic order had less need for women's participation. As the government gradually withdrew its commitment to guarantee employment to all graduates, unemployment among school-leavers rose rapidly. The expectation that women would enter the workplace thus became a burden on the state rather than an asset.

The national view of women's work began to shift, and the definition of women as playing primarily a domestic role gained ground. Justifying ideologies based on sexual division of roles began to appear, supported by the newly emerging Islamic fundamentalist ideology which is based on the central role of the family and thus, emphasizing women's private role to the detriment of their public role. Some passages from the Quran were taken out of context and reinterpreted in a misogynistic way to justify male supremacy. The impact of these interpretations was made possible by adding a qualifying provision to Article eleven of the 1971 Constitution which declared the state's commitment to help reconciling women's family obligations and their equality to men in the public sphere. The addition held, 'provided that this did not infringe on the rules of Islamic Sharia'. Thus, the new Constitution represented an important divergence from the secular discourse of the sixties and created opportunities for Islamic groups to oppose women's rights (Hatem 1992: 241). Ultimately all of this negatively affected women's perceptions of themselves and their public role.

Through the 1980s, the Open Door Policy became increasingly institutionalized, ultimately leading to the current Economic Reform Policy based on the Structural Adjustment Programmes (ER-SAP). Despite the relative success of this policy on the macro level, it has had a negative impact on the welfare of the poor, and vulnerable groups such as women and children (Hassan 1995; El-Baz 1996).

Poverty increased in Egypt during the 1980s. According to one study, 51.1 per cent of urban households and 47.2 per cent of rural households are now living below the poverty line (Korayem 1987: 40). This situation has a greater impact on women; the scarcer the key resources, such as health care and education, the less likely women are to have access to them. This poverty affects social classes which were not previously among the poor: the majority of civil servants, unemployed graduates (particularly those with intermediate level education, who usually come from very poor backgrounds), and persons working in the informal sector. Among these categories women are hit most because of their basic disadvantaged position in the society – thus justifying the concept of 'feminization of poverty'.

Another important point to be considered in the context of women's group formation, is that women in Egypt are of course not a homogeneous category. Thus, tackling gender inequality as a national issue should not mystify the existing inequality between the different categories of Egyptian women. The differentiation is based on class affiliation, unequal access to social, economic and political opportunities, as well as rural–urban disparity. Moreover, these differences are accentuated by the ER-SAPs. This situation results in different, sometimes conflicting, needs, awareness, aspirations, and thus the potential allies and possible forms of action which are beneficial for the different groups of women. This issue is very important for defining priorities and line of action when forming women's groups.

A comprehensive outlook regarding women's development and liberation should include different priorities for different groups in different stages of social development. For poor disadvantaged women poverty alleviation and greater access to social, economic and cultural opportunities, while raising their awareness of their rights and social roles, should receive priority. Regarding privileged gender-aware women, their priority should be the struggle for greater participation in policy-making processes through which they can guarantee formulation of gender-sensitive public policies which, in turn, would help to put women in the mainstream of the development processes. However, an awareness of and commitment to the needs of the poor unprivileged women by the privileged ones are essential conditions for linking all the women in society in the struggle for gender equality.

Women and Education

Although there has been an improvement in school attendance and literacy in Egypt over the past three decades for both men and women, the adult female population is still characterized by high illiteracy rates. The gender gap in education may decrease over the coming years, although when resources are scarce, male education takes precedence over female education.

Illiteracy is very unevenly distributed in the Egyptian population, which clearly represents an inequality of development opportunities within the same society. According to the 1986 census, 62 per cent of adult women are illiterate, compared to 38 per cent for men; 76 per cent of rural women are illiterate, compared to 45 per cent of urban women. Illiteracy is highly correlated with age: for girls from 10 to 14 it is 27 per cent, for women from 25 to 29 it is 66 per cent, for women from 45 to 49 it is 84 per cent, and for women from 60 to 69 it is 92 per cent.

For enrolment in basic education, some official sources state that 98 per cent of school-age children are enrolled (Halluda 1994: 86). Other sources believe the real figure is closer to 80 per cent, and even lower in villages and rural areas, where poor parents tend to withdraw their female children from school as soon as they are old enough to help around the house or earn extra money through outside work (El-Nashif 1994: 1).

While the urban gender gap is 1 per cent, the rural gap is 18 per cent. The gap increases with poverty reaching 56 per cent in poor villages in Upper Egypt (Fergany 1993).

Although the gender gap in school enrolment rates at the primary level may not be high, the gaps in completion rates and literacy between men and women are substantial since gender barriers present themselves as girls get older. Thus, the enrolment rates decline gradually as education continues. The lower social value of girls' education causes a high drop-out rate among those who come from poor families. The rate of drop-out prior to consolidation of literacy skills is high for both sexes, and this causes relapse into illiteracy.

As of 1990, twice as many girls drop out as boys (El-Nashif 1994: 3). The reasons for leaving school are gender-related. Failure to study accounts for 19 per cent of girls and 53 per cent of boys leaving school. Economic factors account for 66 per cent of girls dropouts and 43 per cent for boys. This means that girls who are economically able to continue their education are unlikely to drop out (Azer and Ramzi 1992: 37). Families are obviously more prepared to withdraw girls than boys from school when economic circumstances are hard. Structural adjustment has increased the cost of education, thus discouraging poor people from educating their children, especially daughters. There are also cultural factors which affect the level of girls' education, though these are amenable to change when economic and political factors favour female education.

Women in the Economy

Although Egyptian women have been working productively for thousands of years (Nour El-Din 1995: 9) and the law governing women's work was issued more than fifty years ago, their work is still a controversial issue and a subject of debate among different groups in Egypt. It has thus been possible for bold campaigns to be launched seeking restriction of women's rights and opportunities for work. Several arguments are used to justify forcing women back to their traditional domestic role (El-Baz 1992a).

Egyptian women account for a small but visible share of the professional class, including doctors, engineers, lawyers, university professors, scientific researchers, artists, composers, writers, as well as the more traditional roles as teachers and nurses. Excellence and ingenuity are not restricted to professional women. When Egyptian women cannot find wage employment in the modern sector, they create productive roles in the informal sector, in food production or domestic service (Toubia 1994: 44).

The official definition of economic activity is such that the 1986 Egyptian census discounts most women's work, such as unpaid work in agriculture and other family enterprises, as well as women's economic activities in domestic work and elsewhere in the informal sector. However, the Labour Force Sample Survey (LFSS) of 1988 adopted a more comprehensive definition of economic activity and new survey implementation procedures. It thus provides a more accurate picture of women's employment in Egypt, including unpaid and household-based economic activities which are not carried out entirely for household consumption. However, the level of female economic participation is still less than that of men, and economic opportunities for women are fewer. In addition, 71 per cent of unpaid workers are women. According to the LFSS women's activity rate is 26.6 per cent. It reaches 18.8 per cent in urban and 32.5 per cent in rural areas. Women's economic participation is 35.4 per cent. According to the same survey, women's economic participation in the government is 29.5 per cent, public sector 13.1 per cent and in the private sector 39.3 per cent (CAPMAS 1990).

Contrary to common belief, women's participation in agriculture is greater than that of men, reaching 53 per cent. In addition, women are overloaded with other chores inside and outside the house, especially in villages lacking household water and sewer connections. One study of rural women showed female work days of 16 to 19 hours (Shoukry 1988: 77). Women work longer hours than men, but most of their work is invisible, and recognized neither by the society nor by the women themselves as real work. Women are defined by society within the private domain, while men are defined within the public domain.

The consequences of invisibility are serious. If these women are not recognized as workers, they are certainly not given access to the training, credit and technology necessary for participating in the development process. This invisibility is also reflected in statistical, class, geographical and gender bias.

According to census data, the unemployment rate rose from 7.7 per cent in 1976 to 14.7 per cent in 1986; 10 per cent for males and 25 per cent for females. However, unemployment is seen by policy-makers as a problem concerning young educated males and solutions presented are usually at the expense of female employment, such as legislation offering women half-time employment for half salary as well as early retirement (Roemberg 1991: 4).

The problem of female unemployment has been accentuated by the reluctance of the growing private sector to recruit females, in an effort to avoid the social cost of their labour, such as maternity leave. 47 per cent of working women were employed in the private sector in 1976. By 1986, this figure was reduced to 30 per cent (CAPMAS & UNICEF 1991: 10). The situation is likely to be aggravated by increasing privatization under the Economic Reform Policy and the Structural Adjustment Programme.

With the decline of work opportunities in the formal sector, women are increasingly participating in the informal sector. However, they work under no social or legal protection. Their work is not included in formal statistics, and they receive no support services. Recent studies in Egypt (Badran 1994; Handoussa 1994) have shown that in 1993 between 15 and 20 per cent of households were exclusively dependent on women's incomes. However, public policy and social services have not yet taken this into account.

The rapid increase in the female labour force is mostly due to economic necessity rather than changing social attitudes. And, in fact, both society as a whole and the working women themselves are developing a more conservative attitude towards women's work by considering women's domestic role as her natural and main role. Thus, many young female graduates would prefer to have rich husbands rather than get jobs. The lack of facilities for working women contributes to the promotion of these tendencies. Za'louk has shown that 84.5 per cent of males and 78 per cent of females believe that women with small children should not work (Za'louk 1990: 17).

Women and Health

The past decade has seen an increased awareness of the relationship between the status of women and women's health. Gender-specific data on morbidity and mortality indicate that women are exposed to disproportionately higher risks of death and ill health, mainly because of their disadvantaged position in society. These risks are affected by high illiteracy rates, heavy work loads, repeated pregnancies, scarce economic resources and limited access to good health care.

This gender-based discrimination affects girls and women throughout the life-cycle. Beginning at her birth, the baby girl is often a disappointment to her parents. If she survives, the female baby may suffer from abbreviated nursing, inadequate feeding to malnutrition and ultimately to an increased risk of death (UNICEF 1990: 17). Child mortality rates for babies between one month and less than one year are 28 per 1000 for girls and 24 per 1000 for boys (Beijing National Report 1995: 39). Many other health indicators show similar gender effects.

The paucity of gender-specific health data makes a full assessment of the health situation of women difficult. The lack of information is in itself a gender issue. Maternal mortality rates (MMR) are considered the ultimate indicator of the poor health status of women across countries and within regions of the same country. Egypt has a national MMR of 320 per 100,000 which is high when compared to the rate in developed countries which is 15 per 100,000. However, it is better than the less developed countries where MMR reaches 590 per 100,000 (UNICEF 1993a: 80).

Anaemia is very common among women of reproductive age, especially among the poor. The reproductive years (15 to 49) are the time of highest risk of morbidity and mortality related to anaemia and it is a major gender inequality issue (Toubia 1994: 26).

Early marriage and adolescent fertility from 15 to 19 years are known to affect women's health status and reproductive outcomes throughout their lives. Early marriages can also reduce a woman's chances of education, training and employment since marriage tends to confine them to their domestic role. Although the legal age of marriage for girls is 16, in many rural and poor urban communities girls are still married under the legal age, due to poverty or ignorance.

The percentage of adolescent marriage in Egypt is reported to be 15.3 per cent, but the true figure could be much higher, because doctors often issue age assessment certificates to enable families to marry girls under legal age.

Maternal education is a strong determinant of indicators such as marriage age, number of children born, under five mortality, and use of contraceptives. There is a connection between the total fertility rate and problems of reproductive morbidity and maternal mortality.

It should be noted that the quality of family planning services is not always good, and the availability of a variety of contraceptive methods is limited. Many unwanted pregnancies end in self-induced abortion performed in hazardous and unsanitary conditions because of the illegality of abortion (Roemberg 1991: 7). Abortion is prohibited in Egypt except in cases where pregnancy threatens the life of the mother or the child. No consideration is given to the mother/parent decisions based on economic, psychological or emotional reasons. The doctor who defies the law is penalized. The government is very strict on this issue because of Islamic beliefs.

An important issue in women's health is women's acceptance of discomfort, pain and weakness as a normal part of being a woman. A study on reproductive morbidity showed that rural women suffer from reproductive tract infections, anaemia, and pain during menstruation but are reluctant to seek medical help even from female doctors (Zurayk 1991).

Female circumcision is still widespread in Egypt, causing many psychological and health problems for women. Although it was prohibited in government hospitals by a ministerial decree, it is still widely practised, especially among uneducated and traditional families. However, the practice seems to have developed independent cultural values which influence the attitude of the girls' families in the rural and poor urban areas. If the girls are not circumcised, the families believe, they would be stigmatized and they may not get married. Thus, families in these areas would be ashamed not to circumcise their daughters. Estimates of its prevalence range from 50 to 80 per cent of the population.

Some people present female circumcision as a requirement of Islam, but this is denied by the Grand Mufti of Egypt. His argument is based, among other things, on the fact that it is not practised in Saudi Arabia, one of the most conservative Islamic countries. The issue was raised dramatically at the 1994 International Conference on Population and Development in Cairo, which embarrassed the Egyptian government. Subsequently, a ministerial decree was issued to limit its practice to doctors in hospitals – whether government or private. The government refrained from prohibiting it completely in order to avoid confrontation with the traditional groups, especially the Islamic fundamentalists who hold the idea that female circumcision is obligatory and that it was established through a saying by the Prophet. Nonetheless, they cannot explain why the Prophet Muhammad himself did not circumcise his daughters.

Some Egyptian PVOs have become active in educating the public concerning female circumcision. The Cairo Family Planning Association has produced programmes for television and radio and broadcast them during prime time on several stations in Egypt. As a result of anti-cirumcision campaigns a ministerial decree prohibiting it altogether was issued. However, this does not guarantee the abolition of this practice in the immediate future unless it is accompanied by awareness raising campaigns to change this cultural tradition.

Legal and Cultural Constraints on Women's Participation

Apart from the Personal Status Law, which is based on a conservative interpretation of Islamic Law, the Egyptian legal system is quite advantageous for women. Egypt was the first Arab country to ratify, albeit with reservations, the Convention for Elimination of All Forms of Discrimination Against Women in 1987. The Constitution stipulates equality between the sexes, as do other laws. In line with the ILO convention, Egyptian law grants women equal access to employment and training opportunities while simultaneously protecting her role as a mother. Women employees have the right to paid maternity leave and unpaid child-care leave. Companies employing more than 100 female workers must provide nursery facilities. Women are protected against working in physically or morally hazardous occupations. This rule, in addition to the practice of excluding women from judiciary posts, are considered by Egyptian feminists to be gender discriminating policies.

Furthermore, a new unified labour law is currently under preparation for application within the context of economic reform policy. Business-men represented on the committee formulating the legislation have put pressure to abolish the concessions given to women in the existing law (Hassan 1995: 6). Women's PVOs are already campaigning against the new law. It is also worth noting that despite the existing legal equality, in practice various forms of gender discrimination exist, such as job advertisements exclusively for males or failing female applicants after they have been interviewed.

The current Personal Status Law is an important source of inequality and insecurity for Egyptian women. For instance, men have sole author-ity over divorce, which is often used as a threat even when not a reality. Polygamy has become more difficult due to deteriorating economic conditions, but it remains the man's legal right. Although the Personal Status Law was amended in 1979 to give women increased rights in their marriages, this law was partially revoked in 1985 due to socio-economic problems and conservative attitudes among the judiciary. Another law (Law 100 of 1985) was passed which had less concessions for women than the previous one.

This dichotomy between the liberalism of the secular civil laws and the oppressive Personal Status Law curtails women's abilities to function in the public sphere. It is one of the most important gender inequality issues which concern women's PVOs as part of their struggle for liber-ation. This situation prevails in most Arab countries except Tunisia, under the impact of Bourguiba's modernization, and South Yemen under social-ist rule, where the Family Law was made more favourable to women.

Other gender inequality inheres in the nationality law, which denies Egyptian women married to foreigners the right to pass their nationalities on to their children while granting this right to the man.

In some situations Egyptian women are treated as minors. According to the Ministerial Decree 63 of 1959, the Egyptian married woman is granted a passport only through the written approval of her husband or male guardian. This means that she cannot travel abroad for whatever reason without her husband's consent, which he can withdraw at any time. The husband also can prevent his wife from working outside the house if he proves to the court that her work interferes with her domestic duties. Although, according to Islam women can protect their rights by stipulating them in the marriage contract after agreeing with the husband, this prerogative is rarely used by Egyptian or Arab women. A recent attempt by the Ministry of Justice, under the pressure of some women's PVOs, to add contractual terms to the official formula of the marriage contract which would make both partners aware of their rights, was strongly opposed by religious leaders, men and some women. . . !

In assessing the impact of cultural factors on the position of women in Egyptian society, Islam as the dominant religion should be taken into consideration. However, one should differentiate between Islam as a religion and a culture and the Islamic fundamentalist movements, which are basically political movements. Although the latter have spread their conservative outlook towards women in society, a momentum producing an antithesis is taking shape through progressive men's and women's organizations and groups. These groups are fighting the Islamic fundamentalists through either secular arguments or more progressive interpretation of Islam using many verses of the Quran which treat men and women as equal. However, while the fundamentalists are active all over the country and among the lower middle and poor classes, the impact of these progressive groups is very limited. They exist mostly in the urban areas and their activities are still within intellectual circles. In addition to the conservative religious outlook, the traditions of women's seclusion, especially in remote rural areas, prevent women from going out of the house except when it is strictly urgent. As a result, their access to social and economic opportunities is very limited.

The government demonstrates vacillating policies and behaviour. While they announce their belief in women's equality, they refrain from eliminating discriminatory laws for fear of confrontation with the Islamic groups in the society.

Controlled by the government, the media is also playing ambivalent roles in relation to gender issues. Although women outnumber men in most of the media, particularly in television, it is clearly uncommitted to gender equality. Thus, the image of women in the media is quite traditional. Women's role is defined as wives and mothers, and working women are presented as failures. Moreover, extremely conservative religious speakers who are opposed to gender equality are frequently invited to appear on television. Enlightened Islamic scholars who emphasize gender equality in Islam are never invited to appear. This attitude negatively influences women's perception of themselves and their social roles.

Women's Participation in Politics

Women's participation in politics is very limited. On the one hand, this relates to the general weakness of political participation in Egypt. Although the country has adopted the multi-party system since the seventies, one party, headed by the President, has monopolized political power for the last 23 years irrespective of what the people want. A very low voting rate reflects people's belief that the election results will always be determined by the government. On the other hand, the high illiteracy rate for women, their huge responsibilities in the absence of support facilities, and their perception of the traditional 'domestic-public' division of roles adversely affect their level of awareness of their social rights and roles. As a result, they become generally uninterested in using their political rights. However, women's votes are usually used by the candidates of the government's party, especially in the villages, to increase their votes.

Although women's participation in politics concerns mainly the educated elite, promotion of their participation is essential for any successful effort for gender equality. In this domain, women can influence the decision-making processes and thus work to effect changes in gender-discriminating laws and policies. The trickle-down effect of these activities will eventually have an impact on the less advantaged women in society who would then have the opportunity to participate fully in societal affairs.

After a long struggle since the 1920s, Egyptian women gained the constitutional right to vote and to stand for political office in 1956. According to the electoral law, voting is mandatory for Egyptian males, and optional for Egyptian females. In 1979, further legislative reforms were made to reserve thirty seats in parliament and local councils for women. These seats were cancelled in 1987, on the ground that this policy contradicts the constitutional principle of gender equality.

In the first parliamentary election in 1957, two women won seats in Parliament. The battle was not easy, and they had to use religious arguments by citing examples of the public roles of prominent Muslim women during the early days of Islam. During the 1964, 1969 and 1976 parliamentary elections, the number of women who ran for and won seats ranged from two to eight (Abdel-Kader 1992: 25). After issuance of the 1979 law, the total number of women in the 1979 and 1985 parliaments was 35 and 36.

In 1987, after the cancellation of the women's seats and a switch from individual candidacies to party election lists, the anti-woman position of the various parties appeared either in the exclusion of women from party lists altogether or putting them at the end of the list. The number of female MPs decreased again. Although the individual electoral system was reinstated, women's representation in the People's Assembly changed from about 9 per cent in 1979 to around 2.2 per cent in 1992. In the 1995 election, women's representation in the Parliament reached 2.25 per cent including four women appointed by the President. An important factor affecting women's political representation is the voters' apathy towards gender issues. Women who won the seats were those who addressed themselves to social and economic problems.

As for the Shura (Senate) House, women's representation increased from 3.3 per cent to 4.7 per cent in 1992. However, female members of this council were not elected but appointed by the government (Beijing National Report 1995: 9).

Women have held key decision-making positions since the time of Nasser, who was extremely supportive of women's political rights. The first woman minister was appointed in 1962, and women came to assume positions of responsibility in trade unions, where they struggled to overcome the problems of working women and to provide them with different facilities (Abdel-Kader 1992: 86).

Sadat's regime was equally supportive of women's political rights. It was he who issued a decree reserving 30 seats for women. However, changes in social mores and values under the influence of the Open Door Policy and the emerging Islamic fundamentalist ideologies minimized the political roles that could be played by women.

Although the official policy announced by Mubarak's regime is supportive of women's rights, in his programme for democratic reform the thirty parliamentary seats were cancelled in 1987. This affected not only the position of women in Parliament, but also their positions in local and popular councils. Women's membership in these councils declined from 11.2 per cent in 1979 to 1.2 per cent in 1992. As for village councils, women's participation declined from 6.2 per cent in 1979 to 0.5 per cent in 1992 (Beijing National Report: 11).

What is critical here is not the absolute number of women participating in the decision-making process, but rather the quality of these women, their understanding of and commitment to equal gender relations in society. In the case of Egypt where real democracy, in the sense of circulation of power and participation in decision-making, does not exist most of the women who reach this level are backed by the government and thus, more inclined to support the status quo.

Women in Civil Society

Civil society is the aspect of social life which is distinct and removed from the realm of the state. It is based on the existence of a community of free individuals who are able to form non-state associations which interact with the state to promote citizens' participation vis-à-vis the state's influence (Zaki 1995: 1 & 4). Women's participation in civil society in Egypt reflects their weak participation in public life in general, as well as the weakness of civil society in Egypt.

All the political parties have women's committees. Apart from the Women's Progressive Union (a branch of the left Progressive Unionist Party) which has put women's socio-economic and political rights on the party's agenda, most of the women's committees play a marginal role in their parties.

As for women's participation in trade unions and syndicates, the difference is that although trade unions are considered non-governmental, they are mostly controlled, or at least tamed, by the government through the Minister of Labour. For professional syndicates, female membership is commensurate with their numbers in the profession, but women's representation in the leadership is not. However, a woman became the secretary-general of the journalists' syndicate, and two women have become members of the Council of the Lawyer's Syndicate. This was possible, despite the syndicates' partial control by Muslim Brothers, due to its political nature and the negotiated agreements between the Islamists and nationalist candidates during the election to share the votes. Most of the other syndicates are fully controlled by the Muslim Brothers, and thus women are excluded from leading positions.

The situation analysis of Egyptian women highlights a number of points:

- Continuous impoverishment of women deprives them of social and economic opportunities and increases their responsibilities for survival; thus it crushes their abilities to organize themselves or to participate in societal processes.
- Although gender equality is legally and constitutionally stipulated, to a large extent, in practice gender inequality is dominant. It will, further, increase as a result of the deteriorating social and economic conditions under which women and girls are the first victims.
- The impact of conservative cultural values, Islamic fundamentalist ideology and distorted female images in the media, hinders the development of women's awareness of gender equality. Thus, they

continue to submit to the inequalities inherent in the sexual division of labour and perceive them as natural and unchangeable to the detriment of their public roles.

- A polarization of class structure has occurred as a result of the economic Open Door Policy and the Structural Adjustment Programmes. This situation has created contradictory interests and new forms of inequality among Egyptian women, resulting in conflicting socio-economic agendas. This is bound to affect women's group formation, especially if the strategic goal is to create a strong and democratic national women's movement representing Egyptian women and fighting their battle for equality and liberation.
- Politically, the 'Hyde Park Corner' pattern of democracy practised by the regime in Egypt has alienated the majority of the people – especially women – from participating effectively in the political and decision-making processes as well as in public life in general. Women who do participate generally adopt the government agenda, vacillating accordingly in their concern for gender issues.

Women in Private Voluntary Organizations

Private Voluntary Organizations (PVOs) could be viable channels for people's participation only in a democratic context. PVOs can confront the state's monopoly of political power and the business sector's monopoly of economic power. Politically, PVOs can exert pressure through participating in policy formulation and decision-making processes to realize the interests of different social forces. Economically, PVOs can become a tool for more equitable allocation and distribution of resources than the market mechanism can realize.

The issue of women's PVOs is especially important in the context of ER-SAPs which minimize the role of the state. PVOs are the best feasible channels for mobilizing women and mainstreaming them in the development process, and thus, narrowing the gender gap.

The assessment of the role of women in Egyptian PVOs is faced by the problem of paucity of gender-specific data demonstrating women's level of activities in the PVOs. This is partly due to the fact that the PVO Law 32 of 1964 and affiliated decrees tightly circumscribe the fields of activities in which PVOs can work, and do not include women's activities in the approved list. Consequently, there is no formal or clear definition as to what could be considered a women's PVO (El-Baz 1995: 5). It is, however, informally considered to be a society which is established by a group of women, whose board includes women, and which declares its main activities as the promotion of women's conditions. Thus, societies recognized as women's PVOs are classified under one of the activities of the two main categories of PVOs in Egypt, i.e. social care and development. According to the informal definition, the number of women's PVOs in Egypt is about 200. It should be noted, however, that this omission reflects gender discrimination and lack of awareness on the part of the policy-makers of the necessity of integrating women as an essential component in the development processes through the activities of PVOs. Otherwise, the activities of women's PVOs should have been officially acknowledged as a separate and distinct field among PVO activities.

The Egyptian PVO movement goes back to the nineteenth century. The first one was formed in 1821. Women's PVOs began at the turn of the century, inspired by the anti-colonial movement and the spread of the European enlightenment ideas for women's emancipation. The first women's PVO (mabarrat Mohammed Ali) was formed as a philanthropic organization by a group of women led by Huda Shaarawi who became the leader of the first women's movement during the anti-British 1919 revolution. In 1923 she formed the Egyptian Women Association, the agenda of which included National and Women's Liberation issues.

The historical inception of Egyptian PVOs was based on the philosophy of charity and philanthropy. Thus, it attracted mainly women from the upper classes who could afford to volunteer their time and money. This elitist orientation continues to influence, to a certain degree, PVO membership and activities. It is reflected in the exclusion of women from poorer classes and remote areas from the PVOs' activities except as recipients of aid.

The number of PVOs registered in the Ministry of Social Affairs (MOSA) up to 1991 is 13,526. They are divided into social care associations, 74 per cent and community development associations (CDAs), 26 per cent. Recently the CDAs, as the nearest form to grass-root organizations, became an important subject for national and international agencies as viable channels for mobilizing and raising the consciousness of both men and women as well as for providing services to the community (Huber 1994: 81). About 71 per cent of the PVOs are urban based while 26 per cent operate in the rural areas and 4 per cent in the reclaimed desert areas (MOSA 1993). A positive correlation was thus observed between the number of PVOs and the level of socio-economic development of the areas concerned.

Women's Power in PVOs

Women's power in PVOs is measured by their different levels of participation, hence their power in decision-making and agenda setting. The majority of Community Development Associations (CDAs), especially in the rural areas, are run only by male volunteers who may direct several activities for local women. However, the activities remain confined to the level of rendering services while women are not really participating in running the organization or setting the agenda (Huber: 73). Although some CDAs have been specifically set up for helping women through income-generating projects, they tended to adopt traditional female activities such as, sewing, knitting, poultry, and so on, which are usually low profit and low technology. This results, generally, in economic unsustainability, and so the projects dissipate after the initial funds end without increasing women's abilities. Most of these projects have failed, so far, to build women's income-generating capacity in order to become economically independent (El-Baz 1992b: 45).

Despite the early participation of women in the PVO movement, their participation is still much less than that of men, especially in the decision-making bodies. This could be explained by the socio-economic, political and cultural constraints affecting women's general participation in activities outside their home, especially unpaid voluntary activities.

A sample survey of 1084 social care PVOs carried out in 1988 showed that the rate of female membership was 22.4 per cent compared to 77.6 per cent for men, while for board membership it was 18.8 per cent compared to 81.2 per cent for men. The gender gap is even wider concerning women's membership in social aid PVOs where it goes down to 18.5 per cent and 10.6 per cent for board membership. In cultural and religious PVOs, female board membership reaches the bottom rate of 7 per cent (CAPMAS 1992: 1—26). However, the female membership of motherhood-childhood and family planning PVOs increases to 26.4 per cent and 41 per cent. It was also observed that the female rate of participation in PVOs differs according to the socio-cultural and eco-nomic environment. Thus, it is higher in Cairo and Alexandria than the other governorates, especially in Upper Egypt and border governorates which are less developed. In the newly established environment PVOs, which are usually based in urban areas by educated and enlightened people, the female board membership has risen to an impressive rate of 68 per cent (Kandil 1995: 12).

Regarding the age of women participating in PVOs, it was observed that the majority join after the age of forty when they are free from child-raising responsibilities (El-Baz 1989: 55). Thus youth participation is limited, especially in the more traditional organizations.

Legal Constraints on Private Voluntary Organizations and Forms of Resistance

Despite the urgent need to organize women in Egypt, the prospects are not promising as long as the PVOs are legally controlled by Law 32 of 1964 which restricts the freedom of citizens (male and female), to form independent organizations. The law gives the government a strong hold over establishing, managing, financing, and/or terminating any PVO which does not abide by the detailed regulations of the Ministry of Social Affairs (MOSA). Law 32 further stipulates that no PVO is allowed to engage in political or religious activities. The law, in fact, is suppressing the PVO movement in Egypt by appropriating the essence of this form of organization, i.e. independence from government control.

The law dates back to the sixties when socialism and central planning were adopted by the state, which assumed a greater role in terms of control as well as of providing the people with material and social needs and services. Thus, even if this law was compatible with the system then, the radical transformation to the free market economy and to the multi-party political system – which presupposes more democratization and promotion of the civil society – makes the change of Law 32 imperative. Nonetheless, the regime in Egypt seems to insist on having a strong hold over civil organizations. To contain the campaign by civil society activists for changing the Law 32, the government has introduced a few amendments which did not change the restrictive provisions of the law nor decrease the government control over PVOs.

In the last decade a number of women's PVOs were organized by women activists. In order to avoid governmental control, they registered themselves as non-profit civil companies. The government, however, tried to control their activities in various ways, including declaring them as illegal forms of organization. In the case of those organizations practising any activities specifically stipulated in the Law 32 and affiliated decrees (according to rule 92/2 from the law), their members will be fined and/or imprisoned. Further, being declared illegal, the non-profit civil companies do not have the right of receiving foreign funds (Ministry of Justice, 1995).

Another form of avoiding government control is adopted by some women's groups who do not register themselves separately but work under the umbrella of one of the well established organizations, such as women's committees in the Arab Lawyers' Union, the Egyptian Committee of Afro-Asian People's Solidarity and recently, the Lawyers' Syndicate.

Other initiatives have been taken recently by women's informal groups. A booklet on Egyptian women's legal rights was prepared and published by an ad hoc gathering of women under the name of 'Women's Group Interested in the Woman's Question'. Also a book informing women about their bodies (Woman's Life and Her Health) was published by another group formed for that purpose (Roemberg 1991: 15).

Another interesting example of informal groups using different operational methods is that organized by the political Islamists. Making use of their popularity among university male and female students, they encouraged women on the campuses to organize themselves in groups which provided the members with social support and social services, such as free transportation, mimeographed lecture notes and medical care. The leaders of these women's groups were always men. Women were excluded from the leadership of their own groups on the grounds that male leaders knew more about Islam than women. Thus, despite the visibility of women in the Islamist movement, they were usually operating on the lowest levels. The formation of sexually segregated groups did not change the fact that leadership was the sole preserve of men even in women's groups (Hatem: 245). These Islamist women's groups played an active role in recruiting other women for the movement, especially among those who come from the newly impoverished classes. Solving their immediate material problems was the key to winning them over. They are strongly committed and innovative in their different ways of reaching people especially at the grass-root level (Hatem: Ibid).

When the government started, bound by ER-SAP, to reduce its expenditure on the social services provided by the state, political Islamists of both sexes penetrated the PVO movement and replaced the government in providing social services, especially in the fields of health and education as well as employment and income-generating activities. Through this process, motivated by their political aspirations, they advocate ideas which are hostile to gender equality and based on a rigid traditional sexual division of labour. Their gender ideology has spread among a vast number of Egyptian females; mostly not through real conviction, but through providing practical solutions to their problems. Although radical women's activist groups are aware of and alarmed by the Islamists' influence on women in Egypt, they have been unable so far to confront them and neutralize their impact on society. First, because they have not managed to build a social base and, second, unlike the Islamists, they do not work within the context of a large movement with sufficient resources for providing the people with needed services.

In the context of assessing the ability of women's PVOs to confront the gender-inequality on the objective and subjective levels, one can distinguish between women's PVOs and women-related PVOs (Khafagy 1992). The first type developed in the 1980s out of concern for gender equality and the empowerment of women. The members and the leadership of these NGOs are mostly educated, urban, politically minded, women and men whose intellectual vigour and command over foreign languages enabled them to interact with foreign donors and international women's PVOs. Thus, the agenda of some of them is influenced by Western feminist views. They emphasize the priority of certain topics such as reproductive rights which, though extremely important, should be viewed within a developmental context. Their activities are mostly advocacy through research, seminars and workshops which produce an intellectually progressive understanding of women's issues that is highly appreciated by middle and upper middle-class educated women. They have limited contact with grass-roots women – mainly through researching their problems. Although most of them are ideologically committed to social justice, thus strongly sympathetic with the problems of poor women, none of these PVOs has succeeded in incorporating those women in the organization as active agents for social transformation. Though they are not representative of Egyptian PVOs in general, they can play an avant-garde role in the emancipation of women (Arends 1993).

A different example of a women's PVO, established by a group of professional women working in development, is the Association for the Development and Enhancement of Women (ADEW), whose mandate is to promote the empowerment of women in low-income communities by facilitating access to credit and by providing legal assistance. In doing this they focus on women who are sole supporters of their households. A concrete project to assist such women was that women loan applicants guarantee each other's loans, thus removing the constraints that lack of collateral often poses. The legal assistance component of the project consists of helping women to obtain ID-cards, which is often a complicated process if they do not have birth certificates. The PVO consists of approximately twenty members who believe that the development and promotion of gender relations in society starts with the grass-roots women who are crushed by poverty so that they are not only deprived of their gender rights, but are also deprived of their human right for survival.

Women-related PVOs are those which offer different services, some of which are for women. In these PVOs women hardly have any decision-making power. These organizations concentrate on women's problems rather than gender relations and maintain a traditional outlook toward women's roles in society. They do not question the position of women within the society and they avoid political issues. Many of the women-related PVOs can be found outside Cairo and several of them were established by government officials, and thus are closely linked to the MOSA. Women-related PVO members usually have a poor knowledge of foreign languages which affects their abilities to interact with inter-national PVOs, or obtain funds from foreign donors. It is worth noting, however, that the members of these PVOs have much more contact with grass-roots women. They could be considered a continuation of the traditional philanthropic PVOs. The type of activities and services they offer reflects the traditional sexual division of roles, e.g. sewing, embroidery, nurseries, family planning, and so forth. Although some of these PVOs are controlled by women, the absence of awareness of gender issues is bound to limit their impact on women's position in society.

It is worth noting, however, that the successful PVOs networking achieved through the preparation for the ICPD and the International Women's Conference has brought many organizations of both types together to work on women's issues emphasized by both conferences. These processes have revitalized women's PVOs on the national level and brought to their attention several gender issues which they were not aware of before. Preparations for the two conferences also attracted the youth to the PVOs movement. Young males and females are dynamically active and eager to learn more about gender relations in the Egyptian society. This is especially useful for injecting new blood into the PVO movement, as well as socializing the new generations into the traditions of gender equality.

It is also observed that some of the old PVOs such as the Coptic Evangelical Organization for Social Services (CEOSS), not necessarily gender based, have developed their approach to a more comprehensive and progressive one. They provide programmes to help change oppres-sive family relations to a more participatory relationship. Some of them succeeded in organizing men and women in local communities based on hierarchical elected bodies starting from the level of the street committees. These experiences, nevertheless, are still on a very limited scale and cannot be treated as a general phenomenon.

It is important to note that apart from women's advocacy PVOs, whose work is not directed to a specific target group, all other PVOs (especially those registered with MOSA) are promotional PVOs working with specific target groups, i.e. beneficiaries. The relationship between these PVOs and their target groups is paternalistic and mostly a patron-client relationship. The target groups do not participate on any level except as recipients of aid or services.

Despite the important work that the promotional PVOs do by helping the target groups to improve their standard of living, real and effective transformation of the target groups – especially women – cannot be achieved without their participation as actors through grass-root organizations. This applies in particular to poor women who are marginalized socially, economically and politically.

Some Observations on Women in Private Voluntary Organizations

1. The general undemocratic climate, based on the mutual distrust between the people and the government, prevents the PVO movement from being transformed into a dynamic force for societal change. The traditional women's PVOs registered in MOSA accept the government control and work within a plan decided by the Ministry.
2. On the other hand, the radical women's advocacy PVOs are confronting the government and fighting against its attempts to control and dominate them. The difference of views concerning the role of the government and gender relations has created a gap between the two types of PVOs. Coordination between them might help to radicalize the traditional women's PVOs and may also bring the radical ones into contact with grass-roots women, who represent the majority of the female population.
3. Ideological differences between women's advocacy PVOs create a certain degree of tension among them. Although most of them agree to see the women's question within the societal context, in addition to women's specific gender problems, the difference in priorities makes agreeing on a minimum programme of action difficult. This rigid attitude has undermined frequently the attempts to form a national women's organization.
4. Although networking and coordination between women's groups is extremely important, it is still difficult in Egypt. There is a great deal of competition among individuals as to who should lead or who takes the credit. The spirit of team-work is not very common. One factor has been functional in this direction, i.e. the transformation of the women's question from a subject of serious struggle for liberation to an academically remunerative topic. This attitude was encouraged by the willingness of some donors to generously fund women's activities irrespective of its real value for women's liberation.
5. Foreign funding has become a controversial issue among women's PVOs. Traditional PVOs welcome foreign funding without question

and do not mind the donors' interference. Radical women's PVOs have split over this issue. Some decided to accept foreign funds with no interference from the donors. Others refused on principle because they believe that donors always have their own agendas. They have succeeded so far in funding their activities from membership fees and some supporters' donations.

Conclusion

Despite the stipulated constitutional and legal equality and the state's declared support for women, the situation of women in Egypt is characterized by gender inequality. Their share in the economic, social and political opportunities is much less than that of men. This situation is reinforced by various factors. The form of social and economic organization is more beneficial to women when it is based on a strategy of full mobilization of human resources. Therefore, the new Economic Reform Policy based on Structural Adjustment Programmes, which has less need for mass mobilization, is negatively affecting women's opportunities for participation. However, although the first type of socio-economic organization is necessary for promoting gender equality, it is not by itself sufficient. Its positive effect has been undermined in the Egyptian context by the existing sexual division of labour which confines women's role to the private sphere where they are subject to the inequality and insecurity implicit in the Family Status Law. This, among other things, effectively denies any possibility for gender equality in the public sphere which, in turn, reduces women's access to the decision-making bodies and limits their influence in removing existing gender discrimination. This situation is made worse through the impact of the fundamentalist conservative interpretation of Islam to justify gender inequality. Despite this gloomy picture, some positive signs of women's dynamism is appearing in the form of new militant women's groups, and more vitality in women's traditional PVOs. However, a serious effort by gender-aware women should be made to create a more enabling environment for women to form their own organizations. This should, of necessity, take into consideration the different priorities of the various categories of women in Egypt while establishing the common ground for a powerful movement capable of achieving gender equality and liberation.

References

Abdel Kader, S. (1992), *The Situation Analysis of Women in Egypt*, Cairo: Central Agency for Population, Mobilization and Statistics (CAPMAS) & UNICEF.

Arends, I. (1993), 'Egyptian NGOs and their Perspective on Women and Development,' Cairo: Unpublished paper.

Azer, A. and Ramzi, N. (1992), *Child Labour*, Cairo: UNICEF.

Badran, H. (1994), 'Ni'sa Maso'ulat' (Responsible Women), Cairo: National Symposium, CAPMAS.

El-Baz, S. (1989), 'Al'munazzamat Al'ahleya Al'arabeya Ba'yn Al'waq'i Wa'ltomouh' (Arab NGOs Between Reality and Aspiration), Proceedings of the Arab NGOs Conference, AGFUND, Riyadh.

—— (1992a), 'Makanat Al'mara'a Al-Misreya Fi Al'mugtama'a' (The Status of the Egyptian Woman in Society), *Al-Ahram Daily*, 14 March, Cairo.

—— (1992b), 'Rural Women Project: An Impact Evaluation Study,' UNICEF, Egypt.

—— (1994), 'Amal Al'mara'a Wa Ishkaleyat Al'mo'sawat Ba'yn Al'ginsayn Fi Misr' (Women's Labour and the Problem of Gender Equality in Egypt) in *Al'mara'a Al'misreya Wa Al-Adala Al-Igtima'eya Wa Al'Iqtisadeya*, Cairo: Dar Al-Thaqafa.

—— (1995), 'Al'muna'zzamat Al'ahleya Al'misreya Wa Imkane'yat Al'tatwir: Nadhra Istrategeya' (The Egyptian NGOs and Possibilities for Promotion: A Strategic View), *Al-Qahira*, 154, Cairo.

—— (1996) 'Institutionalized Children in Difficult Circumstances: A Study of Institutions and Inmates,' Cairo: UNICEF.

Beijing National Report (1995), The National Women's Committee, National Council for Childhood and Motherhood, Cairo.

CAPMAS (1986), *National Census*, Cairo.

CAPMAS (1990), *Labour Force Sample Survey* (LFSS), Cairo.

CAPMAS & UNICEF (1991), *Women's Participation in the Labour Force*, Cairo.

CAPMAS (1992), *Ihsa'a Al'gameyat Al'khayreya Al'mo'ana* (Statistics of the Supported Philanthropic Societies), Ref. No. 74-12321/88, Cairo.

Fergany, N. (1993), 'Taq'yeem Al'ingaz Fi Ta'aleam Al'mar'a Fi Misr' (Achievement Evaluation of the Women's Education in Egypt), Seminar on '120 Years of Women's Education in Egypt,' Supreme Council for Culture, Cairo.

Halluda, A. (1994), 'Al'mar'a Al'misreya Fi Al'amaleya Al'ta'alimeya' (The Egyptian Woman in the Educational Process), First Women's National Conference, the National Committee for Women, Cairo.

Handoussa, H. (1994), 'Al'mar'a Fi Al'qita'a Al'rasmy wa Al'gheir rasmy' (Women in the Formal and Informal Sectors), First Women's National Conference, the National Committee for Women, Cairo.

Hassan, A. (1995) 'A'thar Al'takyif Al'ha'ikaly Wa Al'islah Al'Iqtisady Ala

Al'mar'a Fi Misr' (The Impact of ER-SAPs on Egyptian Women), Egyptian NGOs Document for the Women's Forum, Cairo.

Hatem, M. (1992), 'Economic and Political Liberalization in Egypt and the Demise of State Feminism,' *International Journal of Middle East Studies*, 24.

Huber, S. (1994), 'Gender Analysis of Participation of Women and Men in NGOs: The Case of Egyptian NGOs,' in Bonser and Ringeling, eds, *The Role of NGOs in National Development Strategy in Arab and the Middle East Countries*, Brussels: International Institute of Administrative Science.

Kandil, A. (1995), 'Al'mar'a Al'misreya Fi Al'munazzamat Al'ahleya' (Seminar on Egyptian Women in the Public Sphere), Centre for Political Studies, University of Cairo.

Khafagy, F. (1992), 'Needs Assessment Survey of NGOs in Egypt,' paper given to the African Women Development and Communication Network (FEMNET), Cairo.

Korayem, K. (1987), *The Impact of Economic Adjustment Policies on the Vulnerable Families and Children in Egypt*, Cairo: Third World Forum, Middle East Office, and UNICEF.

Ministry of Justice (MOJ) (1995), 'Memorandum: The Legal Status of the Unregistered PVOs According to the Law 32 of 1964,' 22 January, Secretariat of Legislative Affairs, Cairo.

Ministry of Social Affairs (MOSA) (1993) *Al'mu'ashirat Al'ihsa'eya Fi Magalat Al're'aya Wa Al'tanmeya Al'igtima'eya* (Statistical Indicators for Social Development and Care), Cairo.

El-Nashif, H. (1994), *Basic Education and Female Literacy in Egypt*, Cairo: Third World Forum, Middle East Office.

Nour El-Din, A. (1995), *Women's Role in the Ancient Egyptian Society*, Supreme Council for Antiquity, Ministry of Culture, Cairo.

Roemberg, R. Van. (1991), 'An Overview of Women in Development in the Arab Republic of Egypt,' Cairo: Unpublished paper.

Shoukry, A. (1988), *Al'mar'a Fi Al'manatiq Al'rife'ya Wa Al'hadareya: Dirasa Li Hayateha Al'a'eliya Wa Li Amaleha*, Cairo: Dar El-Ma'arefa El-Gami'eya.

Toubia, N. (1994), *Arab Women: A Profile of Diversity and Change*, New York: The Population Council.

UNICEF (1990), *Sex Differences in Child Survival and Development, Evaluation Series No. 6*, Regional Office for the Middle East and North Africa, Amman.

UNICEF (1993a), *The State of World's Children Report*, New York: Oxford University Press.

UNICEF (1993b), *Report on the State of Women and Children in Egypt*, Cairo.

Zaki, M. (1995), *Civil Society and Democratization in Egypt: 1981–1994*, Cairo: Ibn Khaldoun Centre.

Za'louk, M. (1990), 'Women in the Labour Force, Preliminary Report SG/1, Labour Information System Projects,' Cairo: CAPMAS.

Zurayk, H. (1991), 'A Study on Reproductive Morbidity in Rural Giza, Description of Study and Analysis of First Phase,' *Safe Motherhood*, 6, July–October.

8

Feminism and Contemporary Debates in Egypt

Nadje Sadig Al-Ali

Introduction

Two years ago I attended an extraordinary discussion in a relatively new and small women's centre in Cairo. The centre, which is mainly frequented by secular-orientated[1] and leftist women and men, had invited one of the youngest and increasingly prominent Islamist women to present her view on women's issues. Heba Rauf Ezzat, a graduate of a German high school in Cairo and currently a teaching assistant in the political science department at Cairo University, has become known as a 'feminist reformist' within the Islamist movement.

After her eloquent talk about women's political role from an Islamic perspective, a discussion took place which differed from any of the numerous heated debates I had witnessed previously in this centre. Despite obvious disagreements between the mainly leftist audience and the Islamist speaker, the general atmosphere was one of curiosity, respect and an attempt to actually listen to each other.

Without trying to read too much into this particular incident, I suspect that it was not so unique in its display of potential common ground across seemingly opposite constituencies. What made this dialogue possible was a shared discursive universe and set of meanings about 'the West' and 'Western feminism', as well as about the threat of imperialism, perceived to be particularly manifested in foreign funding. Constructions of 'the West' as a dominant, essentialized 'other' are not only prevalent in Islamic discourses, but are also central to secular leftist and nationalist discourses. 'Conspiracy theories' and perceiving 'the West' to be responsible for Egypt's social, political and economic problems lie at the core of many debates in contemporary Egypt.

The literature on Egypt and my own observations suggest that the recently coined concept of *nassawiyya* (feminism) is being associated with the West – hence alien and suspect – within Islamic and leftist discourses alike. This perception has been largely internalized by many contemporary women activists who appear to be as much engaged in trying to assert their 'Egyptianness' as in struggling to increase their rights as women (Badran 1994). However, the symptoms and content of what is being resisted – generally labelled *al-hagma al-thaqafiyyah* (the cultural attack), in which the West is perceived to impose its norms and values – requires serious reflection. I suspect a layer of meanings attached to the notion of 'Western hegemony', which might be deciphered by looking at the ways and contexts in which it is used.

The event at the women's centre raises a number of interesting questions about the political and ideological topography in which contemporary feminist activists struggle. What major debates influence women struggling to improve their rights? What are the main points of reference against which contemporary feminist activists define themselves? I would like to argue in this paper that the context of women's rights activism in Egypt can only be understood by reference to a number of debates and the way they intersect: a) modernity and Westernism; b) the nature of civil society; and c) secularism and minorities. However, these various debates and discourses do not represent analytically separate categories but do interpenetrate with each other. The aim of this chapter is to map out some of the current issues and discussions, which are significant in shaping the complexities of interests and solidarities of feminist activists today.

It is my argument throughout this chapter that women's groups have to engage with the state and various constituencies in civil society in their battle for women's civil rights, often being caught in a web of interests, discourses and solidarities. But it is also these women who, by challenging the various discourses, might have the possibility to disentangle the web and emerge as a democratizing force in contemporary Egypt.

In the first section of the chapter I will outline the major debates within historical analyses of the Egyptian women's movement in order to shed light on the continuities and disruptions of the significant parameters and discourses. I will briefly address the changing nature and orientations of the Egyptian state and its diverse gender policies during the reigns of Nasser, Sadat and Mubarak. Finally, I will attempt to summarize the debates about Westernism, national unity, secularism and civil society, as well as provide a brief overview of the terrain of contemporary women's activism.

Debates on the History of the Women's Movement

The tendency to frame the women's struggle within the wider struggle of national liberation presents a continuous thread in the historical analyses of the women's movement in Egypt. The main angle of analysis constitutes the tension in the bond between nationalist and women's liberation due to the common practice among male nationalists to subsume the latter in the frame of the wider political struggle (Philipp 1978; Badran 1988; Ahmed 1992).

This background is critical to an evaluation of contemporary women's activism since it still informs the major parameters of discourses and debates today. Often it involves the forging of a strict separation between the 'modern, secular and westernizing voice' on the one hand and the 'conservative, anti-western and Islamic voice' on the other. Leila Ahmed, for instance, associates the westernizing and secularizing tendencies of the upper and upper-middle classes with the dominant voice of feminism for most of the century. She contends that it was only during the past decades that an 'alternative voice' gained ground by seeking a means to articulate female subjectivity and affirmation within a native, vernacular, Islamic discourse (Ahmed 1992: 197).

This clear-cut division between seemingly divergent voices obscures the overlappings, contradictions and complexities of discourses and activism that took place against a background of anti-colonial and anti-imperialist struggle. Earlier, Mervat Hatem argued (1986) that even Huda Shaarawi, who has been described as secular and Western-oriented, defended Islam on nationalist grounds. She tackled women's issues with regard to the question of how a new Muslim synthesis could be achieved to respond to the demands of the time. The attempt to blur dichotomies between westernizing and traditional strands of the feminist movement characterizes the most recent publications on its history (Baron 1994; Badran 1995).

Feminist discourses and activism during the period of post-colonial state formation, and even up to the first half of the twentieth century, have repeatedly been identified with Huda Shaarawi and the Egyptian Feminist Union. However, Badran's latest work encompasses a wider variety of voices and activists. By giving Nabawiyah Musa, the first woman to obtain a secondary school certificate and a promoter of education for women of modest middle-class backgrounds, equal weight in shaping the feminist movement after 1923, Badran challenges the common view (Abdel-Kader 1987; Ahmed 1992; Khater and Nelson 1988) that, in its beginnings, the movement was elitist and only included women from the upper class. Khater and Nelson (1988), for example, view the first phase of feminist activism as merely elitist and philanthropic in character. They argue that it was actually during the period from 1945 until 1959, which was to be neglected in many studies (Berque 1972; Jayawardena 1986; Khalifa 1973; Al-Sabaki 1987; Vatikiotis 1985), that the women's movement came of age.

Badran contests some of Khater's and Nelson's arguments by emphasizing that diversification in ideology and political consciousness was already characteristic of the earlier movement. However, with regard to her claim that the movement associated with Huda Shaarawi and Nabawiyah Musa already transcended elitism, Badran's work does not persuade. According to Badran herself, the eleven founding members of the EFU were mainly from wealthy landowning families, raised within harem culture (Badran 1995: 96). Moreover, a look at the magazine *L'Egyptienne* which was published by the EFU reveals that all its writers were either from the Egyptian elite or Western women. In addition, Amina Al-Said's autobiographical reflections on her association with Shaarawi and the EFU also leave the flavour of a powerful elitist atmosphere.

It is undeniable, however, that the discourses and activities of feminists took a different direction in the 1940s and 1950s (Ahmed 1992; Botman 1987; Khater and Nelson 1988). Doria Shafik's Bint el-Nil (Daughters of the Nile) Union was created in 1948 as an initiative for a new and invigorated Egyptian feminist movement whose primary purpose was to proclaim and claim full political rights of women. It also promoted literacy programmes, campaigned to improve cultural, health, and social services among the poor and enhance mother and child care (Shafik 1955: 191). The campaign for women's political rights was linked to the campaign for social reforms (Khater and Nelson 1988: 470).

Fuelled by the monarchy's incompetence to deal satisfactorily with economic austerity after the Second World War – and the resulting political extremism – some women became critical of the Bint el-Nil Union as too bourgeois and conservative. Having adopted a communist outlook, these women believed that women's liberation must be subsumed within a larger struggle for social, economic and political justice. Leftist women like Inji Aflatoun, Latifa al-Zayat and Soraya Adham tended to direct their efforts towards a more general political class struggle which focused simultaneously on national independence and women's liberation (Botman 1987; Khater 1988).

Egyptian feminist activism receded under the rule of Gamal Abd al-Nasser as an outcome of the state's monopolization of women's issues, especially through the activities of the Ministry of Social Affairs.

Although voluntary work has a long history in Egypt, it was only during the Nasser regime that the role of NGOs (Non-Governmental Organizations), PVOs (Private Voluntary Organizations) and LCDOs (Local Community Development Organizations) came under sharp focus, since the regime tried to undermine both independent welfare and political activities. Many laws and regulations, culminating in Law 32 of 1964[2] (still in effect today), were formulated to organize and categorize the various activities carried out by all voluntary organizations. These laws oblige women activists to operate either as informal groups or as officially registered organizations which are subject to the control of the Ministry of Social Affairs.[3]

While there is a tendency in recent scholarship and political discourse to define Nasser's regime merely in terms of its authoritarianism and repression of opposition and independent groups, the state's commitment to social egalitarianism nevertheless included women. Egypt's 1952 revolution inaugurated a new age for women by altering the class structure and by the ideological, legal and practical inclusion of women in the new state.[4]

Nevertheless, the impressive accomplishments of the Egyptian state in education, employment and social mobility, which accounted for the progressive nature of Nasser's regime, were accompanied by the preservation of the conservative Personal Status Laws of the 1920s and 1930s (Hatem 1993: 233). Still, women did gain some economic, social and cultural strength through their increased participation in education and employment.

While independent feminist activism only reappeared at the beginning of the 1970s – coinciding with the beginning of Sadat's era, the rise of *infitah* (open door) policies, and the increased emergence of Islamist movements – this new generation of feminists actually gained their intellectual, social and professional experience under Nasser.

Feminist Activism in the Post-*Infitah* Period

It has been acknowledged that women were affected in different ways by Sadat's *infitah* policies. Their integration into the economy, which had been part of Nasser's 'state feminism', was replaced by high rates of unemployment and inequality of opportunity in the workplace.[5] On the other hand, labour migration, especially to the Gulf countries, did not only provide economic betterment and improved standards of living for many families, it also forced women to take over tasks that were previously carried out by their husbands (Hatem 1992). While a number of women might have gained autonomy due to the migration of male household-heads, some studies point to the demoralizing social and emotional effects of migration on working-class women (Graham-Brown 1981; Hatem 1992: 238).

Work opportunities for women declined as sharply as equal pay; as men more aggressively sought the fewer jobs available, women were increasingly shut out of the workplace. In parallel to the economic pressures on women, more conservative discourses emerged which promoted women's return to domesticity (Hatem 1992).

Sadat's *infitah* policies cut sharply in two ways simultaneously: it opened the door, to the well-placed few, to extravagant wealth, glib corruption and rampant consumerism. On the other hand, the rest of the population suffered from *infitah's* broader implications – high inflation, chronic shortages of basic goods and housing, reduced employment opportunities and poor working conditions – intensified all the more by the state's reduction of investment in public service and job creation.

Women basically lacked independent representative organizations of their own and were dependent on the regime's particular priorities. The beginning of the UN Decade for Women in 1975 induced the regime, which was searching for stronger ties with its new allies, particularly the United States, to promote gender issues. However, despite the progressive laws of 1979, the state lacked an overall programme to ensure women's rights and did not encourage independent feminist activism.

The Personal Status Law of 1979 granted women more legal rights in marriage, polygamy, divorce and child custody; it was implemented by presidential decree along with another law that introduced changes to women's representation in parliament. The presidential decree created conflicts among women of different political persuasions and put them into a difficult position vis-à-vis this progressive law. Obviously, the common nickname 'Jehan's Law' delegitimized the reformed Personal Status Law by indicating the authoritarian and personalized manner by which it was passed. As the activist Shahida El-Baz remembers: 'All of us did not want this law to be abolished. We all preferred changes to take place in a democratic way, but within the context of state dynamics at that time it was a great achievement.'

However, in 1985, during the national discussion of the Personal Status Law, the already antagonized *al-haraka al-nissa'iyya* (the women's movement) experienced an actual split. While Nawal El-Saadawi defended the law and campaigned to maintain it, the Ittihad Al-Nissa'i Al-Taqadummi (Progressive Women's Union affiliated with the leftist

Tagammu party), argued that it was passed unconstitutionally by Sadat and should therefore be annulled. In this debate, nationalist leftist women, who opposed Sadat's policies of *infitah* and rapprochement with Israel, could be found in the same 'camp' as the Islamists and the Al-Azhar who were enraged by the reformed Personal Status Law. While the Islamist constituency certainly differed in motivation from the leftist women, the fact that these obviously conflicting forces argued against the 'radical feminist' trend represents one incident where a 'common enemy' led to the forging of a curious alliance.

At the same time, this episode reflects the heterogeneity and frictions among women representing different political convictions and ideologies and who hold conflictual interpretations of the actual content of *qadaya al-mar'ah* (woman's issues) and how to go about it. While El-Saadawi criticized women's organizations affiliated with political parties, Fathia Al-Assal, head of the Ittihad al-Nissa'i al-Taqadummi at the time, opposed the separation of women's issues from the liberation of society as a whole (Khater 1987: 17). In addition, the two camps differed in the way they sought to mobilize women, accusing each other of working with elite women only (ibid: 18).

Within contemporary Egyptian discourses, Nawal El-Saadawi, who emerged as a prominent and courageous activist for women's rights ever since the publication of her book *Al-Mar'ah wa Al-Jins* (Woman and Sex, 1971), is being affiliated with the new radical movement of *nassawiyya* (feminism). In the 1980s, the Jami'yya Taddamun lil-Mara al-'Arabiyya (The Arab Women's Solidarity Association or AWSA), was founded by El-Saadawi. The general objectives of the association were based on the integration of the struggle for women's rights within the struggle against imperialism, Zionism and economic exploitation.

AWSA participated in the campaign against the amendment of the Personal Status Law in 1985. It organized a number of meetings, issued statements and submitted modifications of the draft law to the People's Assembly. It launched a campaign to publicize the dangers linked to birth control methods used in Egypt. AWSA also organized a number of cultural seminars about women between 1982 and 1987 (Toubia 1987).

The reasons for the banning of AWSA by the Ministry of Social Affairs in June 1991 have been the subject of much debate. What can be said with certainty at this point is that Nawal El-Saadawi and AWSA were an easy target for both the Egyptian government and anti-feminist forces within Egypt. Not only was its feminism highly confrontational and outspokenly critical of Islamist positions on gender, but El-Saadawi's 'autocratic rule' within the organization and the involvement of her family in AWSA also alienated many Egyptian women and men. Nevertheless, many contemporary activists state that Nawal El-Saadawi's books and lectures were crucial in shaping their initial ideas about women's oppression in Egypt.

The reemergence of organized women's rights activism, after its virtual absence during the Nasser period, has been linked mainly to the continuing battle over the Personal Status Law and the taking up of formerly taboo issues such as contraception and clitoridectomy (Ahmed 1992: 214). However, it is important to note that Sadat's policy of manipulating Islamic groups as a means to weaken popular leftist forces led to an increasing Islamist revival which also galvanized women. Both public and private life has been extensively permeated by conservative Islamist forces which vary from what is generally called *al-Islam al-Muassasi* (institutional Islam) of the Al-Azhar to the moderate strands of political Islam represented by the Akhwan Al-Muslimin (Muslim Brotherhood) and finally the extremist Gama'at al-Islamiyya (Islamist groups).

Among their many manifestations in public life are the establishments of Islamic schools, hospitals, banks and social welfare organizations. In the realm of the 'private' a growing observance of religious rites and a stress on 'Islamic values' has particularly affected women. Islamists believe that the emancipation of women is tantamount to a radical and unacceptable change of the fundamental values of Egyptian society. Their claim is made all the more vociferous by their constant harping on the deterioration brought about by corrupt Western liberalism. In addition, by asserting that they violate the principles of the Shari'a (Islamic law), Islamists deny international human rights conventions' claims to absolute equality between men and women (Zaki 1995: 214).

The Current Context of Feminist Activism

The increased confrontation with the Islamists over the implementation of the Shari'a pressured the Mubarak regime initially to legislate and implement more conservative laws and policies towards women (particularly in the realm of personal status) and to diminish its support for women's political representation. While Islamist forces still constitute a powerful constituency within the contemporary Egyptian state, there has been increasing pressure on the Egyptian government to adhere to UN conventions concerning women's rights. Economic dependence on USAID and other international donor organizations (IMF and the World

Bank) compels the current regime to present itself as abiding to the values and ethos of democracy, human rights and women's rights – as promoted by Egypt's financial and political 'benefactors'.

Despite Mubarak's official pro-democracy policies, repressive measures have not only been directed towards Islamic militant groups and Communists, but also towards women activists. A number of laws continue to regulate the establishment of voluntary groups, associations and organizations under the supervision of the Ministry of Social Affairs. The influence of the international community became more pressing during the preparations to the United Nations International Conference on Population and Development in Cairo (September 1994) and the International Women's Forum in Beijing (September 1995). One year prior to the ICPD, Egyptian NGOs seemed to experience a breakthrough in their tension-stricken relation with the government as the latter recognized and supported an elected NGO Committee for Population and Development (NCPD). Nevertheless, throughout the preparations for Beijing, the Mubarak regime's consistent equivocation concerning independent women's rights activism flared up once again during the ongoing debate over Law 32.

It is important to stress that the flurry of pro-feminist activism during the recent past – and articulations of new perspectives and demands on such issues as women's political participation, women's equality in the workplace, and the more sensitive issues of women's reproductive rights and violence against women – took place in a context where the government felt pressured by international constituencies to prove its commitment to women's rights. Moreover, resources and people were mobilized around both the ICPD and Beijing. In some instances, individuals seem to have grouped only temporarily in response to funding possibilities generated by international agendas and dissipated after both conferences ended. However, some issue-oriented networks, such as the Women's Media Watch, the Female Genital Mutilation (FGM) Task Force and a network of organizations working on a project concerning Women and Violence not only persist, but have maintained momentum.

Moreover, the various preparations, activities and experiences of the past two years, which were mainly related to the ICPD and Beijing, have had some positive effect on a number of participants. In my meetings and interviews with activists, I have been sensing a rejuvenated confidence and motivation, despite the overall atmosphere of crisis and defeat which is persistent among all of Egypt's intellectuals and political activists. Even if it is too early at this point to describe a particular trend, I do sense a development away from Badran's earlier observation (1994) that, in contrast to previous generations of feminists in Egypt, many women who are engaged in the struggle for women's rights are reluctant to publicly affirm their conviction as feminists (206).

Nevertheless, women activists do run the risk of being stigmatized as anti-religious and anti-nationalist by Islamist movements and conservative nationalist forces, as well as by leftist nationalist women activists. Feminists have been increasingly accused of collaborating with Western imperialism by importing alien ideas and practices and circulating them throughout society. In the light of these very intimidating charges, it is not surprising that many women activists have internalized these accusations, and themselves equate *nassawiyya* (feminism) with a Western concept, alien and alienating to their social, cultural and political context. However, in my interviews with secular-oriented women activists – which I started after Beijing – many more women than I expected rejected the notion of feminism as a Western movement right away and took pride in their struggle.

According to my observations, 'secular-oriented pro-feminist groups' involve members who enter the realm of feminist activism from a variety of backgrounds and experiences, such as development work, human rights activism, former membership in the Egyptian left, or the commitment to the campaign for increased democratization of Egyptian society. Although there is a degree of interpenetration and overlap in the various constituencies, it is important to highlight the broad and diverse base of feminist activism.

While the arena of secular-oriented women's organizations has yet to be fully mapped out, it can be said that it is composed of a heterogeneous group of women with different motivations and interests: Al-Mara' Al-Gidida (The New Woman's Group), Nur (Arab Women's Publishing house), Rabtat Al-Mar'ah Al-Arabiya (the Alliance of Arab Women), Gamaiyat Al-Tanmiya Wa Al-Nuhud Al-Mar'ah (The Association for the Development and Enhancement for Women), Ma'an (Together), Ittihad Al-Nissai' Al-Taqaddummi (Progressive Women's Union) and the group who published *Al-Huquq al-Qanuniyya li al-Mar'ah al-Misriyya bain al-Nadhariyya wa al-Tatbiq* (The Legal Rights of the Egyptian Woman in Theory and Practice). While all these groups are located in Cairo, we find Jam'iyat Bint al-Ard (The Society of the Daughter of the Earth) in Mansoura.

For the time being, I am able to remark that the various groups differ with respect to their ideological background and orientation, their proclaimed aims, their activities and organizational structures, and their national and international affiliations. The terrain of political engagement ranges from charity and social work, to consciousness-raising through seminars, conferences and discussion groups, research activities, campaigning and the publishing of pamphlets, magazines and books.

As heterogeneous as the groups and their individual members might be, they are united by their middle-class background and their commitment to retain and expand their civic rights and equality before the law and their secular orientation. I assume that they are also united by their fear of growing Islamist militancy, but their actual positions vis-à-vis the various Islamic tendencies and discourses are variable. The various groups and even individual activists in one particular group differ as to what strategy to employ to counter Islamist rhetoric concerning women. The majority of women today believe that the only feasible way to reach Egyptian women and men is to reinterpret Islam and stress women's rights within the frame of Islam. Only a few women oppose this strategy and refuse to argue on the same ground as Islamists, which they view as destined to backfire.

In addition to the groups mentioned above, there are also several women's units or committees affiliated to human rights organizations and a number of individual women activists who can be described as secular-oriented and pro-feminist. Some work independently through their specific professions (writers, journalists, artists), some cooperate with human rights organizations, while others are loosely affiliated with a number of women's organizations (e.g. Mona Helmi, Salwa Bakr, Nadia Farhah, Iqbal Baraka, Shahida Al-Baz, Amina Shafiq and others).

Outside of secular frameworks, we find an increasing number of Islamist women activists who have managed to gain a voice within the mainstream Islamist discourse as well as criticize and challenge their male counterparts for misinterpreting Islam. However, the most celebrated women have remained ambiguous about what constitutes an adequate role of women within an envisioned Islamic state and society: Zeinab Al-Ghazali, the most prominent Islamist woman and founder of the Jama'at al-Sayyidat al-Muslimat (Muslim Women's Association, 1924), and Safinaz Kazim, a journalist and former leftist who committed herself to Islam in the 1970s. While Al-Ghazali and Kazim find no contradiction between women's public and private lives, they have remained antagonistic to feminism (Badran 1994: 209).

A new generation of Islamist women has been more outspoken and confrontational about the way they view women's role in an Islamic state. They stress Islam's compatibility with UN-stipulated standards of women's rights and point to persisting traditions of pre-Islamic times as being responsible for the discrimination against women (Ahmed 1992). Zeinab Radwan, for example, a professor of Islamic philosophy at Cairo University and author of the book, *Islam and Women's Issues*, told me that she would spread her convictions through newspaper articles, in public lectures, TV programmes and in lectures at Cairo University. In her view, the movement of *tahrir al-mar'ah* (woman's liberation) initiated by Huda Shaarawi only addressed issues such as education and veiling, but failed to address women's rights and position in the family, which she sees as clearly defined by Islam.

Heba Rauf Ezzat, the young Islamist woman I mentioned at the beginning of this chapter, is certainly the most outspoken in the call for launching an Islamic women's movement. Feeling closest to the more moderate Akhwan Muslimin, rather than some of the more radical tendencies, she clearly expresses her objective to change society from within in order to realize her vision of an Islamic state. *Ijtihad*, the reinterpretation of the sources of religion and traditional values and the examination of Islamic history are the methods chosen by Rauf to evolve an Islamic theory of women's liberation.

While Rauf rejects being labelled a feminist since 'feminism negates religion' (Badran 1994: 213), she does not categorically dismiss feminism, but acknowledges that women did not really obtain their rights in Islamic societies which explains the successes of 'Western' feminist movements within Egypt (ibid: 214). Rauf does not only criticize men for producing mainstream Islamist discourse, but also Islamist women like al-Ghazali and Kazim for considering women's liberation a Western idea, which prevented them from making their own interpretations about women's problems (MERIP Nov/Dec 1994).

Feminist Activism and 'the West'

The renewed pro-feminist activism is taking place in a climate in which women have been at the centre of and most vulnerable to the 'cultural reconstructions' of Islamist discourses, in both their moderate and extremist forms. The notion of women as 'bearers of authentic values' has been a powerful force in many national and ethnic processes (Kandiyoti 1991), and holds in Egypt as it does elsewhere in the Muslim and non-Muslim world (Shoukrallah 1992). However, the perception of women as bearers of authentic values is not only significant in Islamist discourses, but also in the discourses of secular nationalists and leftists.

While early feminists like Huda Shaarawi were struggling with 'a

West' perceived to be outside of the Egyptian nation (British colonialism), contemporary struggles with *al-hagma al-thaqafiyya* (the cultural attack) and *imberiliyya* (imperialism) are of a far more complex nature. They also tackle 'the West' within the Egyptian national fabric and what appears to be about 'the West' often conceals discourses about social classes. The *nouveau riche* and 'Westernized Egyptians' are labelled *khawagas* (foreigners) just like the tourists who roam the country.

However, as Lila Abu-Lughod (1993) shows in her analysis of two popular TV serials ('The White Flag' and 'The Journey of Mr Abu al-'Ela al-Bishry'), moral values are often not ascribed along an opposition between an authentic indigenous identity and Westernization, but along two classes who have appropriated different aspects of Western culture: the *nouveau riche* villains and the honest and modest educated heroes and heroines. While the latter experience upward social mobility through education or come originally from an upper class, the nouveau riche includes businessmen with little education who have exploited the economic changes brought about by Sadat's *infitah*.

At the same time as Western products and lifestyles have been increasing, criticism and opposition to Westernization continues to grow more fiercely. The mass media in general launch counter-attacks to these trends, stressing the corruption and barbarism of Western civilization, its disrespect for the family, its promiscuity, its suppression of religious and spiritual values, its epidemic AIDS affliction, drug addiction and broken families.

Anti-Westernism and anti-imperialism are obviously related to discourses about Egypt's past. The Nasserist undertones and anti-imperialist slogans of newspaper headlines reveal a certain nostalgia for 'Egypt's glorious days' associated with the Nasser period. A similar nostalgia has been detected by Abu-Lughod with regard to television serials, which 'invoke the period of socialist ideals and nationalist vision through charged symbols of the Nasserist era, like the great singer Umm Kulthum or the Aswan High Dam' (1993: 29).

Disappointment with the 'peace process', generally perceived by Egyptian intellectuals to have worked at the expense of Palestinians and Arabs, has revived anti-Israeli sentiments. Recently, debates on the 'Middle East Market' (Sid-Ahmed 1994) and the 'nuclear non-proliferation treaty' (NPT) further increased the rejection of the 'normalization' process with Israel initiated by Sadat. Israel's strong link with 'the West', in particular its political links with the United States, but culturally with Europe and 'Western civilization' (Sid-Ahmed 1994: 8) expands the ground for anti-Western discourses.

My own research findings indicate a widespread practice within the contemporary women's movement to delegitimize a particular group or project by denouncing it as paying lip service to 'the West'. Those accused tend to differentiate between certain political and economic policies of the United States and particular values and cultural achievements of Western civilizations. The debate between *khosussiya* (specificity) and *alamiya* (universality) is at the centre of many discussions among human and women rights activists in Egypt.

The debate over specificity versus universality takes place within an atmosphere where Western-funded research has become subject to much suspicion. Not only Islamists, but also a number of secular-oriented and leftist intellectuals perceive Western-funded research as serving neo-Imperialist interests, thereby deliberately distorting the reality of Egyptian society. However, other voices (Abdallah 1994) stress the failure of Egyptian national institutions to sustain advanced intellectual life as being responsible for the increase in foreign-funded research within Egypt.[6]

Women's organizations often partake in the tensions around the debate of foreign funding. Secular-oriented women's groups, like all non-Islamist NGOs and associations, tend to be funded by UN organizations or private Western foundations which are accused by Islamist and leftist nationalist constituencies (but also by those who were too late in the rush for funding), of promoting Western imperialism.

National Unity and Minority Rights

The question of whether and how different feminists must negotiate through or around national political discourses is related to the question of how far, if at all, the various groups perceive themselves as marginalized within the current prevailing national discourses. While foreign donors fear accusations of giving preference to the Christian minority and thereby often avoid them altogether, many women activists, Muslim and Copt alike, stressed to me the parallel between the way women and Copts are treated as minorities within the national fabric. The scarce political representation of both women and Copts after the November/December 1995 elections is often evoked to illustrate this parallel.

The Copts' position within the national collectivity appears to be a rather vexed issue at the moment. It is linked to the crisis of secularism in contemporary Egypt, which, after the assassination of the secular human rights activist and writer Farag Foda in June 1992 by Islamic militants, has become muted and gone 'underground'. In the mid-1980s there was still a lively debate with numerous exchanges, revolving around the question of whether secularism could be reconciled with Islam. That debate has become muted. Secularist intellectuals like Farag Foda, Fu'ad Zakariya, Muhammad Nur Farhat and Husain Ahmad Amin argued publicly for a secular state with Islam being restricted to a creed and to spiritual and moral values; they argued against the Islamists' claim that secularism is unique to the European experience (Flores 1993: 34).

Today many secular intellectuals feel threatened and abstain from openly articulating their views and positions. Some thinkers and writers formerly associated with secularism such as Hasan Hanafi, 'Adil Husain, Anouar Abdel-Malek, to name just a few, now subscribe to political Islam (Al-'Azm 1981). Whether the individual motivations are based on conviction, accommodation, opportunism or fear needs to be analysed carefully. Even if those intellectuals who used to hold secularist views do not represent a homogeneous trend, the common denominator among them is a turn towards Islamism and an interpretation of Islam as the core of an 'Eastern' heritage which they must defend against Western cultural imperialism (Flores 1988: 28).

What is obvious is that the crisis of secularism coincides with crises related to the national identity being threatened from 'within and without'. The 1994 conference on minorities, organized by the Egyptian Ibn Khaldoun Research and Development Centre, is a case in point. The conference, which was to discuss ethnic and religious minorities in the Middle East, included a panel on Egyptian Copts. The conference organizer was severely attacked for undermining Egyptian national unity and paying lip service to foreign interests. The famous political analyst Mohamed Hussain Heikal, for example, actually initiated the discussion by stating that major international powers may exploit the 'illusion' of a Coptic minority to strike at Egypt's sovereignty, possibly even militarily, under the cover of protecting minority rights (Zaki 1994: 29).

Civil Society and Feminist Activism

Constructions of a homogeneous West and a monolithic Western feminism take place in an atmosphere of tensions between *mu'asara* (modernity) and *asala* (authenticity), which seem to be reified on a daily basis by Egyptian intellectuals, artists, politicians and the media (Zaki 1995). The heated battle over the issue of modernity – mainly between a few secular intellectuals and a much greater number of Islamists – involves the debate over the political system in Egypt.

Authenticity has been commonly linked to the implementation of the Shari'a , while modernity has often been linked, particularly by liberal Egyptian intellectuals, with political development that progresses from authoritarianism to pluralist democracies (ibid. 1995). In this sense, Egyptian intellectuals tend to differ from Western critiques of modernity which view it as a project of authoritarianism (Mitchell and Abu-Lughod 1993).

Within this debate, secular-oriented intellectuals have repeatedly stressed that Islamists have become so powerful primarily because of an existing political vacuum. The argument that strengthening civil society will offer non-extremist and non-violent ways of political participation has put pressure on the government to loosen state control in favour of the expansion of civil society. Consequently, the concept of civil society has emerged as a catch-word within Egypt, as well as among foreign researchers.

In a recently published book entitled *Civil Society and Democratization in Egypt: 1981–1984* (1995), M. Zaki emphasizes that Egypt, unlike most Middle Eastern countries, has a long history of voluntary associations. However, he also points out that these associations have not been geared towards the attainment of the kind of individual freedoms and rights that characterize Western societies. For example, because widespread chronic poverty affects civil society and depletes its resources, many of the associations and organizations of civil society in Egypt compete over state support 'needed to procure basic goods and services, as well as maintain a modicum of freedom to pursue their material interests without undue interference by the government' (ibid: 43).

Zaki paints a bleak picture in his evaluation of civil society in Egypt today. Religious, welfare and charity organizations, as well as professional syndicates and labour unions are described as lacking the main ingredients that strengthen political democratization. Collective decision-making is virtually absent in most associations which are largely run along autocratic lines. Issue-oriented associations, like the Egyptian Human Rights Organization, which supports civil liberties and draws attention to authoritarian encroachments on civil society, and several organizations dedicated to the preservation of the environment and the defence of women's rights, remain only a very small percentage of Egypt's civil society.

Like most scholars, who examine the make-up and effectiveness of civil society in Egypt, Zaki largely ignores secular feminist associations. His discussion of the status of women is framed into the general discussion of religious and minority rights. Throughout Zaki contrasts the general weakness and political ineffectiveness, that he attributes to the overwhelming majority of associations, to the overall strength of Islamic associations.

Islamic private voluntary associations run major schools, hospitals and charitable organizations. Mosque-associated organizations provide social services such as nurseries, medical clinics and educational centres. The dense network of Islamic organizations and associations has replaced the state in many of its social welfare services (Zaki 1995: 63). Moreover, Islamic associations have benefited from a preferential treatment with regard to authorization and funding by government officials (Zubaida 1992).

A number of scholars have explored Islamist organizations and their role in Egypt's 'civil society' (Marty and Appleby 1993a, 1993b; Zubaida 1992; Zaki 1995). Without minimizing the significance of the rising tide of Islamism, I believe that scholars themselves have been actively, if unwittingly, engaged in muting those groups and individuals that have opposed or reacted to Islamism. While I agree with Zaki that feminist activists represent only a small segment within civil society, such a superficial examination of these groups and their effectiveness reflects the general trend of ignoring women's organizations. First, they are treated in the chapter on minorities and are then marginalized within that chapter in favour of the Copts, who are discussed much more thoroughly. In fact, the seven paltry pages focusing on women really makes the civil society analysed in the book a very male-centred civil society.

The tendency to disregard women's roles and contributions is based on the assumed split between, and gendering of, public and private domains (Pateman 1989; Joseph 1993). In the context of Egyptian women's rights activism this split takes on a reverse expression: *qadaya al-mar'ah* (women's issues), a term widely used to refer to the various forms of discrimination against women, predominantly addresses issues related to the 'public sphere'. It is obvious that many contemporary women activists have internalized the traditional male modernist-nationalist discourse concerning women's rights in the context of the modernization of the nation. Women's political participation, education and work rank high on the agendas of most groups. However, issues touching upon what is perceived to constitute the private sphere, such as women's reproductive rights or violence against women, are widely considered as Egyptian cultural taboos. Only very few women, like those belonging to Al-Mara' Al-Gidida (the New Woman), have taken up these sensitive issues. They have carried out research and campaigns and now try to implement their findings through several projects. Being considered 'radical feminists' at best and as blindly following 'Western agendas' at worst, these activists are actively engaged in the attempt to expand the concepts of *qadaya al-mar'ah* and *huquq al-mar'ah* (woman's rights) and thereby to overcome the forged boundaries of 'the public' and 'the private'.

Conclusion

My current research among contemporary women's organizations and activists suggests that some of the debates, tensions and conflicts of the 1980s have not only been carried over to the 1990s, but have actually developed into a polarization and fragmentation of women's rights activism. For example, the ongoing controversy of how to operate – either as independent women's groups or being affiliated with political parties – has become part of the debates about civil society and democratization.

Another ongoing debate has been the question of whether *qadaya al-mar'ah* (women's issues) constitutes a concern independent of a wider struggle for social justice. Whether conceptualized as *al-haraka al-nissa'iyya* (the women's movement) or *al-haraka al-nassawiyya* (the feminist movement), women's rights activism has increasingly been linked to the debates about *asala* (authenticity) as opposed to *al-hagma al-thaqafiyya* (the [Western] cultural attack).

In these various struggles and debates, Islamists and leftist-nationalists often reveal parallels concerning their rhetoric of 'Western imperialism' and 'the Western conspiracy'. While the goals and motivations of these constituencies certainly oppose each other, in effect Egyptian feminists are often attacked from both sides, accused of paying lip service to 'the West', as well as fostering imperialism by accepting foreign funding.

As I have tried to show throughout this chapter, an attempt to grasp the content of what is actually being opposed involves a disentangling of various interlinked and interspersed debates and issues. For example, discourses about 'the West', whatever form they take and however they are transmitted, reveal much more about contemporary Egypt than what is actually meant by 'the West'. Parallel to orientalist discourses about 'the East', these discourses actually reflect social, economic and political malaises within Egypt, in which, of course, different Western constituencies are often deeply implicated.

The struggle for women's civil rights in Egypt puts those activists who are at the forefront of the battle in a nearly untenable position. Caught between Islamist, government, and nationalist discourses and interests, they are constantly under attack, and often attack one another in their attempts to gain legitimacy and secure resources. Nevertheless, some activists are challenging these homogenizing discourses by constructing new terms of reference. It is within this confrontation that women activists are emerging as a force of democratization in contemporary Egypt.

Notes

1. A 'secular-oriented' tendency refers to the belief in the separation between religion and politics, but does not necessarily denote anti-religious or anti-Islamic positions. Secular-oriented women do not support Shari'a as the main or sole source of legislation; rather they also refer to civil law and human rights conventions, as stipulated by the United Nations, as frames of reference for their struggle.

2. Law 32 restricts the formation and activities of voluntary organizations (e.g. community development associations, village associations, educational and medical charities, women's societies, sporting, art and music societies, and political pressure groups, such as women's or human rights associations) with regard to their fields of activity, number of members allowed, number of organizations within a particular region, record keeping, accounting and funding. Law 32 also gives the government authority to intervene by striking down decisions by the board of directors or even dissolving the entire board. The Law itself has been the object of a human rights campaign in Egypt.

3. The approval of the Interior Ministry is required for public meetings, rallies and protest marches. The Ministry of Social Affairs has the authority to license and dissolve 'private organizations'. Licences may be revoked if such organizations engage in political or religious activities. For example, since 1985 the government has refused to license the Egyptian Organization for Human Rights (EOHR), on the grounds that it is a political organization.

4. Not only did the 1956 constitution and its revised 1963 version declare that all Egyptians are equal regardless of gender, but labour laws were changed to guarantee state sector jobs for all holders of high school diplomas and college degrees irrespective of gender (Hatem 1992: 232). Moreover, in 1956 the state granted women the right to vote and to run for political office. The educational system was reformed to increase enrolment, both for primary

and secondary education which particularly affected female participation in higher education (Ahmed 1992: 210). Hatem has labelled the state's formal or legal or ideological commitment to women's rights as well as informal state policies and programmes which introduce important changes in the productive and reproductive roles of women 'state feminism' (Hatem 1993).

5. Women were often not hired on the grounds that the provision of maternity and child-care leave, stipulated by the progressive laws of the 1950s and 1960s, made their labour expensive.

6. While the notion that foreign governments use financial aid to get access to information or to encourage certain constituencies is not new, in recent years there has been an increased awareness and criticism of foreign research grants given to Egyptian organizations. Financial support for Egyptian research bodies is multi-faceted, extending into the public, private and academic spheres, and touching on a wide range of topics. The scarce Egyptian resources on the one hand, and limited foreign funding on the other have resulted in an atmosphere of competition which breeds rivalry and envy.

References

Abdallah, A. (1994), 'A Case of Compounded Identities,' *Al-Ahram Weekly*. 10–17 November.

Abdel Kader, S. (1987), *Egyptian Women in a Changing Society 1899–1987*, Boulder & London: Lynne Rienner Publishers.

Abu-Lughod, L. (1993), 'Islam and Public Culture: the Politics of Egyptian Television Serials,' *Middle East Report*. January–February: 25–30.

Ahmed, L. (1992), *Women and Gender in Islam*, New Haven and London: Yale University Press.

Al-'Azm, S. (1981), 'Orientalism and Orientalism in Reverse,' *Khamsin*, 8: 5–26.

Badran, M. (1988), 'Dual Liberation: Feminism and Nationalism in Egypt, 1870s–1925,' *Feminist Issues*, Spring 1988, 8 (1): 15–34.

—— (1991), 'Competing Agenda: Feminists, Islam, and the State in Nineteenth and Twentieth Century Egypt,' in D. Kandiyoti ed., *Women, Islam, and the State*, Philadelphia: Temple University Press and London: Macmillan.

—— (1994), 'Gender Activism: Feminists and Islamists in Egypt,' in V. M. Moghadam, ed., *Identity Politics & Women: Cultural Reassertions and Feminisms in International Perspective*, Boulder, San Francisco and Oxford: Westview Press.

—— (1995), *Feminists, Islam, and Nation: Gender and the Making of Modern Egypt*, Princeton, New Jersey: Princeton University Press.

Baron, B. (1994), *The Women's Awakening in Egypt: Culture, Society and the Press*, New Haven and London: Yale University Press.

Berque, J. (1972), *Egypt: Imperialism and Revolution*, London: Faber.

Botman, S. (1987), 'Women's Participation In Radical Egyptian Politics 1939–1952,' in *Women in the Middle East - Khamsin*, London & New Jersey: Zed Books.

Flores, A. (1988), 'Egypt: A New Secularism?' *Middle East Report*, July–August: 27–30.

—— (1993), 'Secularism, Integralism and Political Islam: The Egyptian Debate,' *Middle East Report*, July–August: 32–7.

El-Gawhary, K. (1994), 'An interview with Heba Ra'uf Ezzat,' *MERIP* (Middle East Report), November–December: 26–7)

Graham-Brown, S. (1981), 'Feminism in Egypt: A Conversation with Nawal Sadaawi' in *MERIP Reports*, 95: 24–7.

Hatem, M. (1986), 'The Enduring Alliance of Nationalism and Patriarchy in Muslim Personal Status Laws: The Case of Modern Egypt,' in *Feminist Issues*, 6 (1): 19–43.

—— (1992), 'Economic and Political Liberation in Egypt and the Demise of State Feminism,' *International Journal of Middle East Studies*, 24: 231–51.

—— (1993), 'Toward the Development of Post-Islamist and Post-Nationalist Feminist Discourses in the Middle East,' in J. Tucker, ed., *Arab Women: Old Boundaries, New Frontiers*, Bloomington and Indianapolis: Indiana University Press.

Jayawardena, K. (1986), *Feminism and Nationalism in the Third World*, London & New Jersey: Zed Books.

Joseph, S. (1993), 'Gender and Civil Society: An Interview with Suad Joseph,' *Middle East Report*, July–August: 23–6.

Kandiyoti, D., ed. (1991), *Women, Islam and the State*, Philadelphia: Temple University Press.

Khalifa, I. (1973), *Al-Haraka Al-Nissa'iyah Al-Haditha* (The Modern Women's Movement), Cairo: Dar al-Kuttub.

Khater, A. and Nelson, C. (1988), '*Al-Harakah Al-Nissa'iya*: the Women's Movement and Political Participation In Modern Egypt,' *Women's Studies International Forum*, 11, 5: 465–83.

Khater, A. (1987), 'Egypt Feminism,' *The Middle East*, February 1987: 17–18.

Lotfi Marsot, A. (1978), 'The Revolutionary Gentlewoman in Egypt,' in L. Beck and N. Keddie, eds, *Women In The Muslim World*, Cambridge, Mass. & London: Harvard University Press.

Marty, M.E. & Appleby, R.S. (1993a), *Fundamentalisms And the State: Remaking Politics, Economies, and Militance*, Chicago & London: University of Chicago Press.

—— (1993b), *Fundamentalisms and Society: Reclaiming the Sciences, the Family and Education*, Chicago & London: University of Chicago Press.

Mitchell, T. and Abu-Lughod, L. (1993), 'Questions of Modernity,' *Items*, 47, 4: 79–83.

Nelson, C. (1984), 'Islamic Tradition and Women's Education in Egypt,' *Women & Education,* London: Nichols Publishing Co.: 211–25.

—— (1986), 'The Voices Of Doria Shafik: Feminist Consciousness in Egypt, 1940–1960,' *Feminist Issues,* Fall 1986: 15–31.

—— (1991), 'Biography and Women's History: On Interpreting Doria Shafik,' in N. Keddie and B. Baron, eds, *Women in Middle Eastern History: Shifting Boundaries in Sex and Gender,* New Haven and London: Yale University Press.

Pateman, C. (1989), *The Disorder of Women,* Cambridge: Polity Press.

Philipp, T. (1978), 'Feminism and Nationalist Politics in Egypt,' in L. Beck and N. Keddie, eds, *Women In The Muslim World,* Cambridge, Mass. & London: Harvard University Press.

Al-Sabaki, A. K. B. (1987), *Al-Haraka Al-Nissa'iyah fi Misr bayn al-Thawratayn* (The women's movement in Egypt between the two revolutions 1919–1952), Cairo: Hay'at al-Kitab al-'Amaa.

Shafik, D. (with Abdou, Ibrahim) (1955), *Al-Mar'a Al-Misriyah min al-Faraunah ila al-Yawm* (The Egyptian Woman from the Pharoahs until Today), Cairo: Matba'at Misr.

Shoukrallah, H. (1992), 'The Construction of the Islamic Alternative: Its Impact on Women, Minorities and the Muslim Community,' Unpublished Master's Thesis. The Institute of Development Studies and The University of Sussex, Brighton.

—— (1994), 'The Impact of the Islamic Movement in Egypt,' *Feminist Review,* 47, Summer 1994: 15–32.

Sid-Ahmed, M. (1994), 'Israel and Middle Easternism,' *Al-Ahram Weekly,* 10–16 November.

Toubia, N., ed. (1988), *Women of the Arab World: The Coming Challenge,* London: Zed Books.

Vatikiotis, P.J. (1985), *The History of Egypt: From Muhammad Ali to Mubarak,* Baltimore, MD: John Hopkins University Press.

Zaki, M. (1994), 'The Denial of a Coptic Minority is a Dangerous Delusion,' *Civil Society,* 29: 26–9.

—— (1995), *Civil Society & Democratization in Egypt, 1981–1994,* Cairo : Dar Al-Kutub.

Zubaida, S. (1992), 'Islam, the State & Democracy: Contrasting Conceptions of Society in Egypt,' *Middle East Report,* November–December: 2–10.

9

From Gender Equality to Female Subjugation: The Changing Agendas of Women's Groups in Kuwait

Haya al-Mughni

In Kuwait, women's groups like all voluntary associations operate under the state aegis. Throughout its existence, the state has attempted to manipulate women's groups to maintain its stability and thereby its permanence. The emergence of feminist groups was initially encouraged to promote modernism. These were later replaced by conservative groups to reinforce the patriarchal structure of society. The depletion of economic resources resulting from the Gulf War generated an even more conservative policy to control women's lives.

Kuwait's voluntary associations cannot operate outside the state's institutional framework. In this context, strict administrative and legislative provisions regulate voluntary groups' activities, limiting their ability to pursue their own interests and influence social change in ways likely to conflict with the interests of the state. The state also retains the decision-making power over who ultimately controls an association. The current control of women's groups by elite and upper-class women is by no means accidental. Linked by common interests, the state and women from privileged classes worked to exclude women from lower classes to hold leadership positions and/or create associations. Moreover, the patriarchal social structures regulating Kuwait's civil society restrict women's participation within state-controlled groups. This leaves Kuwaiti women with little autonomy to organize themselves to pursue strategic gender interests.

Against this background, this chapter will examine the state's changing policies, analysing their impact on women's groups' activities and discourses. It will focus on the period from early 1960 to 1995 as it saw the development of a women's movement for equal rights and the Gulf War, with the latter resulting in much greater control over women.

Family, State and Civil Society in Kuwait

As J. E. Peterson indicates, 'Gulf society remains governed by the central importance of the family, as well as the subordination of the interests of the individual to it' (1990: 307). In Kuwait, the state does not compete with the family institution for control over individuals. Neither does it seek to weaken primary ties and kinship allegiance to enhance the citizens' loyalties. The state and the family represent two sides of the same coin. Households members' submission to the household head is comparable to that of citizens' submission to their head of state (Tétreault and al-Mughni 1995a). The state could be regarded as an extension of the patriarchal authority within the family. Since its emergence in the early 1960s the state has been omnipresent in every aspect of citizens' lives through the provision of basic services including education, employment, social security, health and welfare. The state is also heavily involved in the regulation of marriage, sexuality and gender relations.

Citizens have attempted to carve out a framework where they could evolve autonomously, a civil society including voluntary associations, *diwaniyyas*, cooperative societies and an outspoken press (see Ghabra 1991; Hicks and Al-Najjar 1995). Relationships between the state and civil society have been controversial and, at times, cooperative. The kinship-organized state needs civil society to survive. It has therefore worked to win over social groups and influence the direction of social movements rather than neutralize public life.

State interference in civil society is not absolute. It is limited by the political culture characterizing Kuwaiti society. The *diwaniyya*, a semi-public gathering taking place in the home, operates outside state control. The *diwaniyya* turns into a forum for political opposition when civil liberties are suspended. In 1989 the pro-democracy movement, aimed at restoring the parliamentary life which collapsed with the dissolution of the 1986 National Assembly, grew out of the *diwaniyya*. Adapted from the pre-oil era, this traditional institution – to use Tetreault's terminology (1993) – is 'a protected space' capable of resisting and checking state power. Although some prominent women have recently created their *diwaniyya*, the institution remains part of the male political culture controlled by rigid patterns of gender segregation making women's entry into men's space (the *diwaniyya*) a violation of cultural norms. The mosque is another influential institution where Kuwaiti women play a marginal role. In the late 1970s the mosque was instrumental in the resurgence of political Islam. Unlike the *diwaniyya*, the mosque is however not entirely outside state control. The Friday sermons (*khutba*) and religious classes taking place in the mosques are strictly under the state's surveillance and carefully monitored to prevent them from becoming the cause of political discontent.

State control is more rigidly exercised in the realm of associational life. This includes professional and cultural groups; welfare, educational and religious organizations; recreational clubs; women's, music and drama societies. These associations, which fall under the rubric of 'Public Welfare Organizations' (*Jamiyat nafa'am*), are governed by legislation ensuring ultimate state control over their activities (see Hicks and Al-Najjar 1995). Law 24 of 1962 (partially amended in 1965) gives the Ministry of Social Affairs and Labour the full authority to license an association, dissolve its elected board, or terminate it entirely. Equally, the ministry is legally bound to provide premises and funds to support groups' activities. In addition, associational groups must have an elected board, a written constitution and a paid membership. They are also strictly prohibited from engaging in any activity, be it political or other, likely to endanger the stability of the state.

By 1995, fifty-five voluntary associations were officially registered. Of these, five were women's associations. The first women's voluntary organizations were created in 1963 and for almost two decades remained the only groups to speak and act on behalf of Kuwaiti women.

The Emerging State and the Feminist Challenge

The 1960s political climate was propitious to the creation of the first women's voluntary organizations. State-building, combined with rapid modernization, spurred women's emancipation – namely their education and involvement in the public realm. Women's integration in the national economy was particularly needed to increase Kuwaiti participation in the labour force and reduce the country's dependence on foreign labour. The newly emerging state made education available to women from primary school through university. As a result, the female literacy rate increased from 27 per cent in 1965 to 85 per cent in 1993. Similarly, women's participation in the labour force increased from 2 per cent to above 25 per cent in the same period, reducing the state's dependence on foreign workers, in services such as health, education and social work (Shah 1994; Shah and al-Qudsi 1990).

Nevertheless, putting an end to the traditional practice of female seclusion was not an easy task for the newly emerging state. According to Abdullah (1973), the concern for family honour was so ingrained that, when the first comprehensive census was conducted in 1953, male household heads refused to disclose any information about female members. Men from leading merchant families were the first to allow their women to take off the veil, to study abroad and to engage in paid employment. Others gradually – albeit reluctantly – followed. Changes in women's status among the merchant class also resulted from women's persistent claim for emancipation. In 1961 merchant-class women refused to wear the veil in public even if this meant renouncing their careers. This forced the government to allow women to work without the veil (Nath 1978). These women had earlier burned their veil in the schoolyard causing widespread outrage, and wrote to various local journals and magazines demanding the right to education and employment (Freeth 1956; al-Mughni 1993).

The newly emerging state saw in the creation of women's societies an important means to producing the required changes in women's status through the dissemination of an ideal of womanhood, namely the educated career woman who dutifully participates in state-building. The founders of the first women's groups were educated, held civil servant jobs and dressed in Western-style. They represented the new generation of Kuwaiti women anxious to evolve in the modern world, leaving behind the secluded existence within the windowless courtyards. The Women's Cultural and Social Society (WCSS) was created in 1963 by educated merchant-class women whose rebellion against what they regarded as 'backward' traditions and customs set an example for others (Nath 1978; Sultan 1976). This was precisely what the Arab Women's Development Society (AWDS) – later renamed the Society for the Advancement of the Family – sought to achieve, namely women's liberation from 'backward' traditions. Composed mostly of women from the rising middle strata, the AWDS was created in 1963 by Nouria al-Sadani. She was in her early twenties, working for the Kuwait Broadcasting Station.

Until the late 1960s women's groups did not represent a threat to the patriarchal state. The WCSS directed its efforts towards philanthropic and social welfare activities, extending women's traditional role of support and nurturing into the public sphere. The AWDS aimed at raising women's awareness about the importance of education and work. In 1967 the group opened the first nursery in Kuwait to allow working mothers to join the labour force. A few years later, they organized the First Kuwaiti Woman's Day. It became an annual celebration designed to honour women's professional achievements and role in state-building.

By the early 1970s a radical shift in women's public discourse began to emerge. This was precipitated by several factors. The most important one was the growth of the feminist movement in the Arab world. In 1964 the AWDS had joined the General Federation of Arab Women set up in 1944 by the leading Egyptian feminist, Huda Shaarawi. Egyptian feminists had already begun their struggle to end gender discrimination and improve women's social status. They had achieved some significant gains that Kuwaiti women had only started addressing. Discrimination against Kuwaiti women was widespread as they had few rights and were treated as second-class citizens. They had neither the right to vote nor were they fully entitled to similar state benefits and protection as men. Another factor was the growth of Arab nationalism as a political movement advocating democracy and individual rights. The secular and nationalist groups in Kuwait were receptive to the issue of women's rights. Although they did not advocate full gender equality, these groups were nevertheless in favour of extending some rights to women, in particular the right to political participation.

The first Kuwaiti Women's Conference organized by the AWDS in December 1971 provided the impetus to the development of the women's rights movement. The conference gathered more than 100 women from different social strata, providing them with a valuable opportunity to share their experiences as mothers and paid workers. At the close of the conference, the participants unanimously agreed to put their grievances in writing to the National Assembly. They demanded political rights; equality in all fields of employment; the appointment of women as special attorneys to draft family law; the provision of child allowances to married women; and the restriction of polygamy. Thereafter, a forceful campaign was launched to win public support for women's rights issues. This included intensive public debates, press conferences and lobbying. Alliance with the vocal nationalist groups was also forged to give the campaign for equal rights political weight. Here, women activists politicized gender and brought women's issues into the mainstream of domestic politics. This was the first challenge to male prerogatives and state policies.

In 1973 the AWDS succeeded in forcing the all-male National Assembly to discuss an equal rights bill, provoking the stormiest debates in its history. Opponents of the bill, who formed a majority, used religion to justify male superiority. They argued that Islam gave women *certain* rights but not *all* the rights that men enjoy. According to an observer, the bill was unlikely to pass unless government ministers voted with the supporters of women's rights who, despite their minority status, had dominated the debate.[1] Although the government was ready to ease the employment restrictions imposed on women, it felt particularly concerned about the political implications of women's suffrage. Hence, the National Assembly avoided voting on the bill, referring it to the assembly's Legal Affairs Committee for 'study'.

The fact that the assembly made no decision on the equal rights bill and kept it idle on the political agenda was not seen as a defeat by women activists but rather as a victory. For al-Sadani, 'the mere discussion of women's rights issues was a good result in itself, one that should be followed by more debates in the near future'.[2] Having politicized gender issues, al-Sadani was determined to keep women's interests at the forefront of political debate. After the hearings, she delivered a lecture to Kuwait University's female students where she emphasized:

> These are our rights and we would keep fighting for them until they are granted to us. Our rights would not be lost because a group of bigoted men have ganged up to keep us at the bottom of the ladder in society.[3]

However, Kuwaiti women were divided on the issue of their citizenship rights. Many women, in particular upper-class ones, did not support the demand for the extension of political and civil rights to women. Others were in favour of women's suffrage, but opposed changes in the traditional gender relations (Sultan 1976). In 1975 a new women's group, Nadi al-Fatat (Girls' Club), was formed, initiated and supported by al-Sadani. Although predominantly upper class, the new group was fully supportive of the campaign for equal rights. Together with AWDS, they launched a series of conferences and seminars to increase interest in and support for what many began to fear as a threatening movement likely to bring political chaos and social instability.

By the mid-1970s, as Rumaihi pointed out, 'The superficial "modern" liberation of women turned out to be a bubble that soon burst' (1986: 123). A counter-movement began, encouraged by those whose interests were at stake because of women's claims for self-determination. The government moved towards protecting the patriarchal family and women's subordinate role within it. It urged the media and concerned government departments to 'combat all that threatens the existence of the family and distorts the character of solidarity between its members'.[4] In 1978 the state's official Islamization was declared and the Personal Status Law was drafted without women's involvement or consultation in its drafting (see Tétreault and al-Mughni 1995a). The same year saw increased state intervention to reduce the influence of the secular opposition. The government dissolved the elected boards of many of the voluntary associations controlled by the left and nationalist groups and appointed new ones (Ghabra 1991). Al-Sadani was also removed from the AWDS leadership under the pretext, never proven, of an alleged financial irregularity. When the presidency was handed over to a female government official AWDS members declined any involvement in its activities and the organization was soon dissolved.

With the dissolution of AWDS, women's mobilization to achieve some form of autonomy from patriarchal control and gain citizenship rights was brought to an end. The 1980s saw the emergence of religious women's groups seeking to reinforce female submission. A new woman emerged: veiled, puritanical and anti-feminist.

The Rise of Religious Women's Groups and the Domestication of Women

The proliferation of religious groups was encouraged by the government (Crystal 1992; Hicks and al-Najjar 1995). Of the thirteen voluntary organizations set up in the early 1980s, five were Islamic groups. Two of them were religious women's organizations: Bayader al-Salam (Threshing Field of Peace) and al-Riaya al-Islamiya (Islamic Care Society). The latter was created in 1982 by the wife of the Crown Prince and Prime Minister, Sheikha Latifa Al Fahed Al Sabah. It was given the former AWDS headquarters, marking the end of the short-lived women's rights movement. Licensed a year earlier, Bayader al-Salam was also formed by upper-class women who wanted to save the society from moral decay and the Western values preached by AWDS.

The new religious women's groups played a powerful role in marginalizing feminist voices as well as reshaping the content of women's public discourse to reinforce female submission. Emphasis was placed on the *duties* of women in society as a means of diverting the average Kuwaiti woman from feminist concerns. Women were defined as having a moral duty to strengthen family ties, raise good children and defend the Kuwaiti society's traditions. A whole body of discourse was devised to justify the importance of women's domestic role. Faced with increasing expenditure, general public apathy, and a weakening of family ties, the government needed to bring women back to their traditional role, making them 'better' mothers and conscientious housewives. By the mid-1980s it began to urge women's groups to take an active interest in women's role as housewives to guide them 'towards a sensible level of domestic consumption and the firm establishment of the society's values in childhood education'.[5]

As Longva (1993) points out, the reproduction of a nation and its traditions were at stake. Women's involvement in the labour force increased their reliance on foreign nannies, causing widespread concern over national identity and children's loyalty to their Arab-Islamic culture (Hijab 1988). The mother-child relationship and child-rearing became important issues for all women's groups. The WCSS first addressed the problem of foreign nannies and, as early as 1975, set up a nursery to keep Kuwaiti children away from the influence of foreign maids. Bayadar al-Salam gave women and children year-round religious lectures (*muntadas*), courses in Koran reading (*tawjid*) and lessons about the Prophet's life (*sirat al-nabi*). For Bayadar's leaders, children are 'the seeds of today and the trees of tomorrow'. Thus a proper education within an Islamic environment would ensure their moral discipline and fear of God.

The new women's groups aimed at restoring a moral order, assigning women the role of the guardians of society, its values and most fundamental unit, namely the family. The 1980s slogan 'Good women mean good nations', which gained widespread popularity, was specifically constructed to reinforce the belief that society could only prosper if women were righteous and obedient. This was also raised to bring women to sacrifice their gender interests for much broader national interests. The ideal woman was depicted as a selfless creature, a caring mother and a virtuous civil servant who subordinates her interests to social order. Bayadar al-Salam advised women to wear the veil, be chaste and virtuous. The Islamic Care Society introduced classes in embroidery, dressmaking and oriental cookery as a means of linking Kuwaiti women with their lost past. Although they pursued separate and different activities, the new groups sought to discipline women as well as reshape their social roles so as to end earlier feminist calls for individual rights and gender equality.

Elite and upper-class women had every reason to fear female autonomy. In particular, this would imply locating women outside the family as independent individuals with self-determination in matters of marriage, divorce and personal careers. These women perceived such autonomy as a threat to their political interests because they derive considerable power and prestige from their positions within the family. The family mediates access to resources and social privileges.

The emphasis placed upon women's domestic role served the rationalization of the asymmetrical gender relations in society. It also allowed to minimize the call for gender equality, making gender differences a logical consequence of biological differences. In 1981 a parliamentary deputy, Ahmad al-Tukhaim, presented a bill to the National Assembly requesting amendment of the electoral law to allow women to vote but not hold office. The biological argument was then used to justify women's exclusion from formal political participation. A *fatwa* (legal ruling) was issued by the Ministry of Awqaf and Islamic Affairs declaring that 'The nature of the electoral process befits men, who are endowed with ability and expertise; it is not permissible for women to recommend or nominate other women or men' (Hijab 1988: 151).

Kuwaiti women remained openly divided on the issue of political rights. While the WCSS and Nadi al-Fatat campaigned for women's suffrage, neither Bayadar al-Salam nor the Islamic Care Society supported such right. More than 1,000 women signed a petition thanking the National Assembly for rejecting the bill stating that 'True believing Muslim women support the rejection [of the bill] and disapprove of any debauchery. We ask that the debate on this matter be closed for ever. We have great faith in our country and in our men.'[6] Women from different social strata had joined the religious movement, preaching, lobbying and organizing for the Islamic cause. They rejected what AWDS had called for and supported the return of the veil and with it, the virtuous woman.

Involvement in the Islamic movement had, paradoxically, empowered women. It gave them an active role in the public sphere as *da'iyas* (preachers) and enabled them to gain a much wider access to religious organizations and institutions which were hitherto confined to men. Through their role as law and order enforcers, women gained power over others, not only over women and children but also over men who defy religious teachings and beliefs.

Post-war Period and the Rising Power of Elite Women

In 1991, when the Gulf War resulted in the liberation of Kuwait from seven months of Iraqi occupation, women's protesting voices, censored and marginalized in the 1980s, re-emerged. Kuwaiti women married to foreigners organized themselves to put pressure on the government to provide protection and rights to their husbands and children. They used the premises of the Environmental Protection Society (EPS) as their headquarters and demanded, among other things, government housing and permanent residence for their husbands and children. On the other hand, demand for women's suffrage became more vocal. In 1992, during the elections for the National Assembly, more than 100 women staged protests at polling stations demanding voting rights. One of the main arguments put forward by the supporters of such right was that Kuwaiti women shouldered many responsibilities during the occupation, proving they were mature enough for formal political participation (Shah 1994). Kuwaiti women had, indeed, played an active role in the liberation activities. Many participated in armed resistance and died in prison camps as a result of brutal torture at the hands of Iraqi soldiers.

Women's involvement in the liberation activities did not lead to gender equality. In 1994, Kuwait signed the Convention on the Elimination of All Forms of Discrimination Against Women (CEDAW) with certain reservations. Objections were made to the provisions allowing women political rights, the right to bestow their nationality upon their children and equal rights in matters of child custody (Mayer, 1995). Despite evidence of deterioration in the condition of Kuwaiti women married to foreigners, the government was reluctant to modify its discriminatory policies. In 1993 the all-male board of the EPS prevented Kuwaiti women married to foreigners from using its premises. The same year, the government made public the decision of the Council of Ministers to dissolve all 'unlicensed popular committees' (Hicks and Al-Najjar 1995: 188). This left the Kuwaiti women married to foreigners with no choice other than seeking refuge in one of the existing women's societies, adding further strains to the group's activities and autonomy.

The politics of female marginalization which begun in the 1980s was set in motion. This time, the ideal of womanhood became the caring mother devoted to taking care of the children at home. Kuwait emerged from the Gulf War with a depleted economy, reducing the government's ability to provide welfare services (Crusoe and Kemp 1991; Crystal 1992). This was further exacerbated by an over-staffed public sector and a high level of unemployment among youth, whose rights to work are constitutionally guaranteed. Bringing women out of the workforce was seen as part of a solution to the country's economic and social problems. The Islamist groups blamed the rise in child delinquency and divorce on women's participation in the labour force. In 1995, an Islamist deputy, Khaled Al-Adhwa, submitted a bill proposing the amendment of Article 17 of the Social Security Law to allow working mothers to retire after fifteen years of service regardless of their age. The bill was passed and sanctioned by the government. This was justified in terms of 'the interests of the family and society whereby a mother can devote herself to child care' thereby reducing reliance on foreign nannies whose influence on children can be hazardous.[7] Few women protested; while many welcomed the amendment. As one put it, 'We do not see in it any devaluation of our role in society. Women's role in the family is fundamental to the country's progress as it is upon them that rests the responsibility of raising the future generation.'[8]

The view that women are primarily responsible for the maintenance of an orderly society is shared by all women's groups. In 1994 the women's groups joined forces to coordinate their activities and promote common objectives. They formed the Federation of Kuwaiti Women's Associations (FKWA) and elected the Prime Minister's wife its president. The objectives of the FKWA were defined as 'raising women's awareness of their religion, their identity and their role in the family'.[9] The government recognized the FKWA as the sole representative of Kuwaiti women's groups outside Kuwait. This gave elite women full control over the activities and symbols of women's groups, and the exclusive right to speak officially on behalf of Kuwaiti women.

The Women's Cultural and Social Society (WCSS) did not join the FKWA which included Bayadar al-Salam, the Islamic Care Society, Nadi al-Fatat and the Volunteer Women's Association for Community Services (licensed in 1991). After the war, the WCSS had been trying hard to change its former image as an organization entirely devoted to charity work. In 1993 it elected a new president, Adela al-Sayer, and recruited new members from the educated middle strata. They adopted the cause of Kuwaiti women married to foreigners, demanding that they be given the right to pass their citizenship on to their children. In 1994 they organized the First Post Liberation Conference on Women's Role in Cultural, Social and Economic Development which brought women's rights issues back to the fore. However, the creation of the FKWA isolated the WCSS and reduced its authority. This also left it particularly vulnerable to criticisms and attacks by those seeking to undermine the women's movement for equal rights.

Differences in the articulation of women's issues resulted in increased scepticism about what Kuwaiti women want. The FKWA opts for a narrow interpretation of rights using the Shari'a as its legal framework. As one leader pointed out, 'God-given rights are more important than any other rights . . . When Kuwaiti women say they want political rights, I say they should first understand their rights within the Shari'a.'[10] The issue of women's citizenship rights is cast aside as unimportant and incompatible with Shari'a principles of differential gender responsibilities. This group's leaders urge Kuwaiti women to press for the implementation of the Shari'a and maintain family stability, ignoring the many social and economic problems faced by women in their everyday lives. They blame women – not the state – for existing social problems. By contrast, the WCSS concept of rights is based on entitlements carrying egalitarian implications for gender. Yet, despite such differences in the conceptualization of women's rights, the WCSS remains committed to protecting the traditional patriarchal family and maintaining social order. A wide range of the group's activities are community-oriented, entailing the provision of financial support to needy families and the implementation of state policies. Embedded in this orientation is a specific view of a woman's role in society. As noted earlier, Kuwaiti women see themselves first and foremost as mothers responsible for future generations. The ideal society aspired to by WCSS is one 'in which women enjoy equality and civil liberty'. At the same time, they are protected and supported in 'their mission as mothers, wives and paid-workers'.[11]

Family unity is essential for both the WCSS and the FKWA. The Fourth UN Conference on Women had unleashed a furore never seen before in Kuwaiti society, with the Islamists denouncing the all-female gathering as 'subversive' and a Western ploy seeking to destroy the values of the Muslim community. During the conference, Kuwaiti women's groups joined other anti-feminist groups to stage protests against abortion, gay rights and sexual liberties that they feared would lead to the decline of the traditional family and spawn new social problems. Aligning themselves with Kuwaiti officials, the FKWA made it clear that they will not allow the implementation of 'anything contradictory' to the Shari'a or to Kuwaiti society's traditions and culture. In addition, the leaders cautioned Kuwaiti women to 'earn their rights from society and not from international conferences'.[12] The 'headstrong attitude' displayed by the Kuwaiti women's groups was praised by the religious groups and the government.

Conclusion

The state co-opted women's groups, transforming them from a threat into a vital support for its existence. The dissolution of the AWDS; the lack of a public platform allowing Kuwaiti women married to foreigners and others from lower classes to voice their concerns; the creation of the Federation of the Kuwaiti Women's Associations headed by the Prime Minister's wife demonstrate the degree of state penetration in associational life and the constraints to women's gender activism.

As we have seen, in the early 1960s it was in the state's interests to promote women's emancipation to meet the growing demand for labour. Yet, this move proved far more threatening than anticipated. Not only did emancipated women challenge patriarchy but also endangered the traditional foundations of power and legitimacy as they sought to break away from the traditional gender roles providing stability and order to the kinship-organized society. The closure of the AWDS points to the anxiety and fears of the patriarchal society over women's autonomy and independent status. This anxiety is shared by elite and upper-class women – hence the contradictions in the WCSS's brand of feminism which, on the one hand, advocates political and civil rights for women and, on the other, opposes the right of women to decide on matters affecting their reproductive health and sexuality.

Alliance with elite and upper-class women made it possible for the state to maintain control over women's lives and prevent female disobedience to social norms. Under the label of religion and cultural authenticity, women's submission was reinforced while deviations from established values and norms were punished. In a striking similarity with the right-wing women's movement in the United States (see Klatch 1994), Kuwaiti women's groups sought to reinforce the family's moral authority to maintain the status quo. They are also strongly opposed to women's full independence from patriarchal control, which would disrupt women's role as producers of kinship relations. Hence, although they deal with specific women's issues, their central concern remains the community, its stability and security.

Kuwaiti women's groups must not be seen as mere pawns of official policies, seeking solely to exert control over women's lives. The coalition between groups, the distinct divisions betraying the ambivalence of women's gender activism, and the search for control over women's public discourse are also part of the power struggle between elite and merchant-class women. The WCSS symbolizes the aspirations of the liberal merchant class which pioneered women's emancipation and whose class interests had historically conflicted with those of the Ruling Family (see Crystal 1990).

Notes

1. *Kuwait Times*, 7 December 1973.
2. Quoted in *The Progress of Kuwaiti Women for 11 Years through the Arab Women's Development Society*, AWDS publication, Kuwait n.d.: 77.

3. *Kuwait Times*, 6 December 1973.
4. Kuwait Ministry of Planning, *al-Siyassah al-Ijtima'ya fi Araba' Sanawat* (Social Policy in Four Years), June 1975.
5. Kuwait Ministry of Planning, *The Five Year Development Plan 1985/86–1989/90*, Part I: 56.
6. Quoted in al-Qatan, *Women in Islam*: 149–50.
7. *Kuwait Al-Youm*, 221, 27 August 1995.
8. *Al-Watan*, 2 September 1995.
9. *Al-Qabas*, 13 July 1995.
10. *Arab Times*, 3 September 1995.
11. *Al-Anba'a*, 12 September 1995.
12. *Arab Times*, 30 September 1995.

References

Abdullah, M.H. (1973), *Al-Haraka al-Adabiya fi al-Kuwayt* (The Cultural Movement in Kuwait), Kuwait: Rabitat al-Udaba'.

Crystal, J. (1992), *Kuwait: The Transformation of an Oil State*, Boulder & San Francisco: Westview Press.

—— (1990), *Oil and Politics in the Gulf: Rulers and Merchants in Kuwait and Qatar*, Cambridge: Cambridge University Press.

Crusoe, J. and Kemp, P. (1991), *Kuwait: Rebuilding A Country*, Meed Profile 6, London: Emap Business Information Ltd.

Freeth, Z. (1956), *Kuwait was my Home*, London: George Allen & Unwin.

Ghabra, S. (1994), 'Democratization in a Middle Eastern State: Kuwait,1993,' *Middle East Policy*, 3, 1.

—— (1991), 'Voluntary Associations in Kuwait: The Foundations of a New System,' *Middle East Journal*, 45, 2.

Hicks, N. and Al-Najjar, G. (1995), 'The Utility of Tradition: Civil Society in Kuwait,' in A. R. Norton, ed., *Civil Society in the Middle East*, Vol.1, New York: E.J.Brill.

Hijab, N. (1988), *Womanpower: The Arab Debate on Women at Work*, Cambridge: Cambridge University Press.

Klatch, R. (1994), 'Women of the New Right in the United States: Family, Feminism, and Politics,' in V. M. Moghadam, ed., *Identity Politics and Women: Cultural Reassertions and Feminism in International Perspective*, Boulder & San Francisco: Westview Press.

Longva, N. A. (1993), 'Kuwait and Its Migrant Workers: Exclusion and Dominance in a Plural Society,' unpublished Ph.D. thesis, University of Oslo.

Mayer, A. E. (1995), 'Rhetorical Strategies and Official Policies on Women's Rights: The Merits and Drawbacks of the New World Hypocrisy,' in M. Afkhami, ed., *Faith and Freedom: Women's Human Rights in the Muslim World*, London: I. B. Tauris.

al-Mughni, H. (1993), *Women in Kuwait: The Politics of Gender*, London: Saqi Books.

Nath, K. (1978), 'Education and Employment among Kuwaiti Women,' in L. Beck and N. Keddie, eds, *Women in the Muslim World*, Cambridge, Mass.: Harvard University Press.

Peterson, J. E. (1989), 'The Political Status of Women in the Arab Gulf States,' *Middle East Journal*, 43, 1.

—— (1990), 'Change and Continuity in Arab Gulf Society,' in C. Davies, ed., *After the War: Iran, Iraq and the Arab Gulf*, Chichester: Carden Publications Ltd.

al-Qatan, A. (1987), *Al-Mara'a fi al-Islam* (Women in Islam), Kuwait: Maktabat al-Sindus.

Rumaihi, M. (1986), *Beyond Oil*, London: Saqi Books.

Shah, N. M. (1994), 'Changing Roles of Kuwaiti Women in Kuwait: Implications for Fertility,' paper presented at the WCSS Conference on Women's Role in Cultural, Social, and Economic Development', Kuwait.

Shah N. M and al-Qudsi, S. (1990), 'Female Work Roles in a Traditional Oil Economy: Kuwait,' in R. Frank, I. Serageldin, and Sorkin, eds, *Female Labour Force Participation: Research in Human Capital and Development*, vol.6, Baltimore.

Sultan N. (1976), 'The Professional Kuwaiti Woman vis-à-vis the Situation of Women,' paper presented at A.A.U.G. Ninth Annual Conference, New York.

Tétreault, M. (1993), 'Civil Society in Kuwait: Protected Spaces and Women's Rights,' *Middle East Journal*, 47, 2.

Tétreault, M. and al-Mughni, H. (1995a), 'Gender, Citizenship, and Nationalism in Kuwait,' *British Journal of Middle Eastern Studies*, 22, 1 & 2.

—— (1995b), 'Modernization and its Discontents: State and Gender in Kuwait,' *Middle East Journal*, 49, 3.

10

Women Organized in Groups: Expanding the Terms of the Debate

Nancy Lindisfarne

This project began from the particular: when two Harasiis women started to make woollen tasselled keyrings to help local men find keys dropped in soft Omani sand. The setbacks they suffered in making key holders for sale to tourists came later. Officials from the Ministry of Social Affairs of the Sultanate obstructed the women's receipt of a UNDP grant, refusing to recognize their cooperative as a legal entity on the grounds that

> these illiterate, nomadic pastoral women were like children. They needed to be supervised by the government, as a child is supervised by its father. They were simply not modern or civilized enough to accept the responsibility of being a formal association. They were vulnerable to exploitation and thus it was the government's duty to protect them . . . and at the right time set up and run a craft-type income-generating activity for them but directed by men in government (Introduction, pp. 6–7).

The limits on the autonomy experienced by the Harasiis women, and the official reasons given for the gendered discrimination they experienced frame the problematic for *Organizing Women: Formal and Informal Women's Groups in the Middle East.*

In their introduction, Dawn Chatty and Annika Rabo tackle four key issues pertaining to the organization of women in the Middle East. They consider the relevance of Islam, post-colonial government, rural/urban migration and the relation of centre to periphery and, fourthly, the characteristics of top-down development planning in the region. Their aim is to consider the range of social and legal factors which support or inhibit formal and informal groups of women in specific Middle Eastern communities.

Such a goal is insistently comparative, requiring cross-cultural materials and historical data on specific communities to be analysed within a social science framework. It is also ambitious and ambiguous. Its richness derives from the range and complexity of its conception and the ways such a project anticipates new theoretical and methodological questions and further detailed ethnographic studies.

Three new directions for study strike me as particularly promising. These concern how gendered and other differences are produced; the relation between gender and social class, which is little explored in Middle Eastern ethnography; and an anthropology of organizations. Not that these three areas are easy analytically to separate. Consider the following questions which are raised, directly or indirectly, by each chapter of this volume.

To what extent are women's organizations ethnographically discrete from those of men, or from men as individual actors? How might we theorize people's experience of gendered separation, seclusion or segregation? When are gendered markers, as opposed to those of class or sect, socially significant? How is a notion like 'organizing' understood and evaluated locally. How are different degrees of formality and informality of organization experienced and labelled by participants? How do women's groupings differ in their patterns of leadership, their longevity, their explicit aims and the advantages and disadvantages attributed to them locally?

When a collection of articles raises such a range of intriguing and important questions, it becomes appropriate to examine the issues from another point of view. In this concluding chapter, I seek to expand the terms of the debate. I begin with a brief introductory section which suggests some characteristic problems, and possible goals, of comparative social science. My interest is in finding reliable ways of asking questions which will be productive of new, and surprising, ideas about women organizing in groups.

In a second section, I describe briefly aspects of my own field research into women's organizations in the Middle East.[1] (I use the term 'Middle East' in the same way as Dale Eickelman (1989)). In the ethnographic examples I offer, my theoretical premises are processual, and my focus is on pluralities of identity and the fluidity of organizational forms which define women's participation in women-only groups and networks. In part three, I suggest that an emphasis on process is another way of challenging the unexamined premises and analytical dichotomies – such as women and men, public and private, or orthodox and heterodox Islams – which even now all too often dominate discussions of gender in the region. Then in a final section, I return to the articles in the present collection to pose a series of open-ended questions anticipating further research.

Liberal Circles and Social Science Rhetorics

Any topic for social investigation, such as women organizing in groups in the Middle East, requires us to interrogate carefully our terms of reference. What are the criteria which distinguish the Middle East, or the Arab Middle East, from other regions? What are the heuristic advantages of focusing on women-only groups? And what, in fact, do we mean by 'organizing' or, indeed, 'groups'? As we shall see, the answers to such preliminary questions are surprisingly complex. Moreover, they are answers which may tell us more about ourselves than about women organizing in groups in the Middle East.

Indeed, with such a topic, which is hedged round with potent orientalist and sexist biases, it is perhaps not surprising that scholars have adopted another set of premises to offset or counteract the first: about the benefits, for women, of democratic forms of government, secular, or civil, society and the spread of global feminism. Not that these latter premises are unexpected or necessarily contentious. However, when they are presented uncritically or polemically, scholarship suffers and social scientists are all too likely to produce the kind of circular arguments Fredrik Barth has recently described (1996). Barth spoke of social scientists' fondness for self-serving formulations in which the analytical framework and the social configuration to be explained are isomorphic. For instance, the notion 'structure' has been used to describe the patterns which it was meant to explain. Or, 'norm' has been used to label those aspects of social experience distinguished as 'norms'!

Of course, a degree of circularity is an inevitable aspect of the weak functionalism implicit in all social science. However, when social scientists rely on grossly circular arguments, they seem often to be avoiding unwelcome intellectual or political truths. Indeed, tedious, obfuscating academic prose may be the price an author pays for personal comfort. Stylistically, it reinforces the status quo, and when redolent with rhetorical certitude or based on strongly functionalist arguments, it may obscure the sources and implications of a particular theoretical stance.

I have written elsewhere about anthropological ethics and responsibility, suggesting, as many others have done before me, that we stand to learn far more about ourselves and others when we make our political interests explicit (see, e.g. Cesara 1982: 210 ff.; Lindisfarne-Tapper 1992;

Lindisfarne 1996). Another way of reaching the same place is to focus on the practice of 'naturalization'.

One way of defining social anthropology is as the study of those occasions when anthropologists and others make concrete or reify social relations. It is a definition which obliges anthropologists to attend to the rhetoric of everyday life and insists that processes of reification are always political: that they are attributes of discourses which create and sustain difference and inequality.

Defining anthropology in this way has two important consequences for method and theory. First, it obliges anthropologists to listen to local voices (both our own and those of the people with whom we work); to consider local idioms and rhetoric for their nuances and polyphony, as well as for contradictions *and* those occasions when reification takes place. Secondly, it requires anthropologists to focus on those moments when, through naming and labelling, the fluid and endlessly subtle changing relations between human beings are made to seem eternal, unalterable and incontrovertible. In short, it is a definition which insists that anthropologists study social processes in terms of 'naturalization' and how, in any particular setting, a naturalizing discourse may disguise the political agenda of the speaker.

Women's Organizations – Preconditions

In the mid-1960s, I did anthropological fieldwork among the women of the Shahsevan, tribally-organized pastoralists living in northwestern Azerbaijan. My writing then concerned the social activities and relationships which were the basis of what I then, in those pre-women's movement days, called a 'women's subsociety'. My aim was explicitly comparative (see N. Tapper 1968, 1978; see also R. Tapper 1979). I intended that my analysis suggest conditions under which similar women's subsocieties might be identified elsewhere.

Shahsevan women took part in two definite spheres of social activity. One was based on camps, separate localized groups of households, and the other was based on the *kheyr-u-sharr* relations which bring together women from different localized camps for feasts. *Kheyr-u-sharr* was a notion denoting relationships of reciprocal attendance at life-cycle feasts; it also referred to the personal networks so formed. 'My *kheyr-u-sharr*' meant all those people whose feasts I attended and who attended mine. The more well-liked and influential a woman or man, the wider the circle of the *kheyr-u-sharr*, on which indeed their power and influence depended. Separate camp communities of women did not build up into a larger structure, but *kheyr-u-sharr* relations formed a network which extended beyond the pastoral camps and probably beyond the Shahsevan community itself.

In both camp activities and feasts women were able to maintain and manipulate ascribed and achieved statuses so that similar ranking systems based on a common system of values could be assumed to be found among all Shahsevan women. My argument was that these systems formed a structure, and the women of the Shahsevan formed a society (that is, a woman's organization) of their own. Because these values and ranked positions were exclusive to women and yet dependent on and to some extent complementary to certain features of organization among men, and because I described in detail the ways in which it could be said to be a male-dominated society, I called the structure a substructure and the women's society a subsociety.

I thought it likely then that such women's organizations might be found elsewhere in the Middle East, but only when three conditions were fulfilled:

(i) *some degree of separation of women's activities from men's* (among the Shahsevan this derived from the sexual segregation which characterized all social activities, both day-to-day and ceremonial);

(ii) *opportunity for interaction* (for Shahsevan women, social interaction was made possible not only because of the fairly large residential group but also because they were free to travel, sometimes alone, considerable distances to attend feast gatherings); and

(iii) *a medium of interaction* (which for the Shahsevan women was the dyadic *kheyr-u-sharr* ties, with their implicit reciprocity and obligation of mutual attendance at feasts.

The Separate, Purposeful Interaction of Women

A focus on women-only organizations can only make sense, methodologically and analytically, if the local bases for the separation of women and men are made clear. And, in this respect, it is not enough to talk about 'patriarchy' or 'Islam'. Only in terms of ethnographic specificity – the local idioms and metaphors that construe and naturalize gendered difference and its material consequences – can particular meanings and bases for gendered separation be understood.

For instance, women *and men* may both be subject to the same government controls on social gathering, yet the consequences may be different because of the ways gender is construed in a particular setting. Thus in Syria in recent years there have been laws prohibiting public gatherings without prior government approval (cf. this volume, El-Baz), affecting religious as well as secular congregation. However, for men, as long as the crowd attending Friday prayers did not spill out of the mosque, government officials have dared not restrict such gatherings. However, because government informers were also present, there were distinct limits on what could be said or done within the precincts of the mosque.

For pious women, who rarely attended Friday prayers in the mosque, prayer meetings could be held at home. Such meetings suffered from little direct government interference, in part because of the government's reluctance to risk the outcry and anger which would be provoked by overt surveillance in such a setting. Rather, surveillance of women's prayer meetings has apparently taken another form: tacit official support for certain senior women's prayer leaders whose political loyalty was assured. Because women's prayer groups are hierarchically organized, the censorship and control exercised by the women leaders themselves was deemed adequate to limit the activities of devotees and inhibit subversion (cf. Al-Ali, this volume, p. 189).

Moreover, gendered separation is not itself a sufficient condition for the emergence of a women's organization. There are, unfortunately, many situations in which women in the Middle East and elsewhere find themselves socially isolated from all but the members of their immediate families. One pattern familiar from the regional literature shows class to be an important variable in women's interaction: in rural, feudally-organized areas, women from well-to-do households are far more likely to be isolated from gatherings of women than women of poorer households.

Equally, it is the local terms, and value, placed on regularity of the interaction which is important. In one context, interaction may be defined in formal terms as membership in a bounded organization whose meetings require a quorum of members. Or, it may be of the kinds of contacts Mayer described as aspects of 'action-sets' or 'quasi-groups' (1966).

When I was with the Shahsevan, I kept detailed attendance records from five feasts held over a six-week period. I attended these feasts as the guest of the senior wife of a camp leader. Because of her husband's position she was considered an important woman, but her range of contacts was certainly fewer than had she been an acknowledged women's leader. At the five feasts, my hostess met one hundred and two women, from nine other tribal groups and several villages of the region, yet they represented perhaps only three-quarters of the total number of women she met in the six-week period, for she went to four other feasts as well. Thus, during only a short period of time her range of contacts was considerable: in the course of a year the number of women she would meet could be doubled and possibly tripled.

Moreover, the size and heterogeneity of the group of women gathered together at each feast was very significant. These women could be seen as points in an 'unbounded' social field: or, in Mayer's terms, a 'quasi-group', with the potential to meet face-to-face, as members of an 'action-set' on any particular occasion. Thus the opinions they each formed as members of an action set at any one feast could be spread through other comparable contacts to innumerable women (cf. Shaheed 1995: 96 ff., on the advantages of the network form of the organization Women Living Under Muslim Laws).

Finally, I suggested that the third condition for formation of women-only organizations was a medium for interaction: that is, shared values or goals which could provide reasons for regular and purposeful interaction. Clearly, this requirement can only be judged in terms of the women's own perceptions. Among the Shahsevan, the conversations of women at feasts, and those of the women leaders in particular, were a key part of an information network which determined an important factor in determining social values which concerned the activities of both women and men: about economic and political affairs, marriage arrange-ments, healing and a variety of religious practices.

Lest We Forget the Negative Cases

In a second field study, this time with Durrani Pashtuns, transhumant pastoralists of northern Afghanistan, I intended to pursue my hypothesis about the conditions when women organize via a close comparison of women's relations among the Shahsevan and those among the Durrani. I considered comparatively a range of economic and cultural factors such as religious orientation, the jural autonomy of women, the sexual division of labour, household organization and wider kinship patterns. Yet, in spite of many similarities, among the Durrani the three conditions for a separate women's organization – some degree of separation of women's activities from those of men, regular opportunity for interaction and a purpose for interaction – were not fulfilled.

That is, Durrani women's contacts with men were not as exclusive nor as strictly regulated as those of their Shahsevan counterparts. For instance, no classes of men were distinguished with whom contact for a woman was or was not permissible, and veiling conventions among them were such that a Durrani woman normally did not cover her face to any man of any age or ethnic group while she was, so to speak on her home ground. Moreover, within the household, Durrani women experienced little sexual segregation and women were able to entertain male guests when a man was not present or available to do so.

In effect, Durrani women participated in a wide range of social activities where their primary interactions and indentifications were with their families and with other both-sex social groups in the wider community and not with other women. This seemed to dilute the intensity of women's day-to-day contacts with each other and when, at religious and life-change ceremonies, large groups of Durrani women did gather to the exclusion of men, their interaction was barely structured and quite unlike the Shahsevan women's purposeful participation in *kheyr-u-sharr* gatherings. To be sure, the Durrani women gossiped, match-made and exchanged information of political and economic importance, but the impact of such activities on the group of participants as a whole seemed relatively unimportant, and the women appeared to have little sense of operating in an exclusive and positive feminine milieu.

The fact that the Durrani Pashtun women seemed to lack any exclusive women's subsociety meant, of course, I had to change my research focus. Yet the negative example the Durrani case represented suggested that the conditions I described did have some heuristic value (see Tapper 1980, 1991). Meanwhile, of course, I was left with the problem of explaining the differences between the Shahsevan and Durrani women's experiences, in terms of differences in the degrees of their segregation from men, the character and economic importance of marriage trans-actions and the gendered images of women held by women and/or men.

In the absence of other likely factors, I explained these differences in terms of the numbers, kinds and relative importance of social boundaries which were marked in terms of the exchange, or the prohibition on exchange, of items like food and sex. It was a satisfying explanation in part because it grew out of other, wider ethnographic descriptions of social life among the Shahsevan and Durrani Pashtun. It also fitted in well with a range of other explanations of women-only sociality which were being formulated at the time (see, e.g., Caplan & Bujra 1978). Further, it was an explanation which provoked me to think further about the relation between gendered boundaries and women's organizations.

Considering an Entire Social Field: the Range of Women's Organizations in a Single Setting

Some years after my work with the Durrani, I did further fieldwork on women's experiences of practised Islam in a small town in southwestern Turkey. There a striking contrast emerged between two types of formal women's gathering. Each occurred with considerable frequency in small provincial towns and elsewhere throughout Turkey. One of these gatherings, the institution of the *kabul gunu*, that is, of the women's visiting day, was explicitly and determinedly secular. The other, the performance of the *mevlud*, a celebration of the birth of the Prophet Muhammad, was understood locally as explicitly religious in character.

These two types of women's gathering posed a number of general questions about how local meanings were construed through institutional structures. It was also very clear that they could only be understood as part of wider systems of gendered and ceremonial relations involving both women and men (Tapper 1983; cf. Evers Rosander, this volume).

Seen in this wider context, there seemed to be a key difference between women's and men's activities. Men seemed able to express their equality or inequality vis-à-vis each other in either, or both, secular or religious idioms. However, for women, secular and religious discourses did not offer the same scope for negotiation of the inequalities between them as members of competing families, or their equality, whether before men or God, as members of a gender category.

Thus, the structure of the women's visiting day gatherings depended on the perception of equality between participants, but their content, both in terms of gossip and in the use of material symbols of domestic well-being, was competitive and about the inequalities between the women as wives. Moreover, broader class differences were also reproduced between the bourgeois women who went to visiting days and other, poorer women who did not participate in such gatherings at all. By contrast, the structure of the *mevluds* accepted differentiation between women as wives, but their content, as intense religious experiences which focus on birth and motherhood, was about the equality of all women as a gendered category.[2]

Gendered Differences and Organizational Consequences

As was the case with the Harasiis of Oman (above, p. 2ff.), my Turkish fieldwork suggested that the particular way gendered difference is construed in any one setting may have direct consequences for the definition and character of any related women's organization.

In a subsequent comparison of men's and women's *mevlud* rituals in the Turkish town, Richard Tapper and I sought to break away from the conventional dichotomous analyses which seem to bedevil the anthropology of the Middle East: between women and men, private and public domains and popular religious forms and those which are labelled 'orthodox'.

In Turkey, where the state had limited men's public religious activities, the central religious mystery of salvation was celebrated particularly in the women's *mevluds*, through a particular account of the life of the Prophet. We suggested that an intrinsic relation between gender and what, locally, is termed 'religious orthodoxy' was a characteristic of practised Islam everywhere. In the Turkish case, we noted, on the one hand, that men's day-to-day observance of apparent 'orthodoxy' was problematic. On the other, it was wrong to assume *a priori* that women's religious 'work' was less important than, or peripheral to, that of men. Rather, given the separate, yet parallel, activities of women and men, our analysis required us to give full consideration to *both* women's and men's religious ideas and practices and *the gendered relations between them* (N. Tapper & R. Tapper 1987; see also R. Tapper & N. Tapper 1987).

A corollary of this kind of perspective has wide implications. As with the men's *mevluds* in Turkey, men-only associations (whether explicitly religious or political or not) may often be seen as intrinsically more dangerous to the state than those of women. As a consequence, men-only associations may be more obviously and effectively controlled by the state security apparatus, diverting attention from women-only activities. Out of the limelight because of gendered stereotypes or the way domestic or private domains are locally constructed, women-only organizations may subvert the typically masculinized discourses of the state establishment (as with the *mevlud* in Turkey). Or, they may directly express dissent and resistance for both women and men (cf. Moghadam's appendix on the Palestinian Intifada, this volume).

I explored this idea further in a paper on the differences between women's and men's *ziyaret* visits of respect, such as those made to senior relatives and to saints' tombs (Tapper 1990). Following Parry's argument about reciprocity (1986), it seemed possible that fundamental exchange values were gendered in ways which might systematically account for men's dominant, and negative, attitudes to women's religious (and other) gatherings and activities.

In the Turkish town, women could not participate as men did in the 'pure gift' economy of salvation – as expressed in public prayers, in military service, and in the notions of sacrifice which inform the concept of responsibility in religious and civic contexts. Nor did women have the same facility of access or degree of control over political and economic resources: they were thus excluded from many forms of charitable work and achievement in the market economy. In all these various secular and religious contexts, gender constructions precluded women's full participation. Their involvement in the range of valued activities was vicarious and dependent on or mediated by men. In this way, the relationship of women to the dominant ideologies and culture of the town was clearly deemed by both women and men as secondary to that of men.

When women were involved in travel outside the home in the company of other women, the rituals of reciprocity in which they engaged had a quite distinct character and were unlike those of men. The women's exchanges were not expressions of the extreme ideological forms of the 'pure gift' or the market. Rather, they combined muted elements of both: the social and temporal aspects of the exchanges were emphasized in what amounts to a give-and-take kind of reciprocity in which vows and offerings were made for favours and involved calculations of personal merit and advancement (cf. Parry 1986: 462).

Considering Processes of Gendering per se

The complex and contingent ways in which women's activities and organizations are defined and experienced is clear from the range of ethnographic examples I have just offered. Such examples should stand as a caution against reifying gendered identities, naturalizing particular women's (or men's) organizations, or, indeed, treating any single organization in isolation. More recently, I have considered further the problems of reifying gendered identities in the Middle East. My interest has been in the extent to which this is an aspect of local accounts of difference and academic reports on the area.

An obvious starting point was the purported homogeneity of so-called 'honour and shame' societies, labelling which is the product of a bias towards the rhetoric of male 'honour' and the hegemonic masculinities this rhetoric supports (1994). My aim was to dislocate this bias. By problematizing gender, it becomes possible to ask how people make gendered differences known to themselves and how gendered identities may then be reified to sustain inequalities.

I began from Strathern's definition of gender as given in *The Gender of the Gift* (1988). For her, gender is an open-ended category, one based on Wittgenstein's idea of 'family resemblances'. Gender is understood as the 'categorization of persons, artifacts, events [and] sequences . . . which draw upon sexual imagery [and] make concrete people's ideas about the nature of social relationships' (1988: ix). Thus, while it seems that the use of sexual imagery is common to human beings everywhere, neither the character of such images nor their relation to social experience are fixed or universal (cf. Cornwall & Lindisfarne 1994: 40). Applying Strathern's approach, I considered how people are gendered through interaction: that is, how anatomical and physiological notions of difference are construed, literally embodied and transformed through sexual intercourse and/or parenthood. My aim was to show, through a range of ethnographic and other materials from the Middle East, how ideas about female virginity and defloration create and confirm a variety of masculine and feminine identities.[3]

The crucial implication of this approach is that any hegemonic discourse about gender necessarily construes subordinate variants and that both dominant and subordinate notions alter over time. Further, it means that the reified categories of 'women' and 'men' (or 'honour' and 'shame') have no essential validity, but must be investigated in terms of their gendered associations with power, difference and inequality.[4] It is a perspective which raises basic issues about when, how and for what purposes women organize in groups and define, collectively if only temporarily, a shared reality.

Organizing Women – Some Premises

Moghadam's study of women's non-government organizations, NGOs, provides us with an appropriate starting point for developing a new perspective on women's organizations, as well as some telling examples of the process of naturalization. Her chapter is divided into three parts: the first examines the factors behind the formation and spread of women's organizations in the region, the second is a typology of women's NGOs and the third focuses on a document, entitled 'Work Approach for the Non Government Organizations in the Arab Region', prepared in Amman in anticipation of the Fourth World Conference on Women which took place in Beijing in September 1995. A variety of labels frame and, in effect, give political weight to Moghadam's chapter as a brief survey of the units chosen for study (the region and the women's NGOs) will show.

Arabs and Others

In Moghadam's title and elsewhere, her regional unit of study is geographic: the Middle East and North Africa. A first step, then, is to ask how women's NGOs of the MENA area (as she styles it) fit with other locally chosen, or externally imposed, definitions. Thus, in what ways can the MENA area be said to coincide with 'the Arab region'? Or, in what ways did the women who drafted the document in Amman think of 'the Arab region', both among themselves and with respect to the audience of women in Beijing? What were their own ethnic and geographical biases, and how did they characterize the biases of others? In short, what are the further political implications of leaving 'MENA' as both a regional and national/cultural epithet unexamined?

The discussions about the history, extent and use of 'The Middle East' as a geographical or cultural label are, of course, well-known (cf. Eickelman 1989). Equally, the orientalist and other racist entailments of the collective term 'Arab' when used to refer to those states which have adopted Arabic as their official language are not irrelevant. These are questions of discourse: of the ways in which social description has material consequences, for both those who do the describing and those who are described. Naming is an act of power.

Typically, behind any act of naming there are a number of often contradictory presumptions. In this case, are there intrinsic differences between 'Arab' women, and 'Arab' women's organizations, and others? How do women's NGOs in the Arab states differ from those elsewhere in the Middle East or further afield? Evers Rosander (this volume) suggests they do not. She deliberately eschews the conventional regional labels which divide North from West Africa so that she can compare both rotating credit and religious organizations among Muslim women in Senegal and northern Morocco. By challenging conventions about regional differences, Evers offers a new perspective on the categories 'Middle Eastern women and women's NGOs' which have been reified through inattention.

Categorical Constraints and Religious Blinkers

Other definitional issues concern what is meant by non-governmental organizations, and which NGOs are deemed relevant to a particular study. Moghadam's focus is on those organizations which attract women participants and may address women's issues; thus, women's NGOs include 'charitable societies, professional associations, development-oriented NGOs and feminist groups' (p. 24). On internal evidence, we can see that Moghadam's typology itself creates a picture of women's NGOs as 'essentially elite, professional, and middle class' (p. 43; cf. p. 33 e.g. where she builds in a distinction based on class). Yet in the way El-Baz (this volume) and others often mention women's and men's associations in the same context, it is not immediately obvious why class-based groups to which *both* women and men may belong, such as the Red Crescent or trade unions, should be excluded from the survey and typology. And what, apart from often unmarked class distinctions, differentiates the various 'informal', but exclusively female networks or associations (such as those discussed by Evers Rosander; and see above, pp. 214–15), from those organizations Moghadam does discuss.

Nor does this usage explain the meaning or usefulness of the distinction between NGOs and private voluntary organizations (PVOs, cf. p. 25). Moghadam's use of 'NGO' explicitly subsumes the term 'PVO' (p. 25), yet, in practice, she also uses the distinction to separate religious charities (particularly Islamist ones) from other service organizations (p. 29, cf. p. 30), and then to attend mainly to the latter. For instance, we learn that women's NGOs have difficulties with 'poor voluntary recruitment (except for religiously-oriented PVOs, where this is apparently not a problem)' (p. 42). That is a fascinating difference, requiring further explanation.

El-Baz does however provide some clues in her chapter. Though she too is a secularly-orientated women's activist, she does not so ruthlessly exclude Islamist's organizations from her survey of Egyptian women's organizations. Following Hatem (1992), she writes,

> . . . despite the visibility of women in the Islamist movement, they were mostly operating on the lowest levels. The formation of sexually segregated groups did not change the fact that leadership was the sole preserve of men even in women's groups. . .. [Yet] these Islamist women's groups played an active role in recruiting other women for the movement, especially among those who come from the newly impoverished classes. Solving their immediate material problems was the key to winning them over. They are strongly committed and innovative in their different ways of reaching people especially on the grass-root level (p. 165).

Of course, a detailed interrogation of terms of reference may sidetrack the argument of a short article, yet questions of definition can reveal the extent to which political differences may be reified and naturalized to support vested interests. Thus, labelling which derives from a commitment to a secular feminism may hide the way Islamist and secular identities are mutually construed and need to be treated in tandem.

Farida Shaheed also writes from a feminist perspective, but explicitly so and from the perspective of the network of 'Women Living Under Muslim Laws' in Pakistan. Her observations have a general relevance.

> The lack of public mobilization of women, other than those professionally employed, on women's issues in the period 1979–88 needs to be examined. The discourse and debate on women – shaped by the religious right – remained almost exclusively urban. Nor, in the main, was it aimed at the majority of poor women, whether rural or urban, whose transgressions of

patriarchal norms, where these occur, do not seem to be perceived as
threatening the status quo. There is no doubt that this decade was the most
retrogressive for Pakistan's women, marked by state-sponsored legislation,
directives, and campaigns seeking to reduce women's rights, to curtail their
access to economic resources, and to restrict both their mobility and visibility.
Yet, ironically enough, in this same decade the largest number of women were
recruited into the formal labor market and the number of women in the
informal sector also grew; female applicants for higher education increased,
as did the number of technical training institutes for women; and, in urban
areas, even as dress codes become more uniform, an unprecedented number
and new class of women started appearing in public places of leisure such as
parks and restaurants (1995: 88–9).

Of their many implications, Shaheed's observations include the insight
that the numbers of women in the work-force and the particular jobs they
get, may be directly related to the gendered rhetoric of recent Islamist
polemics. Yet it is notable that Al-Ali (this volume), writing of Egypt
during the 'open-door' policies of President Sadat and thereafter,
proposes the opposite relation. Women's employment conditions
changed during the period of male labour migration especially to the Gulf
countries; the end of that migration and the subsequent economic
pressures on women were aspects of more conservative discourses and
women's return to more domestic identities (p. 178).

Neither Shaheed nor Al-Ali need be right or wrong. The situation is
far too complex for that. Rather, whatever the particular relation between
Islamist discourse and women's employment in particular settings, it is
clear this is a topic which needs to be examined straight on.

International Associations and Universal Rhetorics

Taking Moghadam's categories – from 'women' to 'non-governmental
organizations' – as givens her contribution must be treated ethnographically. In this light, her discussion seems to support a wider
discourse employed by the donor governments or multilateral funding
agencies: the former either Euro-American states or those Arab states
which are directly supported by the institutions of global capitalism; the
latter – the UN and other agencies – are, of course, also dominated by
similar interests (cf. p. 41ff.).

Framed more critically however, Moghadam's chapter invites debate
about the politics of development and, more specifically, women-in-
development. To take but one example: she describes the consequences
for women's employment and welfare provision in Egypt of the shrinking
of 'the Third World state' due to the 'highly competitive [sic] environ-

ment of international trade and investment, decreases in foreign aid from the North, and structural adjustment policies of the International Monetary Fund (IMF) and the World Bank'. But it is by no means clear why these consequences 'necessitates non-governmental public action' (p. 29). Or, equally, we can ask by whom, and serving whose interests, are 'NGOs . . . expected to play an increasingly large role in the region' (p. 30).

Her argument appears to rest on an assertion made by Nabil Samuel.

> The state can no longer struggle under the burden of production and welfare for the citizens, and is beginning to open up vistas for the private and community sectors to assume their roles in building civil society, participating in production, and shouldering the efforts to offset the negative side-effects of economic restructuring (Samuel, quoted in Moghadam, p. 52n3).

El-Baz in her contribution to this volume makes the same point in similarly distanced terms:

> The Private Voluntary Organizations (PVOs) sector was especially *encouraged* to fill the vacuum resulting from the withdrawal of the state from its welfare functions, of providing social services to its citizens, under the . . . IMF and the World Bank Structural Adjustment Programmes. . .(my emphasis, p. 147).

Perhaps the most interesting questions about non-governmental organizations are exactly those hidden behind Samuel and El-Baz's presumptions. They both write impersonally, as if the discourse of market-driven economics emerged out of the blue and had no interested advocates. But this, of course, is not the case.

Thus, it becomes important to ask – who are the IMF and World Bank managers? And what are the national and class interests of those who are working in Egypt? Moreover, which politicians, businessmen, members of the Egyptian government, civil servants and others have sought to *encourage* (to use El-Baz's phrase) the development of PVOs? In what ways do such recently *encouraged* PVOs differ from those of earlier periods? Which sections or classes of a population were involved in non-governmental organizations earlier and presently? Has women's (and men's) participation in PVOs changed because of the ways the new SAP-induced forms of poverty have altered their lives? As El-Baz writes:

> affected social classes which were not previously among the poor: the majority of civil servants, unemployed graduates (particularly those with intermediate level education, who usually come from very poor backgrounds), and persons

working in the informal sector. Among these categories women are hit most because of their basic disadvantaged position in the society – thus justifying the concept of 'feminization of poverty' (p. 149).

What are the rhetorics and activities associated with present organizations? To what extent are they marked by gendered as well as other class, sectarian or ethnic differences? Crucially, what does *encouragement* mean? That is, how do these organizations come into being and by what activities are they sustained?

Questions of Civil Society and Islamist Tendencies

Further questions concerning the ways Arab women's NGOs are implicated in global politics, require other frames of reference. In Moghadam's historical account of the formation and spread of these groups, she suggests how, particularly in the 1980s and after, donor goverments and multilateral fundraisers 'embraced non-governmental organizations as partners in development' (p. 25; see also p. 26). This focus seems to have been premised on the apparently self-evident virtues of civil society. Thus, in circular fashion, the incidence and character of such 'women's NGOs' offer direct evidence of the existence of a civil society and are themselves a measure of its present and continuing good health and a defence of the 'rise and spread of Islamic fundamentalist movements' (p. 31).

Yet, if these premises are so persuasive, we clearly need to know more about the sources, meaning and interests served by the notion 'civil society' and the ways it is gendered. The considerable unclarity associated with the term is evident in El-Baz's usage.

> Civil society is the aspect of social life which is distinct and removed from the realm of the state. It is based on the existence of a community of free individuals who are able to form non-state associations which interact with the state to promote citizens' participation vis-à-vis the state's influence (p. 160, referring to Zaki 1995: 1, 4; cf. Al-Ali, this volume).

Terms, such as 'the state' and 'civil society' are, in this formulation, reified. Though each term presented is self-evident, independent and monolithic, the dichotomy thus formed is, of course, predicated on their mutual construal. Such a formulation is common in the literature on women's organizations. It works against social investigation: of the organization of the state and the everyday politics of state officials and the extent to which individuals have links and interests which interpenetrate the notionally discrete terms of the dichotomy.

Moreover, such usages need to be situated in a wider arena. Recent, and very considerable, efforts are being made locally, and by academic writers, to link 'feminist' perspectives (as if 'feminism' were monolithic and unproblematic) with 'human rights' (see Moghadam, p. 30, 36ff.). In much of this work, the labelling process – in this case, the creation of a link between the two areas of discourse, typically 'feminism' and 'Islamic interpretation' – seems to be an end in itself. Such efforts deserve to be treated ethnographically as political projects which may have wide implications.

Kandiyoti describes the conventional form these recent discussions often take. Though she does not say so explicitly, she implies that it is 'Western' feminist scholars who are most likely to adopt the kind of strategy she describes. However, as the majority of contributions to the Afkhami (1995) and Yamani (1996) collections demonstrate, regional, national, sectarian or feminist identities are likely to be essentialized as an aspect of the truth, or legitimacy, of *whatever* scholarly perspective on 'civil society', 'feminism' or 'human rights' an author adopts. Consider the following as a possible frame of reference for this process:

> [The] scholarly strategy, especially in disciplines normally mandating actual fieldwork, . . . [of] deconstructing texts emanating from one's own culture – preferably from male authors with imperial connections – is a much safer enterprise than having to engage with the far messier realities of contemporary social life and the perplexing cross-currents evident in the politics of gender in contemporary Middle Eastern societies. But the more serious disservice which some varieties of post-Orientalist scholarship may unwittingly perform resides in the fact they often remain locked into the categories of colonizer vs colonized, East vs West, Islam vs Christendom, Western Self vs Native Other in ways that keep our gaze fixed upon the discursive hegemony of the West. This usually occurs to the detriment of more self-referential analyses of culture and society which should inform local feminist criticism (Kandiyoti 1996: 16–17).

Kandiyoti suggests that it is often Islamists who offer such dichotomous constructions as a 'justification for counter-hegemonic moves', but I would suggest that there are few scholars, Islamist or not, who, as she recommends, recognize *in practice* 'the complexity and heterogeneity of Middle Eastern societies and open up new spaces for social criticism' (Kandiyoti 1996: 17).

Thus, a high evaluation of 'civil society' and an emphasis on 'secular, non-political' women's non-governmental organizations may also be part of such a discourse (cf. Al-Ali, this volume, p. 188ff.; and below, p. 229).

The consequences of such a formulation are complex. As in the account of Moghadam and others, they may exclude Islamist practices from serious consideration. They may also serve to disguise the class interests of academic feminist writers themselves. However, as Al-Ali argues (p. 189ff.), such a formulation may also mute individuals or groups who have opposed Islamism and even revive the long defunct analytic division between 'public' and 'private' domains, rendering 'civil society' a very male-centred entity indeed!

In short, the terms of reference used by Moghadam to examine Arab women's non-government organizations do not self-evidently encourage the conclusion that 'they may serve women's practical and basic needs, or strategic gender (feminist) interests' (p. 33). On the contrary, such a formulaic reification of interests should provoke anthropologists and others to examine in detail the very diversity of women's interests and the heterogeneity of their self-identifications. The reification also suggests that social class, which has all too often been ignored in discussions of gendering of organizations in the Middle East, may be a salient factor for further study.

Redefining the Field of Study

By beginning from the particular, it is possible to raise quite other questions about women organizing in groups. Al-Ali's chapter in this volume starts with an ethnographic description: of a meeting in Cairo in which a mainly leftist audience of women and an Islamist speaker find common ground through 'constructions of "the West" as a dominant, essentialized "other"' (p. 173). Her interest is to describe how local notions of feminism, *nassawiyya*, relate to the political and ideological topography of contemporary activists' struggle. From the outset, Al-Ali's choice of language makes her sympathies clear. Yet by adopting an ethnographic perspective, her personal politics, like those of the women of whom she is writing, are placed within a relativistic framework. More-over, rather than taking the terms of feminist discourses as given, Al-Ali argues that:

the context of women's rights activism in Egypt can only be understood by reference to a number of debates and the way they intersect: a) modernity and westernism; b) the nature of civil society; and c) secularism and minorities. . . . it is also [women activists] who, by challenging the various discourses, might have the possibility to . . . emerge as a democratizing force in contemporary Egypt (p. 174).

In exploring this debate ethnographically, it is obvious that contemporary Egyptian feminisms are formed from the contestation of Islamist and secular positions.

Class and Other Kinds of Difference

Al-Ali's outline of the major debates within an historical analysis of the Egyptian women's movement suggests that contemporary activism has often depended on forging 'a strict separation between the "modern, secular and westernizing voice" on the one hand and the "conservative, anti-western and Islamic voice" on the other' (p. 175). She also notes that there is a continuing tendency to 'delegitimize a particular group or project by denouncing it as paying lip service to [a reified] "the West"' (pp. 186ff.). Social class is often also implicated in the divide: the upper and upper-middle classes being associated with the West, while an unmarked (lower/peasant/working) class identity is treated as 'native, vernacular, Islamic' (see Ahmed 1992: 197, as referred to by Al-Ali, p. 175).

Yet the class basis of the women's movement, and its relation to Islamisms, is of course far more complicated than the stereotypes and rhetoric allow. For instance, the Nasserist state monopolized women's issues, while at the same time creating new class bases for gender relations and undermining both women's independent welfare and political activities. Later, Sadat's 'open-door' policies, which greatly enriched a few and impoverished many, simultaneously 'manipulat[ed] Islamic groups as a means to weaken popular leftist forces' (p. 180).

Presently, Al-Ali's research suggests that women of secular-oriented women's organizations in Egypt are 'united by their middle-class background and their commitment to retain and expand their civic rights, . . . but their actual positions vis-à-vis the various Islamic tendencies and discourses are variable' (p. 183). Moreover, in contemporary struggles, 'what appears to be about "the West" often conceals discourses about social classes. The *nouveau riche* and "Westernized Egyptians" are labelled *khawagas* (foreigners) just like the tourists who roam the country' (p. 185).

Meanwhile, as Al-Ali notes, 'the attempt to blur dichotomies between westernizing and traditional strands of the feminist movement [which] characterize the most recent publications on its history' (p. 175), such as the writing of Baron (1994) and Badran (1995) on Egypt, themselves suggest another political agenda among feminist academics.

In brief then, Al-Ali's effort to understand a range of secular-oriented women's organizations in terms of local debates and activity, points to a host of contradictions between the rhetorics of women's activism, organizational practice and social class. Her work offers a careful, imaginative model for ethnographic research.

Producing Social Differences

The question – how are social differences produced? – is vexed. It requires us to compare like with like and depends greatly on the time-frame within which we situate our explanation. To avoid tautology, we must approach the topic we wish to understand from a right-angle. That is, to understand the gendered aspects of *women's* organizations, the independent factors or variables we consider must necessarily exclude gender. Three case studies from the collection are effective illustrations of this process.

Thus, al-Mughni takes social class as an independent variable to describe the gendered characteristics of the five, out of fifty-five, voluntary associations in Kuwait which are for women. The agendas of women's groups in Kuwait are then analysed in terms of a fundamental change: from the original modernizing ambitions of the women's organizations to their present affirmation of 'the patriarchal structure of society' (p. 195). Yet, as with many accounts of women's organizations, the terms of al-Mughni's analysis are too close to the subject to be explained: a term like 'patriarchy' tells us little about social class, and, for instance, a modernizing agenda may also be patriarchal (cf. Sharabi 1988); while the class interests of the elite and upper-class women who presently control the organizations, may also have been effectively served during the period of the 1960s as well.

Al-Mughni's analysis is instructive, distinguishing carefully between women of the leading merchant families who, in the late 1950s and 1960s, were the first women in Kuwait to unveil, seek rights to education and employment and form the first women's associations to fight against 'backward' traditions and customs. However, in the early 1970s, feminist equal rights demands coincided with wider demands for political partici-pation and thus presented 'the first challenge to male prerogatives and state policies' (p. 199). Shortly thereafter,

> the government moved towards protecting the patriarchal family and women's subordinate role within it. It urged the media and concerned government departments 'to combat all that threatens the existence of the family and distorts the character of solidarity between its members' (p. 200).

Quite properly, Al-Mughni relates this discourse on the family to the right-wing women's movements in the United States (p. 207). Though she verges on treating the state as a monolith, whose official policies are *distinct from* women, or from the elite kinship ties which locate the ruling Al-Sabah family in Kuwaiti political discourse, she gives us a good idea how, for elite Kuwaiti women, class and gender interests intersect and have lead to the rejection of democratic forms on a number of fronts. Thus, the 'patriarchal bargains' made by these women (cf. Kandiyoti 1988), have involved, among other things, the formation of new Islamist women's groups which, with government encouragement, have reshaped the content of women's public discourse (p. 8; see above (on Syria), p. 216). With a nice irony, in Kuwait as elsewhere, the Islamist movement (like the Gulf War, p. 195; cf. Doumato 1995) benefited organizing women in various ways. Yet, the associational gains of this period were later systematically dismantled by the government.

By comparison, as Seikaly's chapter shows, in the Bahraini case, the Al-Khalifa rulers have attempted to reduce a great variety of cross-cutting ethnic and class differences, and popular wishes for democratic reform, into a system of ethnic privilege (the rulers claim to be 'pure' Arabs) and a reified sectarian divide between Sunni and Shii (the Al-Khalifa are Sunni Muslims). This has been reflected in the more recent formations of many women's associations in which, as elsewhere in the country, people have increasingly been distinguished along ethnic and/or religious lines. These ethnic or sectarian organizations have been:

> a major path which absorbed the energies of the new generation of educated, often western educated, and socially conscious women. Whenever official recognition and permits had been barred, women still improvised channels of creating a means of empowerment and unobtrusive methods of expressing social and political commitments (Seikaly, personal communication).

In effect, in the near civil war which continues in Bahrain, the apparent ethnic and sectarian character of women's activism has been a means by which women could be effective political actors. In spite of the official rhetoric to the contrary, for many the central political issues concern ending ruling class oppression and privilege and the institution of a range of civil and democratic rights.

Revisiting the Family

'The family' is another topic where careful ethnographic accounts can forward our understanding. There are at least three distinct ways this is so. First, there is the question of 'the family' as a metaphor. Familial love, loyalty and support, the position of the head of the family and local understandings of authority, food and the use of other domestic imagery – all these are well-known rhetorics for describing the state and other organizations, as well as institutions of governance and power generally.

As al-Mughni notes,

> In Kuwait, the state does not compete with the family institution for control over individuals. Neither does it seek to weaken primary ties and kinship allegiance to enhance the citizens' loyalities. The state and the family represent two sides of the same coin. Households' members submission to the household head is comparable to that of citizens' submission to their head of state. . ..The state could be regarded as an extension of the patriarchal authority within the family (p. 196).

And there are other ways in which defining gendered relations within the family becomes a political project. Consider, for instance, the extent to which, in any particular case, the networks of women organizing in groups may be based on pseudo-kinship or detailed familial ties. Thus, though al-Mughni says little of the class identities of the first women members of the voluntary associations in Kuwait, it is unlikely that they were far removed from kinship and other ties with the very state officials who initially controlled those women's organizations.

Joseph's chapter in this volume makes a similar point: that women's organizations may reproduce familial forms and interpersonal ties. Thus, women's organizations in Lebanon often reproduce the political processes of men's political organizations. Individual women set up 'shops' (*dakakeen*) and remain the head of the organization throughout their lives. Their activities, which are often diffuse, depend on the leader's interests and enthusiasms, and are dependent, for their execution, on the women clients who attach themselves to their patronness. Joseph argues that, structurally, the women's organizations reproduce patriarchal forms and allow women to assume positions vis-à-vis each other which replicate those of men in the men's shops. This suggests that a further step in Joseph's analysis would be to compare ethnographically the range and density of ties with 'shopkeepers' experienced by both the male and female members of the households of a particular neighbourhood.

Joseph insists that though she is writing of women-only organizations engaged, at least some of the time, in women's issues, the women's shops do not contribute to feminist consciousness or feminist processes at all. Rather, as with the Shahsevan women's subsociety (see above, p. 214), the women's associations create access to the wider political process and power for the founder/leader of a shop rather than for women in general.

These women's organizations seem to be fundamentally different in their structure and aims from, say, the secular women's organizations described by Al-Ali for Cairo and much more like those described by Caplan for Madras City in India (1985). It may be that feminist consciousness is more closely related to class identities than to gendered differences per se. Again, it is likely to be the case that the insights we may derive from our explanation of any particular social phenomenon, like the women's shops, depend, at least in part, on our willingness to view it from a right-angle: to reframe it in social terms in a less than self-evident way.

A third aspect of the 'family' metaphor is that explored by Shami, who examines both how the state institutions define the family, and households, for their own purposes. She is also interested in the extent to which everyday experiences of domestic relations confound such definitions. Kandiyoti, citing Tucker (1993), has noted that 'the family, whose centrality is axiomatic in Middle Eastern studies, has hardly been the object of any detailed research that reveals the variability of household formations in the Arab world through time and space' (1996: 17).

Thus, Shami's work is unusual and important. In intriguing and careful ethnographic detail, she offers a comparison of *intra*-household patterns of relationships from two squatter areas in Amman. *Inter*-household relations, on the other hand, are often those constructed or mediated through state agencies. Local usages serve local political interests and households are seen as discrete and bounded. This local understanding recalls Harris's early work on households (1981): how the household, while so often reified as an isolated, autonomous unit, cannot, analytically, plausibly be treated this way. Rather the household is construed through its relationships: of propinquity in neighbourhoods, or economic dependence on wages, domestic exchanges and taxation. Shami also describes how in Amman local discourses often depend on local definitions of a dichotomy similar to that of 'public' and 'private' and she reopens the old theoretical debate in anthropology to understand better local usage. Local understandings of this dichotomy confound the popular, and older anthropological, stereotypes of women as constrained and limited to private, domestic environments. What Shami's work underscores is that in this case, notions of the 'domestic' and the 'private' are not synonymous:

> Women flock the corridors of public offices and use their visibility and physical presence as a means of achieving their aims. . . . Although I did not observe the formation of formal women's groups in these situations, . . . there is, at the very least, the formation of a female front, one that relies on the

supposed individuality of each case while evoking particularly female cultural categories such as motherhood. Thus women constantly invoke the domestic sphere to legitimize their excursions into the public sphere and their incursions into the formal decision-making arena (personal communication).

A neat inversion of this point, in terms of class and gender presumptions, comes from al-Mughni. She too explores the *local* understandings of limits of state intrusion in her discussion of the *diwaniyya* gatherings which, though 'semi-public', take place in the 'protected space' of a private household, an institution formerly associated only with men which some prominent women have recently appropriated for their own use (p. 196).

Again detailed ethnography and a willingness to reexamine tired, and now often self-serving, analytical concepts can produce new questions. For example, we can ask how exactly (in the examples Shami and al-Mughni offer) are women and men regendered through their activities, whether in the state offices or the *diwaniyya*? How do these experiences alter their understanding of other organizational forms and institutional structures? How do these changes relate to their aims and aspirations for themselves, their children and other women in gendered, class or other terms?

Such questions extend the limits of ethnographic, historical and theoretical enquiry. To answer them in new and engaging ways, we need to be self-reflective, and transparent, about our terms of reference and the biases we bring to the enquiry. What indeed is implied by the regional, 'Middle Eastern' label, or one which refers to some essentialized 'Arab' ethnicity? What attributes of formal, or informal organization, tell us most about the wide variety of women-only associations here described? Finally, what are the mechanisms by which people understand gendered difference to be created and transformed in everyday interactions, and what relations of power are constituent parts of these interactions? Such are the questions raised by *Organizing Women*. They are questions which deserve to run and run.

Notes

1. I am particularly grateful for the support I received from the School of Oriental and African Studies for my fieldwork, and for the project awards I recieved from the Economic and Social Research Council (UK): for

Afghanistan (hr1141/1 (with Richard Tapper), Turkey (HR7410) and Syria (R000 23 1533, H524 27 502995). I also wish to thank the Nuffield Foundation for their support with respect to my fieldwork in Syria.

2. A similar case of paired women's gatherings is described by Keirn (1978) who examines the participation of women of a South African township in both voluntary associations and spirit possession rituals. Her description and my ethnography from Turkey prompt a further question: how common are such paired sets of women's gatherings in communities where male dominance was considerable, institutionalized and largely unquestioned?

3. An important aspect of this argument was that while hegemonic versions of masculinity and femininity may frame relations of inequality, hegemonic forms are never totally comprehensive, nor do they ever completely control the behaviour of those who are thus defined as 'subordinates'. That is, there is always some space for subordinate versions of masculinity and femininity as alternative gendered identities which validate self-worth and encourage resistance.

4. This work was an attempt to theorize exactly the process whereby women have challenged apparently absolute cultural definitions, such as those concerning female circumcision (see El-Baz, this volume).

References

Afkhami, M., ed. (1995), *Faith and Freedom: Women's Human Rights in the Muslim World*. London: I.B. Tauris.

Ahmed, L. (1992), *Women and Gender in Islam*. New Haven: Yale University Press.

Badran, M. (1995), *Feminists, Islam, and Nation: Gender and the Making of Modern Egypt*, Princeton: Princeton University Press.

Baron, B. (1994), *The Women's Awakening in Egypt: Culture, Society and the Press*. New Haven: Yale University Press.

Barth, F. (1996), 'Economy, Agency and Ordinary Lives,' Keynote Address at the Fourth EASA Conference, *Culture and Economy: Conficting Interests, Divided Loyalties*, Barcelona.

Caplan, P. (1985), *Class and Gender in India: Women and their Organizations in a South Indian City*, London: Tavistock.

Caplan, P. and Bujra, J., eds (1978), *Women United, Women Divided: Cross-Cultural Perspectives on Female Solidarity*, London: Tavistock.

Cesara, M. (1982), *Reflections of a Woman Anthropologist: No Hiding Place*, London: Academic Press.

Cornwall, A. and N. Lindisfarne (1994), *Dislocating Masculinity*, London: Routledge.

Doumato, E. A. (1995), 'The Ambiguity of Shari'a and the Politics of 'Rights' in Saudi Arabia' in M. Afkhami, ed., op. cit.: 135–160.

Eickelman, D. (1981), *The Middle East: An Anthropological Approach*, 2nd ed. 1989, Englewood Cliffs, NJ: Prentice Hall.

Hatem, M. (1992), 'Economic and Political Liberation in Egypt and the Demise of State Feminism,' *International Journal of Middle East Studies*, 24, 2, 231–51.

Harris, O. (1981), 'Households as Natural Units,' in K. Young, C. Wolkowitz and R. McCullogh, eds, *Of Marriage and the Market: Women's Subordination in International Perspective*, London: CSE Books.

Kandiyoti, D. (1988), 'Bargaining with Patriarchy,' *Gender and Society*, 2, 3: 274–90.

—— (1996), 'Contemporary Feminist Scholarship and Middle East Studies,' in D. Kandiyoti, ed., *Gendering the MIddle East: Emerging Perspectives*, London: I.B. Tauris.

Keirn, S. M. (1978), 'Convivial Sisterhood, Spirit Mediumship and Client-Core Network among Black South African Women,' in J. Hoch-Smith and A. Spring, eds, *Women in Ritual and Symbolic Roles*, New York: Plenum Press.

Lindisfarne, N. (1994), 'Variant Masculinities, Variant Virginities: Rethinking "Honour and Shame"' in A. Cornwall and N. Lindisfarne, eds, *Dislocating Masculinity: Comparative Ethnographies*. London: Routledge.

—— (1996), 'Local Voices and Responsible Anthropology: Finding a Place from Which to Speak,' Workshop Paper presented at the Fourth EASA Conference, Barcelona.

Lindisfarne-Tapper, N. (1992), 'Local Contexts and Political Voices,' *Anthropology in Action*, 10: 6–8.

Mayer, A. C. (1966), 'The Significance of Quasi-Groups in the Study of Complex Societies' in M. Banton, ed., *The Social Anthropology of Complex Societies*, London: Tavistock.

Parry, J. (1986), 'The Gift, the Indian Gift and the "Indian Gift",' *Man*, 21, 3: 453–73.

Shaheed, F. (1995), 'Networking for Change: The Role of Women's Groups in Initiating Dialogue on Women's Issues' in M. Afkhami, ed., op. cit.: 78–103.

Sharabi, H. (1988), *Neopatriarchy: A Theory of Distorted Change in Arab Society*, Oxford: Oxford University Press.

Strathern, M. (1988), *The Gender of the Gift*, Berkeley CA: University of California.

Tapper, N. (1968), *The Role of Women in Selected Pastoral Islamic Societies*, University of London: Unpublished M.Phil. Dissertation.

—— (1978), 'The Women's Subsociety among the Shahsevan Nomads of Iran,' in L. Beck and N. Keddie, eds, *Women in the Muslim World*, Cambridge, Mass.: Harvard University Press.

—— (1980), 'Matrons and Mistresses: Women and Boundaries in Two Middle Eastern Tribal Societies,' *European Journal of Sociology*, 21, 59–78.

—— (1990), '*Ziyaret*: Gender, Movement, and Exchange in a Turkish Community" in D. Eickelman & J. Piscatori, eds, *Muslim Travellers: Pilgrimage, Migration, and the Religious Imagination*, London: Routledge.

—— (1991), *Bartered Brides: Politics, Gender and Marriage in an Afghan Tribal Society*. Cambridge: Cambridge University Press.

Tapper, N. and Tapper, R. (1987), 'The Birth of the Prophet: Ritual and Gender in Turkish Islam,' *Man*, 22, 1, 69–92.

Tapper, R. (1979), *Pasture and Politics: Economics, Conflict and Ritual among Shahsevan Nomads of Northwestern Iran*, London: Academic.

Tapper, R. and Tapper, N. (1987), '"Thank God We're Secular!"': Aspects of Fundamentalism in a Turkish Town' in L. Caplan, ed., *Studies in Religious Fundamentalism*, London: Macmillan.

Tucker, J., ed., (1993), *Arab Women: Old Boundaries, New Frontiers*, Bloomington: Indiana University Press.

Yamani, M., ed., (1996), *Feminism and Islam: Legal and Literary Perspectives*, Reading: Ithaca.

Zaki, M. (1995), *Civil Society and Democratization in Egypt: 1981–1991*, Cairo: Dar Al Kutub.

Index